FAR-EASTERN VEGETARIAN COOKING

FAR-EASTERN VEGETARIAN COOKING

Margaret Leeming &
May Huang Man-hui

Photographs by Anthony Blake

Illustrations by Roy Jennings

COLUMBUS BOOKS · LONDON

Note on serving quantities

In the Far East meals are made up of several dishes of equal importance, rather than being constructed, as in the West, on the principle of a meat dish with vegetable accompaniments. The more important the meal, the more dishes are served. The number of dishes in the meal will largely dictate the number of people each will feed, but as a very rough guide the quantities stated for each recipe should be sufficient for four people.

First published in Great Britain in1985 by
Columbus Books
Devonshire House, 29 Elmfield Road, Bromley, Kent BR1 1LT

Designed by Mavis Henley

British Library Cataloguing in Publication Data
Leeming, Margaret
Far-Eastern vegetarian cooking
1. Vegetarian cookery 2. Cookery, Oriental
I. Title II. May Huang, Man-hui
641.5'636'095 TX837

Typeset by August Filmsetting, Haydock, St. Helens
Printed and bound in Italy

ISBN 0–86287–199–9

Contents

1 Behind the Bamboo Curtain

Far-Eastern vegetarian cookery, with its rich yet subtle blends of flavours and creative use of ingredients, is arguably the best in the world. To us in the West, it can offer a new view of the way in which we serve foods – worlds away from the heaped plates of the Western dining-table – and of healthy eating. Peasant peoples, out of financial and geographical reach of mass-produced, processed foods, grow their own out of economic necessity, and inevitably know only whole food. Many of the recipes in this book, which draw upon both religious traditions and peasant experience throughout the Orient, can stand comparison with the most sophisticated Western dishes – and what is more, a large proportion of them embrace the healthy principles that we have recently begun to rediscover in our own society.

Indian curries, Mexican chilli and Middle-Eastern *hummus* are part of everyday eating for many of us, and we use such migrant ingredients as yoghurt and bulghar wheat without a second thought. From here it is no great step to crisp Chinese stir-fried vegetables, a sweet, creamy Indonesian curry or a Japanese salad delicately flavoured with a sesame dressing. These are just some of the many faces of Far-Eastern vegetarian cuisine.

Also among its glories are the sauces – delicious, seductive and infinitely varied: from the crunchy nut and lime juice sauce that accompanies tiny beancurd-and-egg omelettes from Indonesia, to the sweet and sour sauce, first recorded in the ninth century, that transforms aubergines, or the delicate, understated ginger-spiked sauce in which the Japanese cook pumpkin. Each of these is easy to make, from ingredients readily available in the West.

Sauces, however, are just the beginning. Beancurd (or *tofu*) is one of the richest sources of vegetable protein, and is at last becoming more widely known in the West. Immensely versatile, it can be served just as it is, with almost any other food, or deep-fried, steamed, boiled – even grilled. This chameleon food lends itself to all levels of seasonings: we particularly like fried beancurd with sesame sauce, for its glorious combination of crunchy and creamy textures combined with a nutty sweet and sour flavour. You can serve it in a Western meal if you wish, perhaps with a raw vegetable salad, a hot bean casserole and bowl of stuffed vegetables, or as one dish in a Chinese meal.

Another food, hardly known in the West at present, is the protein made from wheat flour: gluten. This is cheap, easy to make and great fun to handle, since it can be shaped and structured into many different forms. It is used in China to make 'mock meats', which are cooked in the same style as the meats they represent, thus opening up such possibilities as 'spareribs' and 'chilli chicken' to vegetarian cooks. For the Chinese people, always short of meat, the chance of enjoying the dishes of the rich, traditionally containing meat, was a great incentive for the invention of these imitative forms – distasteful and unnecessary as the idea may seem to some Western vegetarians.

One of the most exciting aspects of Far-Eastern vegetarian dishes is the range of exotic food plants they call into play. Over the last thirty years the West has been introduced to a great number of new fruits and vegetables, and many of them have become standard ingredients in our daily cooking. In Britain, for example, aubergines, peppers, avocados, white radish and Chinese leaves were all virtually unknown in the 1950s: now all these are regularly available in high-street outlets. Yet there is still a cornucopia of new possibilities waiting to be explored – crunchy Asian long beans, Japanese seaweeds and vegetable melons from China. The recipes in this book make use of these less familiar vegetables, now reasonably common – though some, admittedly, are available only in season – in the West.

Some of the techniques for preparing these will probably be new to you; the majority are explained in the relevant chapters, but a few which are used frequently throughout the book are described in detail in Chapter 4, 'The Basics of Far-Eastern Cookery'. Ingredients, including the vegetables themselves, are described, and in many cases illustrated, in Chapter 2.

Quantities stated in recipes are sufficient for four people in meals comprising three of four other dishes and a staple of rice or noodles; if only two dishes and rice are cooked the quantities will be sufficient for two people. Measurements are stated in metric, American liquid volume and Imperial: use only one system of measurement in any particular recipe since these are not exact equivalents and are not interchangeable. If you use American liquid measures, use Imperial dry weights.

The recipes come from three complementary and contrasting regions. China lies at the heart of all Far-Eastern cooking and her culture has had a profound influence throughout the region. Japan and Korea originally learnt many of the fundamentals of their cuisines from China, although they later developed their own distinctive styles.

The cuisines of Indonesia and Malaysia have had a more varied background than those of Japan and Korea. The earliest foreign visitors to influence Indonesian culture and cuisine were the Indian Buddhists. They were followed by Hindus, who were also vegetarian, and who were in turn succeeded by Moslems – who brought with them a totally new set of dietary customs, though not necessarily different seasonings or cooking styles. Chinese migrants, who settled in increasing numbers after the beginning of the fifteenth century, brought with them their own flavourings and cooking methods. Indonesia and Malaysia share a cultural inheritance with a common language and similar cuisines, with regional variations. The two countries had close, continuing contacts with Europeans from the sixteenth century onwards – an influence almost entirely lacking in the development of Japanese and Korean cookery.

Two strands of vegetarianism are discernible throughout Far-Eastern cooking: basic survival, as reflected in the diets developed over the centuries by people too poor to be able to afford meat; and the influence of religion – whereby foods and cooking styles were dictated by Buddhist (and Hindu) precepts.

For many people in the West, vegetarianism means meals without meat. This negative concept is in complete contrast to the beliefs of committed Far-Eastern vegetarians, and of most Western whole-food devotees, who regard not eating meat as only one element in a complete system for living. Such a system was first outlined two-and-a-half thousand years ago by Siddharta Gautama – Buddha – whose teachings spread throughout the Far East and beyond and remain influential to the present day. Buddha taught that one should not kill, and by extension that no living animal should be killed for food. Over the centuries, this doctrine was amended in various ways. In the seventh century the Emperor of Japan decreed that the rule relating to meat should be relaxed; a temple record from that time reads, 'If you buy meat, pray to Buddha and then you will be free from sin'. Similar dispensations setting a level of sinfulness according to the type of animal killed and the manner of its killing exist in Burma today, where a shrimp or fish attracts little blame while killing a large animal or eating red meat would still be considered wicked.

Modern-day followers of strict Buddhist rules in China, Japan and Korea totally refrain from eating meat; they drink no alcohol and strive through self-awareness for balance and harmony in every aspect of their lives. However, the greatest number of Buddhists are part-time observers – 'Sunday Buddhists' – who consider eating by strict rule more in the light of a spiritual health-cure than as an everyday activity.

Buddhist vegetarian food is not the only style of vegetarian eating in the Far East. In prehistoric times pressures of population forced some communities to become cultivators and therefore vegetable-eaters, while others, perhaps more aggressive, remained hunters and meat-eaters. The dividing line between the rich and poor was drawn early; in the Far East the peasant poor co-existed until about the seventeenth century with the rich hunting nobility. Even today, in many peasant communities vegetarianism is an economic necessity rather than a conscientious restraint. For example, in Indonesia the peasants eat no meat and only a little salted fish on ordinary days, but welcome beef, mutton and chicken on feast days – which occur about twice a month. In Taiwan and Japan, on the other hand, a curious reversal of roles has taken place during the last thirty years whereby orthodox Buddhist vegetarian cooking has become a luxury afforded only by the rich.

The recipes in *Far-Eastern Vegetarian Cooking* represent all the different styles of vegetarian cooking described in this introduction, and on occasion suggestions are made for crossing national or regional boundaries and mixing one style of dish with another from a different culture. In Chapter 3, on meal-planning, the whole question of mixing styles is discussed – because there is nothing to stop you mixing different kinds of Far-Eastern dishes or, for that matter, including them in Western meals. If, on the other hand, you want ethnic authenticity, you can follow the menus and serving traditions described for each of the different cultures.

2

Eastern Vegetables and Spices

So wide is the spectrum of foods covered in the cuisines of the Far East, which for the purposes of this book stretches from Java in the south to northern Hokkaido (Japan), that while some ingredients are common to many, others are strictly local. For this reason, substitutions have been suggested in certain recipes, and dishes have been selected largely according to their ability to translate happily into a Western context. Thus, while there is a wealth of fresh green vegetables in Indonesia, our recipes include only the four which are easily available in the West: Chinese cabbage, spinach, water-spinach and long beans.

When shopping for specialized ingredients in the West, remember that although labels are, generally speaking, consistent in their own language, translations of ingredients' names into English can vary widely. However, most Far-Eastern grocery stores in the West are arranged with open shelves, so you can spend time browsing among the various commodities. Moreover Western people are increasingly welcomed by Eastern grocers, who are usually very glad to help you find what you want.

FRESH VEGETABLES

Green leaves

Chinese broccoli, sometimes called Chinese kale, used in Chinese cooking. This leafy green vegetable has white flowers and a rather tough stem. Sold all the year round in Chinese grocers, it can also sometimes be bought in Western markets. It is not the most delicate of Chinese greens.

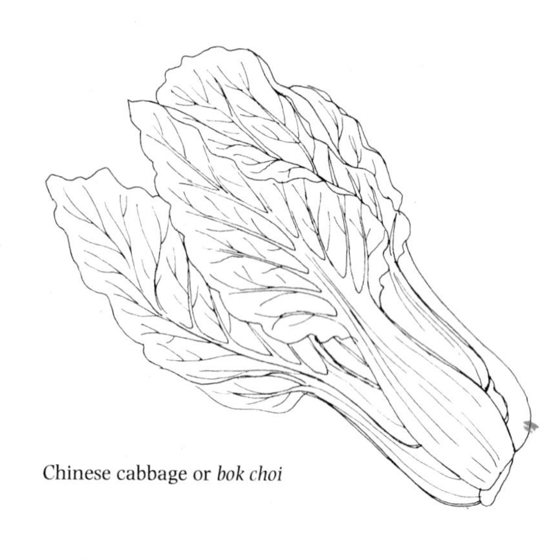

Chinese cabbage or *bok choi*

Chinese cabbage, used in Chinese cooking. These small cabbages are usually known by their Cantonese name *bok choi*. They have dark green leaves and wide white stalks joined near the base of the stem, looking rather like a miniature Swiss chard. The smaller the individual cabbage, the more delicate the flavour.

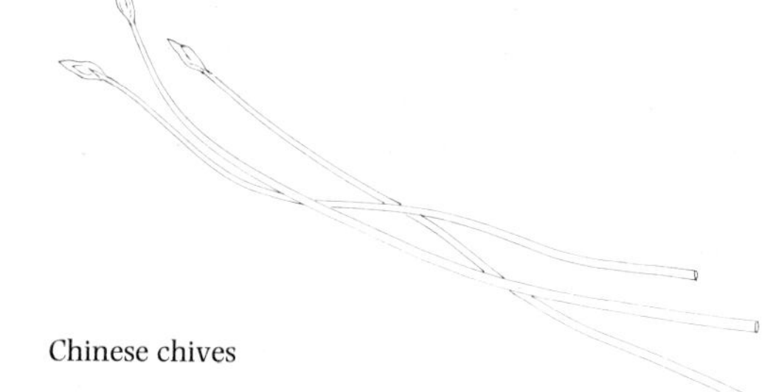

Chinese chives

Chinese chives, used in Chinese cooking. The long green stalks with pointed heads are the flowering stalks of Chinese chives. The leaves of Chinese chives are also sold occasionally in Chinese grocers, either blanched a pale yellow or natural green. They all have a distinctive garlicky flavour. Use the flower heads as a vegetable and the leaves as a seasoning herb. If necessary substitute spring onions or chives and a clove of garlic.

Chinese leaves (Cantonese *bai cai*), used in Chinese, Japanese and Indonesian cooking. This cabbage is a familiar sight in all Western greengrocers, where it is now sold throughout the year. In shape it resembles a cos lettuce, but the light green leaves are thicker and crunchier. Chinese leaves can be kept for several weeks standing upright wrapped in newspaper in a cool, dry place. The thicker, paler-leafed variety is better flavoured than the brighter green, thinner-leafed kind.

Choisam, used in Chinese and Japanese cooking. It is not usually known by its English name of 'oil-seed rape'. This delicately flavoured cabbage has

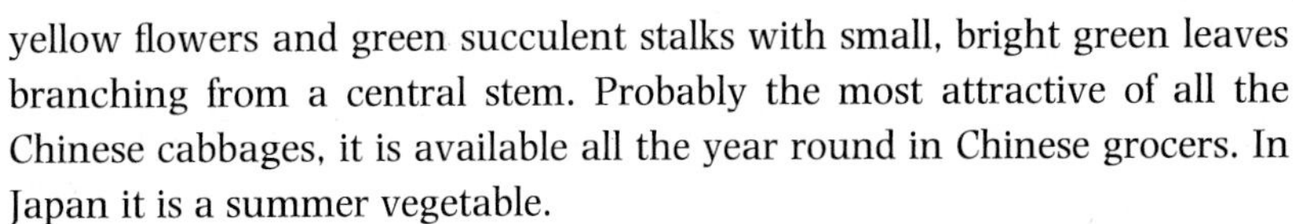

yellow flowers and green succulent stalks with small, bright green leaves branching from a central stem. Probably the most attractive of all the Chinese cabbages, it is available all the year round in Chinese grocers. In Japan it is a summer vegetable.

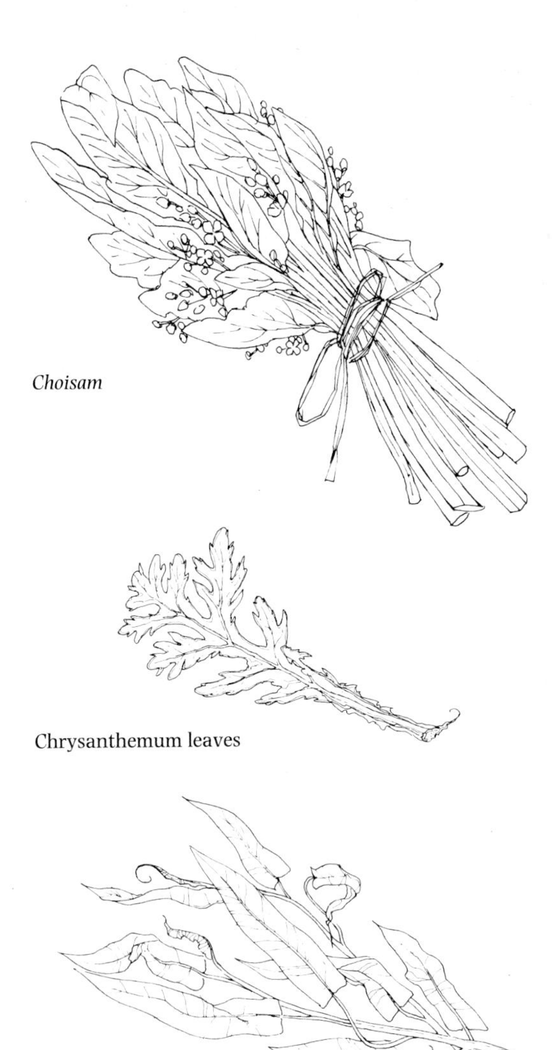

Choisam

Chrysanthemum leaves

Water-spinach

Chrysanthemum leaves, used in Chinese and Japanese cooking. When cooked the leaves of the edible chrysanthemum (*Chrysanthemum coronarium*) resemble spinach in colour and texture, but they have a mildly resinous flavour of their own. They can be bought fresh from Chinese grocers, on occasion, or grown from seed.

Mustard greens, used in Chinese cooking. This rather rank cabbage is occasionally sold fresh during the winter months and as such is strictly soup material. However, it is more usually sold salted (see below).

Purslane, also known as Chinese spinach, used in Chinese cooking. It has either green leaves or green and purple leaves, and is rather like spinach in texture, though a little bit stiffer, with a fresh, leafy flavour.

Spinach, used in Chinese, Japanese and Indonesian cooking. In Japan spinach is picked as a whole, young plant when only about 12 cm (5 inches) tall. It is a form of spinach beet with red stalks, sometimes sold in West Indian markets in the UK as *pallack* spinach. However, it is almost impossible to find fresh, good-quality commercially grown young spinach beet plants on sale in the UK, so substitute either fresh spinach or spinach beet leaves.

Water-spinach, used in Chinese and Indonesian cooking. This variety of spinach is grown on damp or swampy lands everywhere in South East Asia. Sold occasionally throughout the year in Chinese grocers, it has thin, pointed green leaves and hollow stems that remain crunchy when cooked.

Fruit vegetables and gourds

Chayote

Aubergine or eggplant, used in Chinese, Japanese and Indonesian cooking. Chinese and other Far-Eastern aubergines are smaller and sweeter in flavour than the big, purple-black aubergines commonly sold in the West. The usual Chinese variety is thin and light purple in colour, and can sometimes be bought in Chinese grocers. Indian aubergines, which are small, round and bright purple in colour, are commonly sold in Indian grocers. Use whichever kind is available.

Chayote, used in Chinese and Indonesian cooking. This firm, light green gourd with a smooth skin and a soft central pip has very little flavour of its own, but adds an apple-like texture to any dish. There is no need to peel or remove the central pip.

Chillis

Chillis, used in Chinese, Japanese and Indonesian cooking. Several varieties of fresh chilli are sold in the UK, ranging from large, matt-skinned West African chillis with a mild flavour to tiny, shiny-skinned Indian chillis with a fiery heat. Generally speaking, in the UK the sweeter ripe (red) chillis are less often sold than the sharper-flavoured unripe (green) ones. Choose your chillis accordingly, to taste.

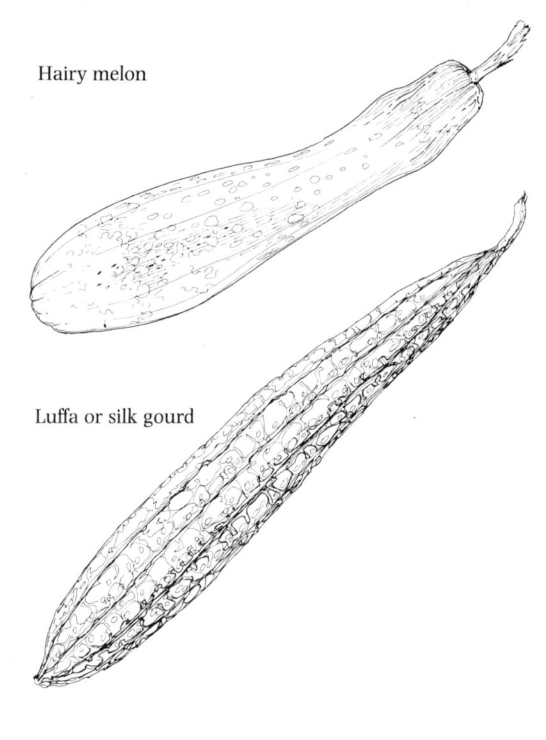

Hairy melon

Luffa or silk gourd

Hairy melon, used in Chinese cooking. These melons, shaped rather like round-ended cucumbers, are a small variety of winter melon, which they resemble in texture and taste. However, their skins are lightly coated with short hairs, and they are about one-eighth the size of a winter melon.

Luffa, or silk gourd, used in Chinese and Indonesian cooking. This dark green gourd has marked ridges running along its length, and as it ages these ridges become more marked and the flavour more bitter. Before using, scrape the edges of the ridges to remove the tough rim.

Mange-tout or snow peas, used in Chinese and Japanese cooking. As the name suggests these bright green, flat pea pods are eaten whole, and add both colour and flavour to soups and simmered dishes.

Persimmons, sometimes called Sharon fruit, used in Chinese and Japanese cooking. These bright orange fruits with smooth skins look rather like tomatoes. They have recently become common during mid-winter in the UK. When ripe their flesh is jelly-like and very sweet.

Winter melon, sometimes called wax gourds, used in Chinese cooking. These large, oval-shaped gourds can weigh up to 20 kg (40 lb), and are usually sold whole. The flesh has a very light flavour, and a marvellous texture which becomes transparent when cooked. They are an expensive vegetable, but when cut can be kept in the refrigerator covered in clingwrap for up to a week.

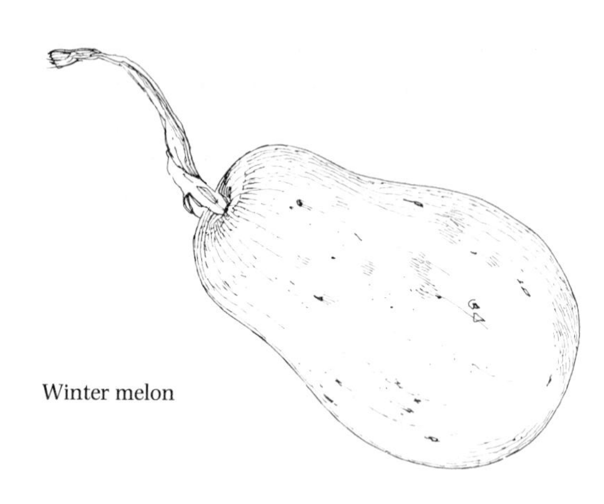

Winter melon

Root vegetables

Burdock, used in Japanese cooking. This long, thin-rooted plant grows wild in the UK but in Japan is cultivated as a vegetable. In form and flavour it is similar to scorzonera and salsify, to which it is related. The distinctive flavour is sometimes said to resemble oysters. Always peel burdock under water to prevent it turning black, and place immediately in acidulated water – 600 ml (1 pint) water and the juice of half a lemon – until required. Substitute either scorzonera or salsify.

Lotus root

Lotus root, used in Chinese and Japanese cooking. This is the jointed tuber of the water-lily, with regularly arranged air spaces running down the length of each section. When fresh it makes a crunchy addition to *tempura.* Peel and slice before cooking. It is sold either fresh or canned in Chinese grocers (use canned for simmered dishes).

Sweet potato, used in Chinese and Japanese cooking. Two varieties are widely available in the UK. One is purple-skinned and orange-fleshed, and is sometimes known as a Louisiana yam, and the other, more floury in texture, is pink-skinned and white-fleshed.

White radish or mooli, used in Chinese and Japanese cooking. These long white roots, looking like overgrown carrots, have a mildly peppery flavour and, when raw, a crunchy texture. Cooked white radish gives body and substance to a dish. When boiling it, change to fresh boiling water after 5 minutes to remove any residual bitterness. White radish is widely available in the West, sometimes marketed as rettish.

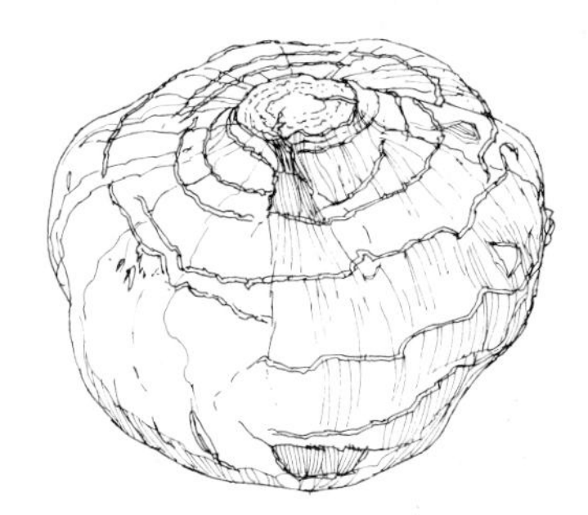

Yam bean

Yam bean, used in Chinese cooking. A light brown, disc-like tuber with strongly marked segments, it has a pleasingly crunchy flesh and can be used in place of bamboo shoots. It is sold fresh during the winter in Chinese grocers.

Yam (called *tarro* in Chinese cooking), used in Chinese and Japanese cooking. Two kinds of yam are commonly on sale in the UK: one is a big tuber from Brazil and the other, sold as edoes in West Indian markets, is about the size of a small potato, with a scaly, slightly fibrous skin. Large yams are cut and sold in portions in West Indian markets in the UK.

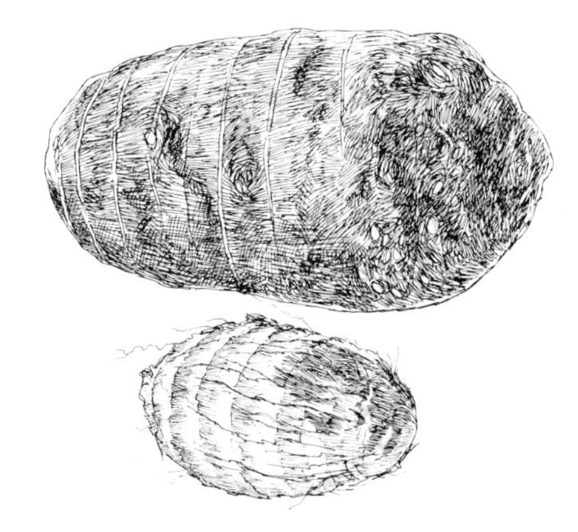

Yam (above) and edoes (below)

DRIED, PRESERVED AND CANNED VEGETABLES

Chinese medlars, also called wolf berries, used in Chinese cooking. These small dried red berries have a bitter-sweet flavour and are expensive.

Dried melon strips, used in Chinese and Japanese cooking. Strips of dried winter melon are used for tying various 'rolled' foods. The Japanese variety is bleached and highly processed; the strips need rubbing with salt and boiling for 10 minutes in clean water before use. The Chinese variety, which is coarser and not bleached, needs only soaking in hot water.

Red dates, used in Chinese cooking. These crinkled, red dried fruits are from the Chinese jujube tree, not a date palm. They need soaking for 3–4 hours before cooking slowly.

Konnyaku, used in Japanese cooking. This is not really a vegetable, but a jelly prepared from a type of sweet potato. It is sold fresh in Japanese food shops and can be kept in cold water for about a week (at most), providing the water is changed each day. Before using, boil in fresh water for 3 minutes, then dry in a pan over moderate heat.

Lily buds or golden needles, used in Chinese cooking. These are the dried flower buds of the tiger lily, and have a slightly acrid taste. Soak for 30 minutes in hot water before using. Traditionally each is tied in a knot before being cooked.

Lily bulb petals, used in Chinese vegetarian cooking. These are the dried petals of the lotus flower. Soak the creamy-coloured small flakes for 30 minutes in hot water before using.

Pickled bamboo shoots, used in Chinese cooking. These preserved bamboo shoots have a pleasant, tangy sour taste which goes particularly well with hot and sour soup. Rinse in fresh water, then blanch in boiling water several times to lessen the sour flavour before using.

Pickled sour plums, used in Chinese and Japanese cooking. These are Japanese apricots preserved in brine. They have a dry sour flavour and are used to flavour rice and other foods.

Pickles, used in Japanese meals. Many kinds of commercially prepared pickled vegetables (Japanese *tsukemono*) are sold in Japanese grocers in the UK, including ones made with cucumbers, aubergines, perilla buds, ginger threads, and snow cabbage. Sold in small packets, they are not expensive and will keep for a long time after opening.

Sichuan preserved vegetable, used in Chinese cooking. This is the preserved club stalk of a variety of cabbage which has a peppery flavour of its own. Its taste is enhanced by the use of spices. Usually sold in cans, it can be removed and stored in the refrigerator in a covered container; it will keep for months. Rinse and slice as required.

Bamboo shoots, used in Chinese and Japanese cooking. The best-quality bamboo is the first growth of shoots which break through the earth early in the new year and is known as winter bamboo. Ordinary bamboo is less tender. Both qualities are sold, canned, in the West.

Baby corn cobs, used in Chinese, Japanese and Indonesian cooking. Sold mostly in cans, baby corn cobs are used as a specialist or novelty food, mainly for appearance. They were developed commercially about 30 years ago in Taiwan, which is still the prime source. They need little cooking and can even be eaten straight from the can.

Mustard greens, used in Chinese cooking. This pickled cabbage is usually sold canned but can sometimes be bought loose. It has more stalk than leaf, with a sour flavour and a firm texture. Once opened, immerse in brine – 600ml (1 pint) water to 10ml (2 teaspoons) salt – and store uncovered in the refrigerator.

Red-in-snow, also called snow cabbage or pickled cabbage, used in Chinese cooking and in Japan for making pickles. It is always sold salted and canned in the West. Take care not to add any salt to a dish which contains red-in-snow. Soak for 4 minutes in cold water to remove some of the salt before using. Once opened, it can be kept in a clean container in the refrigerator for about a week.

Water chestnuts, used in Chinese cooking. These small white rounds have a crisp, nutty flavour. They can sometimes be bought fresh, but are more usually sold canned in the West. Once opened, drain, seal in polythene bags and deep-freeze, or keep in water in the refrigerator, boiling every two days in fresh water.

SEAWEEDS

Agar-agar, used in Chinese and Japanese cooking. A vegetable form of gelatine, made from seaweed, it is transparent, colourless and tasteless. In its Chinese form it is sold in skeins like crepe knitting wool, in its Japanese form in blocks or powder. Both the blocks and the strips need soaking in hot water to soften.

Kelp (Japanese *konbu*), used in Chinese and Japanese cooking. These long fronds of dried seaweed have a mildly iodine flavour when cooked. Use in salads and other dishes in Chinese cooking, and as a flavouring and for stock-making in Japanese cooking.

Nori, used in Chinese and Japanese cooking, is a type of laver. Known as purple vegetable in its Chinese form, it is processed into round sheets with a roughish texture and used only in soups. Japanese *nori* is processed into square, paper-thin sheets, dark green in colour. To bring out the best of its flavour, toast over a high flame for about 5 seconds. Once the packet is opened, keep in an airtight container.

Wakame, used in Japanese cooking. A seaweed with long, thin fronds joined by a tough rim, *wakame* is sold either salted or dried in the UK. When soaked, it greatly increases in size. See page 36 for preparation.

NUTS AND SEEDS

Coconut, used in Indonesian cooking. In Indonesia these hairy brown nuts are the source of both cooking oil and the 'cream' (*santan*) which enriches many dishes. Sold widely in supermarkets as well as Indian grocers, they are available fresh throughout the year, although how fresh is sometimes questionable. See pages 41–2 for making *santan*.

Ginko nuts, used in Chinese and Japanese cooking. These fleshy nuts are occasionally sold fresh in the UK. They should be cracked open and the inner skin removed by dipping in boiling water. Fresh ginko nuts turn a beautiful green when cooked, and have a delicate nutty flavour. Canned ginko nuts, sometimes called white nuts, are cream in colour and have little flavour. Once opened they can be kept in the refrigerator, as long as the water is changed every other day.

Macadamia nuts, sometimes called candle nuts, used in Indonesian cooking. These nuts have a sharp, rather bitter flavour. They are sold dry in small packets in specialist Indonesian and Malaysian stores in the UK. If necessary substitute brazil nuts or almonds.

Peanuts, also known as ground nuts, used in Chinese and Indonesian cooking. Always skinned and usually cooked by deep-frying, peanuts are used to make sauces in Indonesian cooking and for texture and additional nutritional value or as a garnish in Chinese dishes. Peanut butter can be used instead of peanuts in making some Indonesian sauces; use approximately 15 ml (1 tablespoon) peanut butter for 25 g (1 oz) peanuts. Many Chinese prefer oil made from peanuts to other types of cooking oil.

Poppy seeds, used in Japanese cooking; tiny, they are sometimes toasted for use as a garnish.

Pine kernels, used in Chinese cooking. These small, long white seeds, which feature in both sweet and savoury dishes, can be bought at western nut stalls and health-food stores. They are best deep-fried before being included in a dish.

Sesame seeds, used in Chinese and Japanese cooking. Both black and white sesame seeds can be used, although white seeds are more usually used for nut pastes and in Chinese cooking. Sesame seeds should be toasted in a dry pan over a moderate heat until they start to change colour and to 'dance'. They can then be either ground into a paste or used whole. Sesame paste can be substituted for freshly ground sesame seeds, but the flavour is never as good.

FUNGI

Dried mushrooms, used in Chinese and Japanese cooking. Several varieties of dried mushrooms are now on sale in the West. Some are more delicate in flavour and firmer in texture than others. All are expensive. The very best Chinese dried mushrooms have brown, crazed caps and thick, curved gills, while another, less delicate variety has uncrazed black caps and flatter gills (these are perfectly acceptable for most dishes). All kinds of dried mushroom need rinsing well and soaking in warm water for 30 minutes. The soaking water can be used as a stock.

Black fungus, used in Chinese and Japanese cooking. Two main varieties of black fungus are sold in the West. Wood ears, or *muer*, are the biggest and coarsest in texture, black on one side and velvety grey on the other. Black fungus is thinner, in smaller pieces and almost transparent. Both lend a crunchy texture and slightly smoky flavour to a dish. Before using, soak for 20 minutes in warm water, then rinse well.

Black hair, used in Chinese cooking. This costly, hair-like fungus, sold in small packets, is used in traditional vegetarian cooking. Soak in warm water for 20 minutes, then rinse well. Once opened, it keeps well in a dry place.

Golden needle mushrooms, used in Chinese and Japanese cooking. These tiny-headed, long-stemmed mushrooms cannot be bought fresh in the UK, but are sold in packets, preserved in brine. Rinse before using. They do not belong to the mainstream of Chinese cooking, but have been widely used in Japan and Taiwan for soups and one-pot dishes during this century. They need almost no cooking.

Oyster mushroom, or abalone mushrooms, used in Chinese cooking. These fleshy mushrooms are sold fresh during the late summer in specialist food-shops in the UK. They can also be bought, preserved in brine, in small packets from Chinese grocers. Rinse and use as directed.

Silver wood ears

Silver wood ears, sold in packets labelled 'dry white jelly fungus' and used in Chinese cooking. The yellowish transparent bundles of thin leaves expand dramatically when soaked for 30 minutes in warm water. Discard the hard, discoloured centres and use as directed.

Straw mushrooms, used in Chinese cooking. Sold only in cans in the West, these almost ball-shaped mushrooms with their enclosed stalks have a delicate woodland flavour.

EGGS

Preserved duck eggs, used in Chinese cooking. These, the so-called '100-year-old' eggs, are closer to six weeks old. Inside the egg white is a dark, transparent jelly; the yolk is solid and greenish-black in colour. There may be a slight smell of ammonia when the shell is first peeled off, but this will quickly evaporate.

Salted eggs, used in Chinese cooking. These can be either hens' or ducks' eggs. Preserved in brine, they have a sooty black coating and a salty, slightly astringent flavour. Wash off the black soot carefully before use.

BEANS AND BEANCURD

Long beans, used in Chinese and Indonesian cooking. These green beans, which grow to about 50cm (18 inches) long and are nearly cylindrical in shape, have a fresh, crunchy texture and a delicate flavour. Widely grown in the Far East, they are sold fresh in Chinese grocers. Substitute French beans.

Soya beansprouts (above) and mung beansprouts

Mung beansprouts, used in Chinese, Japanese and Indonesian cooking. These beansprouts do not have the intensity of flavour of the soya beansprouts, and are much more delicate in texture. They are preferred by Indonesian cooks for salads. Sold fresh in most Western supermarkets, they do not keep well. Growing instructions are given on pages 140–1.

Silk noodles, or peastarch noodles, used in Chinese, Japanese and Korean cooking. Made from mung beans, these transparent, wiry noodles are served as a vegetable, not a staple, in Chinese cooking. Cut to the required length, then soak in hot water for 10 minutes. Use as directed.

Soya beans, used in Chinese, Japanese and Indonesian cooking. Round yellow beans, they are used for a variety of preparations but seldom eaten as beans. Always sold dried in the UK.

Soya beansprouts, used in Chinese cooking. About double the size of the more common mung beansprouts, they have a strong, nutty flavour and crisp texture. Available from Chinese grocers, they will keep for several days in the refrigerator. They are used particularly for making the best vegetarian stock. For growing instructions see pages 140–1.

Fermented black beans, used in Chinese and Indonesian cooking. These fermented soya beans turn black and have a strong, salty flavour. Sold in packets, they keep for years in the refrigerator.

Natto, used in Japanese cooking. These soya beans, fermented and sticky with a hint of decay in their flavour, are not to everyone's taste. Eaten with rice and *nori* for breakfast or as a salad dressing, they are sold frozen in small packets in Japanese food stores.

Yellow beans, or salted soya beans, used in Chinese and Indonesian cooking. Whole yellow soya beans are preserved in soy sauce, or sometimes crushed into a yellow-bean sauce. The whole beans are better flavoured and a jar of yellow beans keeps for years in the refrigerator. Drain and mash as directed in the recipe.

Beancurd, or *tofu*, used in Chinese, Japanese, Korean and Indonesian cooking. Beancurd in all its forms is made from soya beans. Standard Chinese beancurd, which is lightly pressed, is sold fresh in most Chinese grocers by the square. Use this kind in Chinese and Indonesian recipes. It can be kept for up to 5 days if stored in a cool place immersed in cold water, which should be changed daily. Japanese cotton beancurd (*tofu*), firmer than standard Chinese beancurd, is sold fresh in some Western health-food shops and can be kept in the same way. Silk beancurd (unpressed beancurd) is used particularly for soups. Sold in long-life packets from Japan, it can be kept unopened for several months.

Freeze-dried beancurd, used in Japanese cooking. These squares of beancurd are sold in packets in Japanese grocers and will keep for at least 9 months.

Aburage, used in Japanese cooking. These are flat cakes of deep-fried beancurd, which can be bought ready-made in Japanese grocers in the UK. They can be kept for a short time in the freezer without deteriorating, but quickly go bad in the refrigerator.

Dried beancurd sheets and sticks, used in Chinese cooking. (The Japanese use fresh beancurd skin, but this is not available in the West.) Flat sheets are made from the skin which forms on top of boiling soya milk. This is dried either in sticks or as flat sheets. Soften the sheets by soaking in warm water for about 7 minutes before using; soak the sticks overnight in water. Dried beancurd skin needs cooking for some time before it loses its leathery texture.

Fermented beancurd, used in Chinese cooking. These cubes of beancurd have been mixed either with lees of wine to make red beancurd, or with chillis, sesame oil and salt. A cube of either kind can be used as a relish with rice; alternatively, the juice from red beancurd can be cooked with vegetables to give extra flavour. Red beancurd is sold in earthenware jars and improves in taste with keeping.

FARINACEOUS PRODUCTS

Rice, used in Chinese, Japanese, Korean and Indonesian cooking. A long-grained rice (Indica) is the most commonly eaten rice in southern China and Indonesia, while a stickier, short-grained rice (Japonica) is popular in eastern China, Japan and Korea. (Use short-grained American Rose rice, *not* pudding rice, as a substitute for Japonica.) Always use short-grained rice for *sushi.*

Glutinous rice, used in Chinese, Japanese and Korean cooking. This round-grained, matt white rice, grown mainly for wine-making, is much stickier when cooked than ordinary rice, and is used for both sweet and savoury celebration dishes.

Rice noodles, used in Chinese cooking. These dried white noodles made from rice flour, sometimes called rice vermicelli, come in various thicknesses from fine round strings to flat ribbons. Soften in warm water and use as directed.

Wheat flour, strong white flour, with a 12 per cent protein content, and plain white or cake flour, with 9 per cent protein, are used for gluten dishes as well as for bread buns.

Gluten, used in Chinese and Japanese cooking, is the protein constituent of wheat flour. It creates the spongy texture in breads, by virtue of the elastic networks it forms in the dough when water is added to flour. It can be separated from the starch in flour by washing and then used as a vegetable protein.

Dried Japanese gluten is sold in the UK in flat cakes. Chinese gluten is not dried. (See pages 92–3.)

Wheat starch, used in Chinese cooking. The dry, powdered starch remaining when the protein has been removed from wheat flour is used for thickening sauces.

Noodles, used in Chinese and Japanese cooking. The Chinese use egg noodles and plain noodles made from wheat flour. These are sold both fresh and dried. Japanese noodles (*udon*) are very white and fine, made from bleached white flour with no egg in them. *Udon* noodles vary in thickness: flat ribbons about 5 mm thick are called *kishimen*; *udon* (used here as a specific name rather than a generic) are about 2.5 mm thick; the finest *hyamugi* is 1.5 mm thick and the finest *somen* about 1 mm thick.

Buckwheat noodles, used in Chinese and Japanese cooking. Called *soba* in Japan, these slightly grey noodles made from buckwheat have a pleasing, peppery taste. They are sold dried in some health-food stores as well as in Japanese grocers. A green-coloured *soba*, called *cha soba*, is flavoured with tea.

Kudzu flour, used in Japanese cooking. This very fine flour is used for dry-dusting foods before they are deep-fried and for thickening sauces. It is sold in packets in Japanese grocers. Substitute arrowroot.

Potato flour, used in Chinese cooking. A very fine white flour, sold in Chinese grocers, which makes a smooth, non-sticky thickening for sauces and soups. Take care to dilute well and mix in completely before bringing to the boil.

COMMERCIALLY PREPARED FLAVOURINGS AND SAUCES

Barbecue sauce, used in Chinese cooking. Two varieties of barbecue sauce are sold in the UK. One, made with soya beans, sugar and vinegar, comes from southern China and is also called *hoisin* sauce. The other, made without vinegar, comes from eastern and northern China and is also called sweet bean sauce. Substitute one for the other as available.

Chilli-bean sauce, used in Chinese cooking, particularly Sichuan. A very hot bean sauce, it is made from soya beans, chillis and garlic. Take care not to overheat when cooking or the flavour will become acrid.

Chilli oil, used in Chinese cooking. This fiery hot oil can be made at home by stir-frying 3–4 dried chillis in 30 ml (2 tablespoons) oil over a moderate heat for about 3 minutes. Strain and use as required; this oil will not keep. Commercially-made chilli oil (which can be kept) often still has the chillis in it.

Coconut milk (*santan*), used in Indonesian cooking. Sold in cans, this 'milk' is thicker than the *santan* made from fresh coconuts or dried coconut at home. Dilute as required. Once opened, it will not keep.

Creamed coconut, used in Indonesian cooking. Pure creamed coconut is unsweetened and sold in blocks rather like lard in Chinese and some Western supermarkets. Use as directed on page 42 to make *santan*, or add directly to sauces just before serving.

Mirin, used in Japanese cooking. This is a sweet, almost syrupy rice wine specially brewed for cooking.

Miso, used in Japanese and Korean cooking. This highly nutritious bean paste is made by fermenting soya beans with rice or barley, depending on the variety. It comes in four basic types, and there are many different brands of each type. White *miso* made with rice mould as a ferment is light in colour. Red *miso*, made with a barley ferment, is darker in colour and saltier in flavour. *Hatcho miso*, made only from soya beans, can range in flavour from sweet to salty, and is very dark in colour. There is also a very sweet white *miso* called *kyomiso*. Used in classic Japanese cooking, it is dark cream in colour and is made with a rice mould. The different brands of *miso* vary in degrees of saltiness, so always check and adjust the seasoning of any dish to which you have added *miso*. *Miso* keeps for a long time in the refrigerator. It can be bought in Japanese and Chinese food stores as well as in Western health-food stores.

Rice wine, used in Chinese cooking. Usually made from glutinous rice, this rather coarse-flavoured fortified wine, about 16° proof, is used for both cooking and drinking. Warm to blood heat and dissolve crystal sugar in it to taste before drinking.

Sake, used in Japanese cooking. *Sake* is Japanese rice wine, more refined and with less flavour than Chinese rice wine. (Indonesians, being Moslems, do not use wine in cooking.) Used for drinking as well as cooking, *sake* should be warmed in a carafe in hot water before being served (unsweetened) in tiny glasses.

Sesame oil, used in Chinese and Korean cooking. This nutty-flavoured, delicate oil with a low smoking point is used both for cooking and as a final seasoning. Take care not to overheat or the flavour will spoil.

Sesame paste, used in Chinese cooking. Made from crushed sesame seeds, this is an oily, nutty-flavoured paste with a distinctly smoky overtone. *Tahina*, the Greek sesame paste, can be substituted.

Soy sauce, used in Chinese, Japanese, Korean and Indonesian cooking. This is the basic cooking sauce for both the Chinese and the Japanese cuisine, and is made from soya beans. The best varieties are naturally fermented and then matured for several months. Chinese dark soy – labelled 'soy superior sauce' on bottles from China – is a heavy, richer-flavoured soy sauce. Mushroom soy sauce, a variety of dark soy sauce brewed with mushrooms as well as soya beans, is a good all-purpose soy sauce. Light soy sauce is saltier and lighter in colour than dark soy. It is labelled 'superior soy'. Japanese and Korean soy sauces are thinner and lighter than Chinese ones; the best-known brand in the West is Kikkoman. In Indonesian and Malaysian cooking a dark soy sauce called *kecap manis* and a light soy sauce called *kecap asin* are both used. *Kecap manis* is much sweeter than its Chinese equivalent, and is made with sugar. *Kecap manis* can be bought in some Eastern grocers in the UK; Chinese soy sauce may be substituted.

Tamarind juice, used in Indonesian cooking. Extracted from tamarind pods, it is diluted 1 to 4 with water. Otherwise use tamarind paste (overleaf).

Tamarind paste, used in Indonesian cooking. Blocks of the flesh, fibres and seeds of tamarind pods are sold in Far-Eastern and Indian grocers in the UK. From this is made tamarind juice, a fruity, mildly acidic liquid which is used instead of vinegar in many Indonesian recipes. Instructions for making tamarind juice are given on page 42.

Vinegars, used in Chinese and Japanese cooking. Most vinegars used in Chinese and Japanese cooking are made from rice. White rice vinegar, a colourless, mild-flavoured vinegar, is the standard Japanese vinegar, also used in Chinese cooking. Black vinegar, also made from rice, is very dark in colour but much less astringent than Western malt vinegars. It is used in Chinese cooking. Red vinegar, or red vinegar sauce, is a spicy sweet vinegar used in Chinese cooking.

Wasabi mustard, used in Japanese cooking. This is a hot, fragrant green paste. It can be bought either ready-made in tubes or as a powder to mix with water, when required (as for English mustard). Ready-made *wasabi* does not keep its flavour long once opened and should be kept in the refrigerator.

SEASONINGS

Basil, used in Chinese and Japanese cooking. Fresh sweet basil can be grown from seeds or bought as a herb in summer. Dried basil is not a satisfactory substitute for fresh basil.

Cinnamon stick or bark, used in Chinese and Indonesian cooking. Both the rolled thin sheets and the thicker pieces of bark are milder in flavour than Western powdered cinnamon.

Citrus leaf, or lime leaf, used in Indonesian cooking. Dried leaves (occasionally fresh, too) with a lemony tang can be bought in specialist Indonesian shops. Substitute bay leaves.

Chilli powder or cayenne pepper, used in Indonesian cooking.

Coriander leaves, used in Chinese and Indonesian cooking. Fresh coriander leaves resemble flat-leaved parsley in shape but have a distinctive sour aroma. It is sold fresh in bunches in Indian grocers, usually complete with its roots, and in some supermarkets. Store in water in light as you would a bunch of flowers *or* remove the roots, rinse, dry and deep-freeze. When required, crumble while still frozen into sauces, etc. Frozen coriander may not be used as a garnish. Indonesians often prefer the flat-leaved Italian parsley to coriander. See also *mitsuba.*

Coriander powder, used in Indonesian cooking. Included as one spice among others in curries, it has a clean, fresh flavour.

Crystal sugar, used in Chinese cooking. This sugar comes in lumps of varying sizes, and gives a syrupy, rather unctuous consistency to sauces. It is not as sweet as Western refined sugar. The Japanese use refined caster sugar for most of their cooking.

Cumin, used in Indonesian cooking. This is a pungent, rather astringent powdered spice used in curries.

Dried orange peel, used in Chinese cooking. Usually made from tangerine peel, dried orange peel gives a unique sweet-sour taste to any dish. Use in small quantities, and soak for 20 minutes in warm water to soften before slicing finely. Substitute thinly pared fresh tangerine or orange peel.

Fennel seeds, used in Chinese cooking. Use either the seeds or the powder to flavour slow-cooked foods.

Five-spice powder, used in Chinese cooking. This powdered spice is a blend of star anise, fennel, cinnamon, cloves and Sichuan pepper. Use very sparingly.

Shoot ginger and ginger

Ginger, used in Chinese and Japanese cooking. Fresh root ginger is used for seasoning many types of dishes. The knobbly rhizomes are a light brown colour, and when fresh have a shiny skin. Keep in a cool, dry place. It is also sometimes possible to buy fresh young ginger, the shoots of which are too immature to have formed a skin; particularly delicate in flavour, this is the best type of ginger to use for pickles. Powdered ginger may not be substituted for fresh ginger.

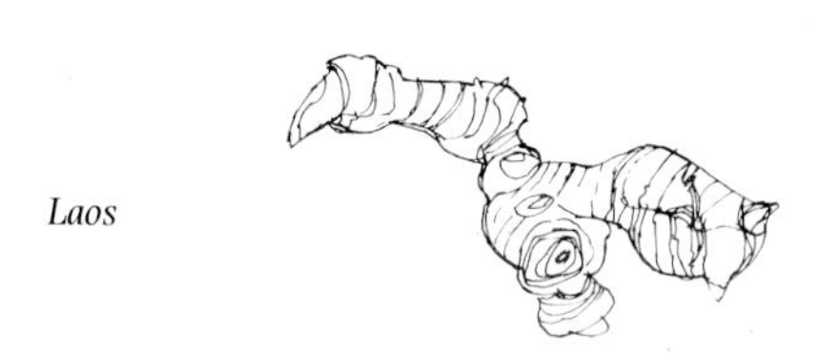

Laos

Laos, used in Indonesian cooking. Sometimes called galingale, it is related to ginger, the form of which it resembles, but *laos* has a sharper and hotter flavour with something of a bite to it. Available fresh on occasion in Chinese and Indonesian shops. Peel and slice before use. Substitute fresh ginger.

Laos powder, used in Indonesian cooking. This is not as hot as fresh *laos*, but is rather bitter in flavour. Use very sparingly. Substitute slices of ginger.

Lemon grass, used in Indonesian cooking. This flavouring, which imparts a lemony tang to dishes, can be bought fresh, dried in small flakes, or in powdered form. Since very little is used at any one time either the dried flakes or the powder, both of which keep well, would be the best buy.

Mitsuba (trefoil), used in Japanese cooking. This bright green herb, belonging to the parsley family, has a flavour somewhat similar to a rather bitter celery. Trefoil is not available in the UK. Possible substitutes are coriander or parsley, though both are very different in flavour if not in form.

Monosodium glutamate (MSG), used in Chinese and Japanese cooking. This traditional Chinese flavour-intensifier has been given a very bad press in the West during recent years, yet MSG is included in a large number of commercially prepared foods sold in the UK. Traditionally, MSG is made by acid hydrolysis of soya beans and other plants. Naturally made, it is a completely harmless amino acid; however, if synthetically produced it may contain some substances which cannot be absorbed by some people. As it is a traditional element of the seasoning spectrum of Buddhist and other vegetarian food in China, its use is recommended (unless it is known to disagree with the diner) in vegetarian soups, where it will impart a richness of flavour that cannot otherwise be matched in a vegetable stock. MSG is usually present in Japanese soy sauces.

Onion flakes, used in Indonesian cooking. Use Western dried onion flakes to make thin slices of fried onion, a standard garnish for Indonesian dishes. (See page 42.)

Sansho pepper, used in Japanese cooking as a dip or final seasoning. This pungent, rather sour powder from the seed-pods of the prickly ash is sold in Japanese grocers. It is used mainly with fried or grilled foods.

Shiso leaves, used in Japanese cooking. Also called the beef-steak plant, *shiso* is a small herb with bright green leaves and a sharp, slightly minty flavour. Sweet basil or mint may be substituted for flavour, but fresh *shiso* leaves are also used to garnish and decorate many Japanese dishes. *Perilla ocimoides* (the beef-steak plant) can be grown from seed.

Sichuan peppercorns, used in Chinese cooking. These are from the native Chinese pepper plant, and are spicier and less hot than black pepper. The dried calyx and seed look rather like a brown clove. Grind in a Western pepper mill. To make salt-pepper dip, put 15 ml (1 tablespoon) sea salt and 7.5 ml (1½ teaspoons) ground Sichuan peppercorns in a saucepan, cook over a moderate heat until they smell good, then use as a dip as directed.

Star anise, used in Chinese cooking, is a star-shaped seedhead resembling fennel in flavour. Use in small quantities.

Togarashi, used in Japanese cooking, is the Japanese version of chilli pepper. One variety, called one-spice pepper, is made with minute flakes, and the seeds, of dried chillis, for which you can substitute chilli powder or cayenne. The other variety is called seven-spice powder, a spicy condiment comprising chilli pepper, black pepper, sesame seeds, poppy seeds, hemp and dried zest of orange peel, powdered *nori*, white pepper and prickly ash. It adds considerable interest to a dish when sprinkled over as a garnish.

Turmeric, used in Indonesian cooking, is a bright yellow spice with a mildly bitter, musty flavour; it gives food a yellow colour.

Yuzu peel, used in Japanese cooking. From a bitter, dry-flavoured orange, this fragrant rind is often used as a garnish or flavouring in Japanese winter dishes. It is sometimes sold frozen in Japanese grocers. Substitute finely pared Seville orange, lemon or lime peel.

TEAS

Chinese black or fermented teas have a full, round flavour, similar to Ceylon tea, and should always be made with boiling water. *Puer* and Fujian *hong cha* are two varieties available in the West. These teas go well with food.

Chinese oolong or half-fermented tea, dark in colour, and rather astringent in flavour. Make with boiling water. 'Gunpowder' is a particular brand of *oolong* sold in the West. This tea also goes well with food.

Chinese green teas, light-coloured and astringent, are a very refreshing drink. Use not-quite-boiling water. These are better not drunk with food.

Chinese flower teas of various kinds, made usually from green or *oolong* tea. Make with not-quite-boiling water. These are best drunk *after* meals.

Japanese bancha, the coarsest grade of Japanese green tea, often drunk with meals. Make with not-quite-boiling water and allow to infuse for only 2 minutes before draining off all the tea from the leaves, otherwise it will become bitter.

Japanese sencha, a superior grade of Japanese green tea usually drunk after a meal. Make with not-quite-boiling water and do not allow to infuse for more than 2 minutes.

Japanese matcha, the green powdered tea used for the tea ceremony.

3

Planning Far-Eastern Meals

Far-Eastern meals have no 'main' courses in the Western sense, but a number of equally ranked dishes that are all served together. There are a few rules of thumb that can be helpful in planning a meal. Always think of it as a whole, and try to arrange for the dishes to complement and contrast with each other. Variations in sauces and levels of seasonings add enormously to the interest of the meal.

It is perfectly possible to combine many of the recipes given in this book with Western meals, either to bring variety to simple family meals or as a novelty at a special dinner. If you are planning a mixed meal of this type, you can of course serve the dishes in courses, avoiding a strongly flavoured starter if you plan to follow it with a more delicately flavoured dish. On the whole, Indonesian dishes, which tend to be highly flavoured, do not fit very happily into most Japanese meals, which are, by contrast, delicately flavoured. However, many of the more highly seasoned Chinese dishes combine well with Indonesian food. We find our families, who like hot food, relish a little Korean *kimchi* with almost any meal, rather than Western pickle.

Almost any stir-fried vegetable (see Chapter 5) can be combined with Western foods, while Japanese salads with their imaginative dressings (ranging from sesame and other nut pastes, creamed beancurd or tangy vinegar and egg mayonnaise to simple blends of soy sauce, rice vinegar and salt) make delicious and unusual side dishes. Japanese tempura, although not a dish to tackle if you want a quick and easy meal, goes well with a Western-style meal. Beancurd and wheat-flour protein both make excellent dishes which can be served in Western meals. We sometimes make Mapo's beancurd (page 80), doubling the quantities for four people, and accompany it with an undressed salad and brown rice, for a meal which is both quick to make and a departure from the usual main courses. For a special occasion lichi and walnut balls would make a very novel dish in a Western-style dinner if you wanted to be adventurous. You could start with a tomato and basil soup, then serve the lichi and walnut balls with crêpes filled with spinach and yoghurt, and baked haricot beans with tomato and onion lightly seasoned with garlic and chilli. You could follow this with fresh fruit poached in red wine, served chilled with almond wafers.

Far-Eastern food takes time to prepare and short-cuts are rarely successful; however, the last-minute cooking is often very quick. Perhaps the hardest thing to do when coping with unfamiliar cooking styles and ingredients is to estimate the time the dishes will take to prepare and cook, and to avoid last-minute panics. We suggest that you start by cooking only one or two unfamiliar dishes at a time.

Choose one hot dish and then, to complement it, select either a cold dish which can be prepared in advance or a hot one which needs no last-minute attention. Add to these a soup and plain rice and you have a basic Far-Eastern meal. When you become more expert, move on to more ambitious menus.

The menus and timetables that follow are offered only as examples of possible combinations of dishes, and to give you some idea of the time it will take to prepare them. They can be followed as they stand, or you can use them to help you plan your own menus. The times given are very approximate, since everyone's circumstances vary, and are meant only as a guideline in planning the preparation of a meal. No time is allowed in the timetables for making stocks or *santan*, washing-up, heating oil or boiling water, nor for collecting the ingredients together or laying tables.

Simple meals of no specific ethnic cuisine

Menu 1

Egg fuyung (page 44: use double quantities for 4 people)
Family aubergines (page 131: use double quantities for 4 people)
Mixed vegetable soup (page 148)
Plain boiled rice

Serve all the dishes together.

TIMETABLE

At least $1\frac{1}{2}$ hours before the meal

- ☐ Wash, cut and soak the aubergines.
- ☐ Wash the rice.
- ☐ Prepare the vegetables for the soup and egg fuyung.
- ☐ Cook the aubergines and leave to cool.

30 minutes before the meal

- ☐ Put the rice on to cook.

10 minutes before the meal

- ☐ Make the soup.
- ☐ Beat the eggs and make the egg fuyung.

Menu 2

Beancurd 'steak' (page 87: use double quantities for 4 people)
Ginger pumpkin (page 70: use double quantities for 4 people)
Three-colour egg soup (page 147)
Plain boiled rice

Serve all the dishes together.

TIMETABLE

At least 1 hour before the meal

- ☐ Press the beancurd.
- ☐ Wash the rice.
- ☐ Prepare the onions, pumpkin and soup vegetables, and the sauce ingredients.

30 minutes before the meal

- ☐ Put the rice on to cook.
- ☐ Put the pumpkin to cook.

10 minutes before the meal

- ☐ Cook the beancurd and keep it warm; make the sauce.
- ☐ Finish the pumpkin.
- ☐ Make the soup.

Menu 3

Curried eggs (page 63)
Red and white salad (page 116: use double quantities for 4 people)
Creamed corn soup (page 151)
Plain rice

Serve all the dishes together.

TIMETABLE

At least $4\frac{1}{2}$ hours before the meal

- ☐ Prepare the salad.

1 hour before the meal

- ☐ Wash the rice.
- ☐ Boil and deep-fry the eggs.
- ☐ Prepare the soup vegetables.
- ☐ Prepare the sauce for the eggs.

30 minutes before the meal

- ☐ Put on the rice.
- ☐ Start cooking the egg sauce.
- ☐ Cook the soup.
- ☐ Add the eggs to the sauce.

Meals which follow national styles

CHINESE FAMILY MEALS

In ancient China grain was food, all other edible substances merely garnishes or luxuries. A good meal had to have both. This feeling for the balance between the two sides of a meal still prevails. A meal of rice, or other grain food, and four dishes is considered ideal (even though there are many in China who could not afford it), together with a thin soup which serves as a drink. In a more elaborate meal, an appetizer of one or two small dishes of vegetables with a vinegar dressing (see Chapter 9) would be included. It does not matter how many people will be eating the meal: the dishes can be made bigger or more rice cooked. The four dishes are chosen for variety of ingredients, size of food pieces, style of cooking and convenience for the cook. All the dishes, including soup and rice are served together. The diners have their own rice bowls, and sometimes their own soup bowls. They help themselves as they please from the serving dishes in the centre of the table. A Chinese meal is a friendly communal affair.

A Chinese family meal for 4

Stir-fried egg and black fungus (page 46)
Ginger spinach salad (page 134)
Silk gourd with mushrooms (page 77)
Stuffed green peppers (page 91)
Three-colour beancurd soup (page 148)
Plain boiled rice (page 154)

TIMETABLE

Two hours before the meal

☐ Prepare and finish the ginger spinach salad.
☐ Make the stuffing for the green peppers.
☐ Prepare all the remaining vegetables; soak the dried black fungus.
☐ Wash the rice.
☐ Make the egg omelette.
☐ Stuff the green pepper pieces.
☐ Prepare all the soup ingredients.

30 minutes before the meal

☐ Put the rice on to cook.

20 minutes before the meal

☐ Cook the silk gourd and mushrooms and keep them warm.
☐ Make the soup and keep it warm in the oven in a serving bowl.
☐ Make the batter for the green peppers; heat the deep fat; deep-fry green peppers.

☐ Finish the stir-fried egg and black fungus.

Serve the four dishes and soup with the rice.

Meals which follow national styles

JAPANESE FAMILY MEALS

A Japanese family meal is very different in style from a Chinese meal. Each diner has his or her individual share of each dish served on a separate plate or bowl. An ordinary Japanese meal has three dishes; one simmered, one a salad, and the last either fried, grilled or steamed. These come to the table as one course together with a *miso* soup – also served in individual soup bowls. In a more formal family meal the Japanese will serve a small *hors d'oeuvre* of vinegared salad (see Chapter 9). Rice in Japanese culture, as in Chinese, is the real food – the other dishes are merely luxuries – and second helpings are available only of rice. Rice is sometimes served separately after the other dishes are finished, with pickles and green tea.

A Japanese family meal for 4

Simmered mixed vegetables with frozen beancurd (page 89)
Spinach and *nori* rolls (page 116)
Egg '*tofu*' (page 103)
White radish and *wakame* soup with *miso* (page 174)
Plain boiled rice (page 154)
Pickles either bought in or made previously
Japanese tea (*bancha*)

Serve the simmered dish, egg tofu *and spinach rolls with the soup. When they are finished serve the rice, pickles and freshly-made Japanese tea (see page 25).*

TIMETABLE

Well in advance of the meal

☐ Make the egg *tofu*, and leave to cool.

☐ Prepare the sauce for the *tofu* and leave to cool.

1½ hours before the meal

☐ Wash the rice and leave to stand.

☐ Make the spinach and *nori* rolls, and prepare the dipping sauce.

☐ Prepare the vegetables for the soup and simmered dish.

☐ Par-boil the carrots and snow peas.

30 minutes before the meal

☐ Put the rice on to cook.

☐ Finish and cook the simmered vegetables and beancurd, and keep warm.

☐ Arrange the pickles on separate dishes.

☐ Make the soup.

Meals which follow national styles

INDONESIAN FAMILY MEALS

The style of Indonesian family meals varies greatly between the towns and the countryside. In the big towns in Java, where on the whole people are more prosperous, even a family meal may start with freshly grilled *satay* bought from a hawker passing in the street. These hawkers carry small charcoal braziers and cook the small skewers of meat to order. They also provide a spicy dipping sauce to eat with them. After the *satay* the meal continues with a range of dishes including some kind of a stew with plenty of gravy and perhaps three other dishes, in addition to rice and a *sambal*. These dishes are always chosen, as in Chinese cuisine, with the aim of providing not only a range of ingredients but also of different cooking styles and levels of seasoning. Simpler family meals are usual in the villages, where rice with a stew and perhaps two smaller side dishes and a *sambal* (hot chilli relish) are the standard meal. These are all served together on large dishes in the centre of the table. The diners help themselves to the dishes as they please and eat the food with a spoon, or with their right hand from their own plates, Indian-style.

An Indonesian family meal for 4

Lodeh of aubergines, string beans and chayote (page 65)
Asinan (soured vegetables, page 114)
Tahu campur (fried beancurd in a spicy sauce, page 84)
Sambal goreng taocoo (eggs in a hot sauce, page 62)
Sambal tomat (tomato-chilli relish, page 138, or bought-in *sambal ulek*)
'Silver and gold' (rice and corn, page 154)

Serve all the hot dishes together with the rice and corn, asinan *and* sambal.

TIMETABLE

Well in advance of the meal
- ☐ Make the tomato *sambal*, unless bought in.
- ☐ Make the *asinan* salad and leave covered in the refrigerator.

2 hours before the meal
- ☐ Prepare all the vegetables.
- ☐ Hard-boil the eggs, cool and shell.
- ☐ Deep-fry the beancurd, potato slices and onion flakes.
- ☐ Prepare the sauce for beancurd.
- ☐ Prepare the seasoning paste for the eggs, and cook.
- ☐ Pre-heat the oven.
- ☐ Prepare the seasoning paste for the *lodeh* and cook.

30 minutes before the meal
- ☐ Put the corn and rice into the oven.
- ☐ Start cooking the *lodeh*.
- ☐ Cook the sauce for the eggs.
- ☐ Arrange the fried beancurd and vegetables on a serving plate.
- ☐ Finish the *lodeh* and keep warm.
- ☐ Finish the eggs and keep warm.
- ☐ Cook the sauce for the beancurd and pour over the arranged dish.

Meals which follow national styles

KOREAN FAMILY MEALS

No ordinary Korean family meal would be vegetarian; there would always be at least one meat dish – usually beef. Therefore the meal we propose is not really authentic, although it follows the framework and style of a Korean meal. The dishes are chosen to represent different cooking methods, as in a Japanese meal. For an ordinary meal four dishes might be served: one simmered, one grilled or stir-fried, one deep-fried and one cold. They are all served together in big dishes in the centre of the table, in the Chinese manner, with only rice and soup in separate bowls. Everybody is provided with a tiny pair of metal chopsticks rather like knitting needles, and a spoon for their soup as well as a small plate for waste items. A Korean meal is never without some *kimchi* (Korean vegetable pickles) and two or three simply cooked vegetable side dishes called *namuru.*

A Korean-style meal for 4

Braised silk noodles (page 77)
Sweet potato balls (page 58)
Mixed vegetable grill (page 56)
Cold beancurd salad (page 132)
Aubergine *kimchi* (page 139)
Mixed vegetable *kimchi* (page 139)
Aubergine *namuru* (page 131)
Cucumber *namuru* (page 130)
Beansprout salad (page 129)
Beancurd and leek soup (page 146)
Plain boiled rice

Serve all the cooked dishes at once with the rice. At the same time, while everyone is eating the other dishes, cook the mixed grill at the table and hand round the freshly grilled vegetables as they are ready.

TIMETABLE

Several days in advance of the meal

- ☐ Prepare the *kimchi.*

Three hours before the meal

- ☐ Prepare the *namuru* and leave to cool.
- ☐ Steam the sweet potatoes and leave to cool.
- ☐ Prepare the egg omelettes for garnish.
- ☐ Prepare all the vegetables.
- ☐ Wash the rice.
- ☐ Prepare the dipping sauce for the mixed grill.

One hour before the meal

- ☐ Arrange the beancurd salad.
- ☐ Soak the dried mushrooms and silk noodles.
- ☐ Arrange the vegetables on a plate for the mixed grill.
- ☐ Prepare the dipping sauce for the fritters.

30 minutes before the meal

- ☐ Put the rice on to cook.
- ☐ Cook the braised silk noodles and keep hot.
- ☐ Cook the fritters and keep hot.
- ☐ Cook the soup.
- ☐ Prepare the grilling ring in the centre of the table.

SERVING AND GARNISHING FAR-EASTERN DISHES

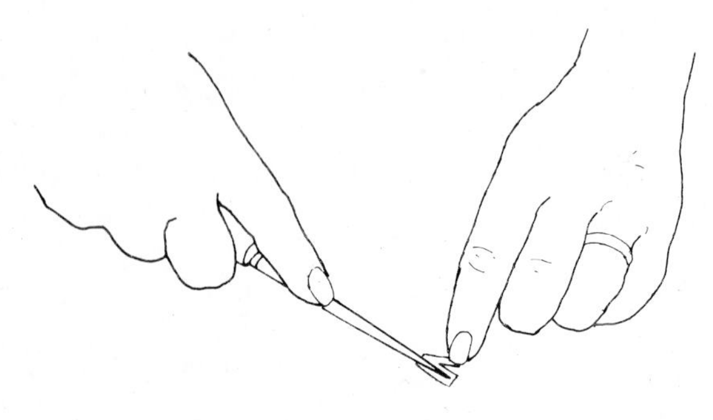

Lemon garnish
1. Make 2 cuts in a thin 1-cm ($\frac{1}{2}$-inch) square of lemon or lime peel as shown.

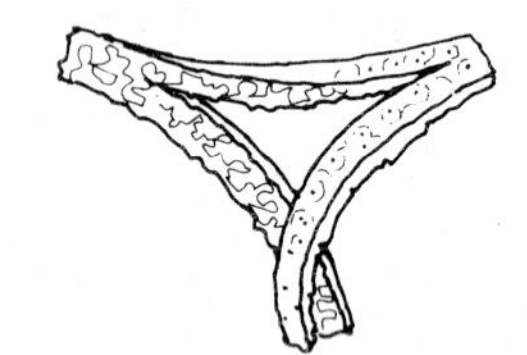

2. Fold into a triangle.

Japanese food is always arranged on individual plates in the kitchen before it comes to the table. Design plays a very big part in the Japanese presentation of food. Attention is given to the shape and form as well as the colour of food, and the plates on which it is served are chosen with care, even for a family meal. Japanese households do not have dinner services as we in the West understand them, but a whole collection of different sets of dishes, bowls and plates of varying sizes and shapes, including oblongs and squares. These are made of a range of materials such as lacquer, wood, roughly glazed pottery and glass as well as porcelain. The cook will select whichever she considers will best suit the food, bearing in mind not only the food itself but also the season of the year and the design of the meal as a whole.

No food is put on to a plate without thought or without appropriate garnish. A curling green leaf may lie beside a piece of beancurd, with perhaps a cone of mustard or grated white radish; a simmered dish may be arranged in a bowl so that the pieces of food lie like a fan, or softer foods, piled up in mounds away from the sides of the bowl, might be sprinkled with sesame seeds or red pepper flakes. *Nori* shreds, *sansho* pepper, shreds of ginger or citrus fruit peel are all used on occasion as a garnish for Japanese dishes. No Japanese plate is ever filled. There must always be space on it as well as food.

Once the meal arrives at the table, there is a formal order for the arrangement of the dishes around the diner – although in family meals this is not usually strictly followed. A formal place setting is described in Chapter 12.

The style of serving Indonesian food is not unlike that of the more familiar Indian foods. The dishes are big, generous and filled to overflowing. The foods on them are arranged rimmed with garnishes such as slices of cucumber and tomato, or scattered with potato crisps and shreds of egg or onion flakes.

Korean food is also served on well-filled plates, with the food very brightly decorated with white and yellow egg threads, shreds of red Korean chillis, coriander and pine kernels. The first impression of any Korean meal is of colour and pattern, often geometric in style.

OPPOSITE *Simmered mixed vegetables and frozen beancurd (Japanese, page 89): airy-textured frozen beancurd cooked with snow peas, carrots and slices of lotus root in soy sauce, sweet wine and stock garnished with shreds of lemon peel.*

DRINKS TO ACCOMPANY MEALS

Alcohol is not usually drunk with ordinary family meals in the Far East. In China the standard family drink is the soup served with the meal. At a special meal, however, where there are guests, a family may serve *huadiao*, a matured Chinese rice wine which is sweetened and warmed to blood heat before being served in tiny cups, or Chinese beer, which is rather like English bitter. In the south of China, tea without milk is frequently served with restaurant meals.

In Japan, tea is usually served either with the meal or at the end of it. However, in well-to-do circles or in family meals at which guests are present it is usual to provide some form of alcohol – either *sake*, Japanese rice spirit, which is drunk warm in tiny cups, or beer, or a Western-type spirit such as whisky.

The Koreans drink rice wine, beer or a tea made from roasted barley and tea, depending on the preference of the family.

In Indonesia, where both tea and coffee are native crops, sweetened tea without milk or sweetened black coffee are usually served with the meal.

If you wish to serve some form of alcoholic drink with an Eastern meal, we suggest either beer or a light dry white wine.

OPPOSITE Kappamaki *(page 119): crisp batons of cucumber surrounded by delicately flavoured* sushi *rice wrapped in sheets of* nori. Norimaki *(page 120): sheets of* nori *rolled round* sushi *rice with a centre of dried mushrooms, egg shreds, melon strips and chrysanthemum leaves.* Inari sushi *(page 121): small pouches of deep-fried beancurd filled with* sushi *rice.*

4

The Basics of Far-Eastern Cookery

The three major cuisines in this book – Chinese, Japanese and Indonesian – have their own national characteristics. Part of the hallmark of each cuisine comes from its specialist ingredients and cooking techniques, without which no cuisine can sustain its identity and authenticity. However, no one has an unlimited store-cupboard of ethnic seasonings, nor an inexhaustible battery of specialist pans and other equipment, so in this chapter we have outlined what we consider are the bare essentials necessary to produce satisfactory results, and what substitutions you can make without sacrificing too much of each cuisine's essential character. (A complete list of all the ingredients used in the recipes appears in Chapter 2.) As you gain experience in East Asian cooking styles you will also accumulate specialist ingredients and equipment which can be used for further experiments. Some ingredients are common to all the cuisines – with minor variations.

This chapter also includes a few recipes for preparing ingredients which, while not basic, appear frequently in recipes throughout the book, together with instructions for cutting and garnishing different styles of dish.

BASIC CHINESE INGREDIENTS

Chinese condiments are now familiar to many of us in the West, and many ordinary supermarkets have a section devoted to a range of Chinese sauces and seasonings.

Soy sauce is basic to Chinese cooking, and without it dishes appear insipid and colourless. There are two varieties of soy sauce; dark soy, which is heavier and more strongly flavoured than light soy, which is saltier, lighter in colour and thinner. Soy sauce is used at every stage in Chinese cooking: in marinades for meats, meat substitutes and steamed dishes; to add flavour to stocks and braises; as a final seasoning in stir-fried dishes; and as a dipping sauce or in a dressing for a salad. It has a rich, savoury flavour and gives a lovely golden colour to foods. There is no substitute.

The Chinese also add small quantities of rice wine to many of their dishes. This both lessens strong flavours and highlights delicate ones. It works particularly well in soups. You can however substitute a dry sherry for rice wine if you wish.

Two other basic Chinese seasonings are ginger and onions, without which it is hard to make dishes taste authentic. Fresh Chinese ginger is sold very widely. It will keep well in a cool, dry place. In Chinese cooking it is sliced, chopped or grated as the recipe directs, and it can be eaten either cooked or raw. Powdered ginger is not a suitable substitute.

Ginger juice is made by grating a length of unpeeled ginger on a medium-gauge grating surface, then squeezing the pulp tightly between the fingers to extract the juice. Discard the dry pulp. Ginger juice is used in both Chinese and Japanese cooking where only flavour, not texture, is required.

Onions in China are of a different variety to those usually found in the West. However, spring onions are perfectly acceptable substitutes and can be obtained throughout the year. Cut into 1-cm ($\frac{1}{2}$-inch) lengths, they are used most frequently for flavouring oil, sometimes together with ginger and other seasonings, before food is fried in it. But spring onions can also be used as a final garnish and added virtually uncooked to a dish – in which case they are chopped very finely. Western onions can be substituted for spring onions for flavouring oil if necessary, but do remember that they must be chopped more finely because of their coarse texture, and that they take longer to cook.

These are the four basic ingredients you will need to cook Chinese food. However you will also often need a good vegetarian stock. One recipe is provided here, and there are several other stock recipes on pages 140–2.

Vegetarian stock

INGREDIENTS

300 ml (10 oz) soya beansprouts
15 g ($\frac{1}{2}$ oz) Western onion
1 slice ginger
2 cloves garlic
10 black peppercorns
30 ml (2 tablespoons) rice wine or dry sherry
5 ml (1 teaspoon) salt
15 ml (1 tablespoon) light soy sauce

PREPARATION

Wash the soya beansprouts and add to 2 litres ($7\frac{1}{2}$ cups, 3 pints) water in a pan. Add the remaining ingredients and bring to the boil. Skim the top of the stock, turn down the heat and cover the pan with a lid. Simmer for an hour. Strain and use as required.

EQUIPMENT FOR CHINESE COOKING

Although there is no need to have any special equipment for Chinese cooking, many people like to use a wok. This is the curved-bottomed pan with flaring sides and a wide top which the Chinese use for almost every cooking process, and which is now available in Western hardware shops as well as Chinese outlets. When used in a Chinese kitchen it sits sunk into the fire on a solid fuel stove and is a marvellous all-purpose pan. In the West, while it is reasonably efficient on a Western-style gas cooker, particularly if steadied by a wire stand, it has serious disadvantages on electric hobs because the round bottom gives too little direct contact with the source of heat. Flat-bottomed woks are now available and are greatly superior for cooking with electricity, but they must *never* be used for deep-frying because the ratio of depth of pan to volume of oil makes them liable to overflow when food is submerged into the hot oil.

Of course, you can use an ordinary frying-pan instead of a wok for stir-frying, but a wok does give you much more space in which to stir-fry a quantity of food, particularly valuable when cooking vegetables.

Chinese bamboo steamers are used in conjunction with a wok. Their interlocking boxes allow many dishes to be cooked over one flame. Metal Western steamers may be used instead, though they do not allow for racking in the same way. The Chinese also steam food on a plate standing on a rack just above water-level in a covered wok, which can also be done using a saucepan. Note that the Chinese usually put foods to be steamed on to plates or in bowls rather than directly into the steamer.

BASIC JAPANESE INGREDIENTS

When starting Japanese cooking it can seem as if there is an endless list of ingredients with strange-sounding names, but in fact there are only a few essential items, and with just a limited number you can make authentic Japanese dishes.

First and foremost for a successful Japanese dish you need the freshest vegetables possible, for much of the attraction of Japanese cooking lies in the fresh flavour of the food. Vegetables which have aged or wilted can never have their original flavour restored, so it is worth while searching out very fresh produce before you start. The aim of Japanese cooks is to bring out the natural flavours in the food, and unlike the Chinese they often cook with almost no seasonings, providing any additional flavour in a garnish or dipping sauce served at the side.

Soy sauce is basic to Japanese cooking, as it is to Chinese. The Japanese brew their own varieties of soy, and in the West Kikkoman brand is the most easily obtainable. This is slightly saltier and less strongly flavoured than any Chinese soy sauce, but a Chinese light soy can be used in its place. The Koreans use a sauce very similar to the Japanese Kikkoman brand.

The Japanese also use a rice wine, *sake*, which unlike Chinese rice wine has almost no flavour of its own. Dry sherry cannot therefore be used as a substitute because its penetrating flavour will overpower the other flavours in a dish. However, vodka diluted to half strength with water can be used as a substitute for *sake* in Japanese cooking. The Japanese also have a sweet wine especially distilled for cooking only, called *mirin*. This gives a richness to dishes without making them sickly, and adds a roundness to the flavour as a whole. You can substitute 1 part vodka, 1 part water and 2 parts sugar for *mirin*: for example, for 15 ml (1 tablespoon) *mirin* use 5 ml (1 teaspoon) vodka, 5 ml (1 teaspoon) water and 10 ml (2 teaspoons) crystal sugar.

Another basic ingredient of many Japanese recipes is sesame seeds, which give a delicate, nutty flavour that goes well with many vegetables. Toasted sesame seeds are made by stirring sesame seeds in a dry pan over a moderate heat until they turn golden brown and start to dance. Tip them out on to a plate or flat board immediately they are ready. You can then crush them into a paste with a rolling-pin or use them whole to garnish a finished dish. Sesame paste, either Chinese or Greek *tahina*, can be used instead of the crushed sesame seeds, but neither tastes as good as freshly toasted and crushed sesame seeds.

The last basic ingredient in Japanese cookery is seaweed. Three different varieties are commonly used.

Wakame has long fronds joined to a central rib and is used in soups and salads. It is sold either dried or salted in the West, and in either case needs soaking for 5 minutes in cold water before the central rib is torn off and the fronds cut into suitable-sized pieces. It must then be either blanched, by having boiling water poured over it, or put into boiling soup for 1 minute only. *Wakame* quickly loses its texture if it is overcooked or soaked for too long.

Nori is laver seaweed processed into flat sheets, in both Japan and Korea, and is one of the most popular seaweed foods. Sheets of *nori* need toasting over a high flame for about 20 seconds to turn them from green to purple before they are used. *Nori* is not used in cooking but as a garnish or a wrapping for other foods. For a garnish it can be cut into thin shreds with a pair of scissors.

The third variety of seaweed used in Japanese cookery is *konbu* (dried kelp). This is used for making stock, called *dashi* in Japanese. However, when *konbu* is heated to boiling point in water it gives the water a very strong iodine taste. Therefore when making *dashi* with *konbu* always take care that the water never actually boils while the *konbu* is in it. *Dashi* is used in a wide variety of dishes; an alternative recipe for it is given on page 142.

Quick konbu dashi

INGREDIENTS

1 piece konbu *about 8 cm (3 inches) square*
600 ml (20 fl oz, 1 pint) water

PREPARATION

Wipe the *konbu* and cut it into quarters. Put it with the water into a pan and bring *very slowly* to boiling point. Just before it starts to boil lift out the *konbu* and discard. Use the stock as required. The quantities in this recipe may be doubled.

Thin omelettes and egg shreds

This is another preparation used for both Chinese and Japanese dishes. It consists of thin slices of cooked egg. The following recipe can be used for either cuisine.

INGREDIENTS

3 size 4 eggs
pinch salt and sugar
oil

PREPARATION

Beat the eggs lightly with the salt and sugar. Heat a 20-cm (8-inch) frying-pan with a very little oil over a moderate heat and pour in one-third of the beaten egg. Tip the pan so that the egg coats the bottom of the pan evenly and cook until set. Then carefully lift the omelette out of the pan and lay out flat to cool. Repeat to make 3 omelettes in all.

To make *egg shreds*, roll the cold omelettes up separately and cut into thin shreds across the roll. Use as directed.

Korean two-colour egg omelettes

INGREDIENTS

2 large eggs
15 ml (1 tablespoon) cold water
oil

PREPARATION

Separate the eggs. Lightly beat the egg whites. Beat the egg yolks with the cold water. Heat an oiled frying-pan and pour in half the egg white. Over a low heat tilt the pan until the egg has covered the bottom, then cook the omelette until the egg is set. Lift out and lay flat to cool. Repeat with the remaining egg white. Then cook the egg yolks as one omelette in the same way. When the omelettes are cool, roll them up separately and cut crosswise into thin shreds. Use as directed.

CUTTING TECHNIQUES

Cutting matchsticks

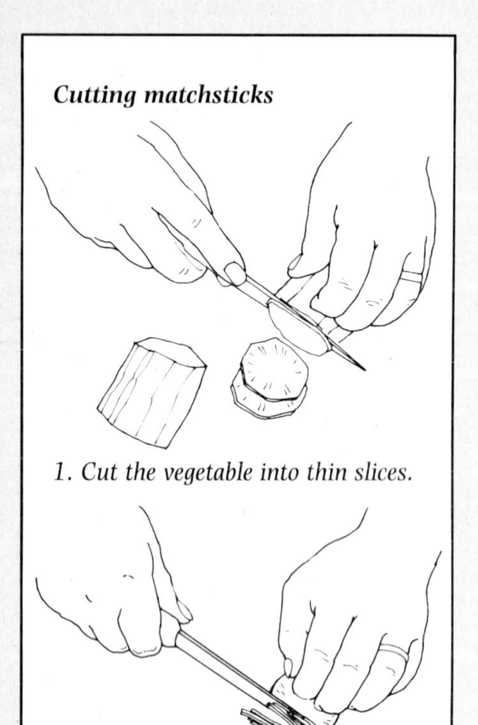

1. *Cut the vegetable into thin slices.*

2. *Pile up the slices and cut into thin strips.*

Cutting batons

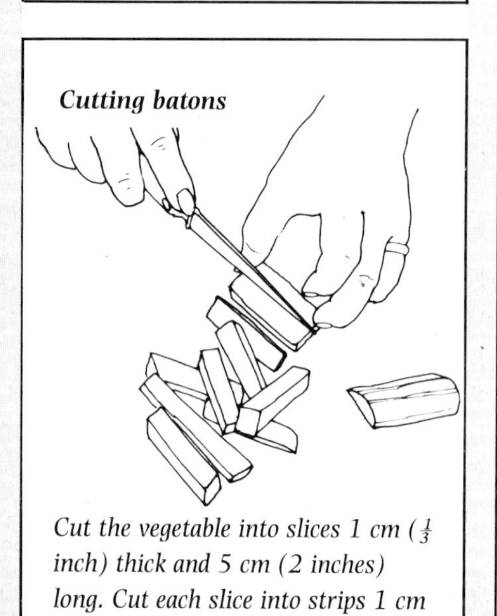

Cut the vegetable into slices 1 cm ($\frac{1}{3}$ inch) thick and 5 cm (2 inches) long. Cut each slice into strips 1 cm ($\frac{1}{3}$ inch) wide.

'Hair'-cutting

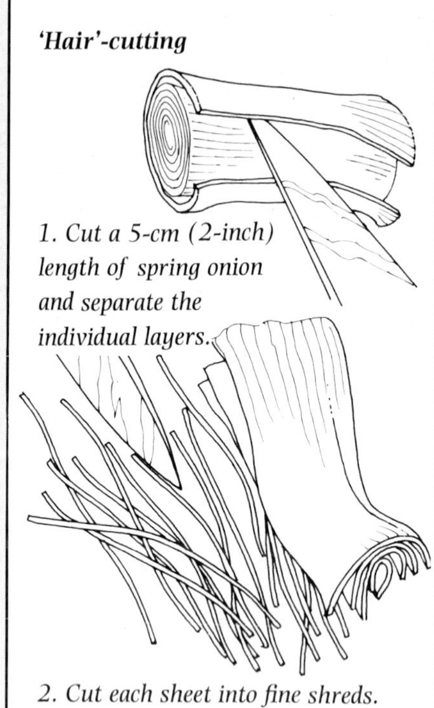

1. *Cut a 5-cm (2-inch) length of spring onion and separate the individual layers.*

2. *Cut each sheet into fine shreds.*

Rolling cut

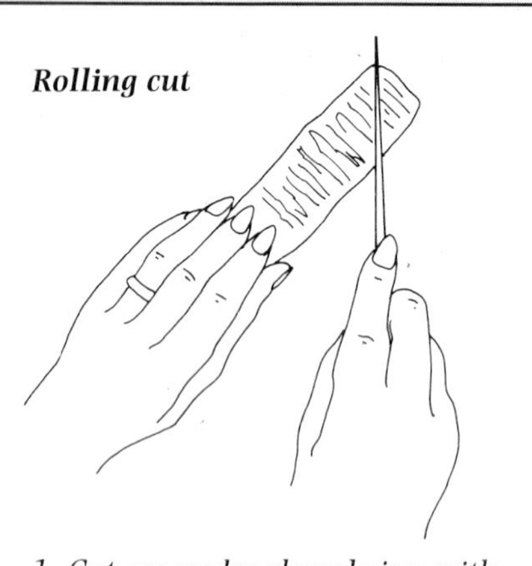

1. *Cut one wedge-shaped piece with the knife held diagonally to the vegetable.*

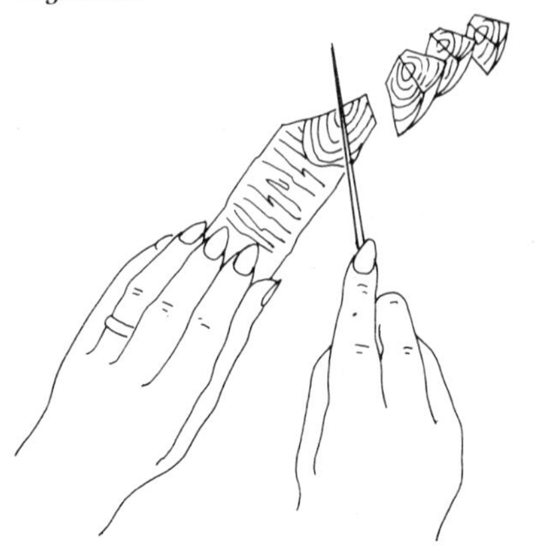

2. *Rotate the vegetable through 90 degrees and cut the next wedge-shaped piece with the knife still held diagonally to the vegetable. Repeat.*

Onion brushes with chilli rings

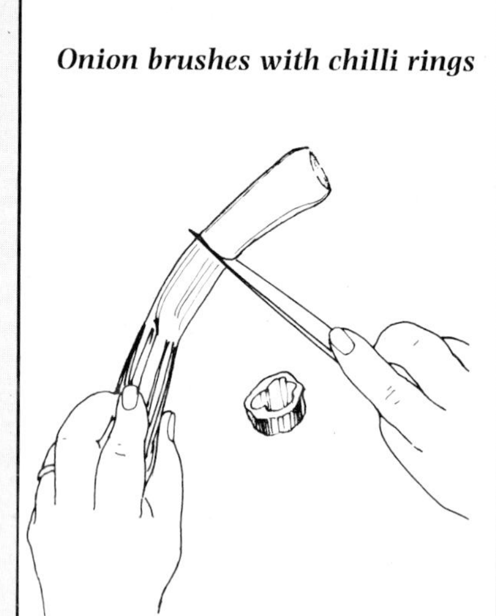

1. *Cut trimmed spring onions into 5-cm (1-inch) lengths. Have ready a ring of fresh chilli 1 cm ($\frac{1}{3}$ inch) wide.*

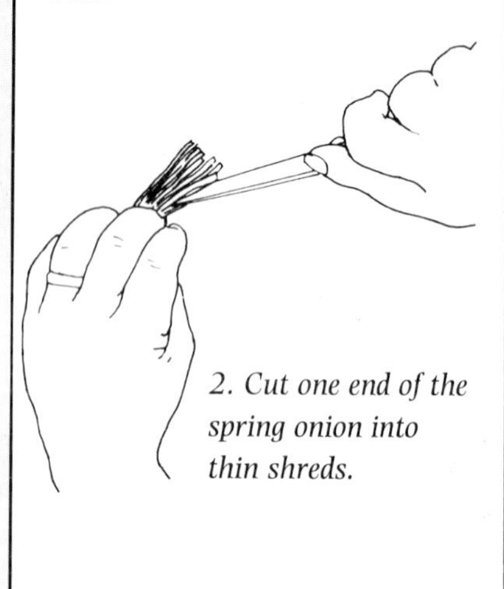

2. *Cut one end of the spring onion into thin shreds.*

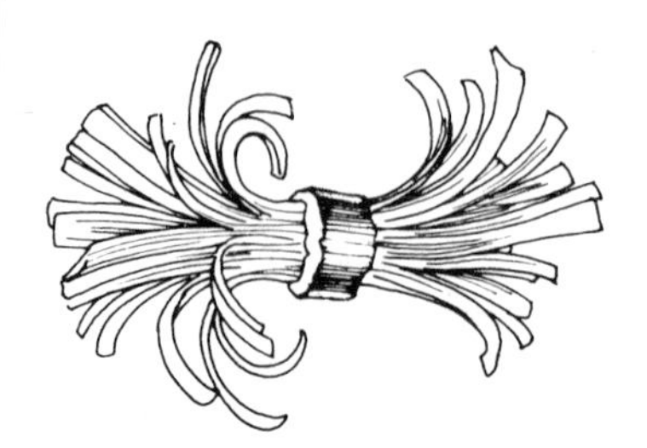

3. *Slide on the chilli ring and cut the other end of the spring onion.*

Cucumber fan

1. Cut a slice of cucumber 1 cm ($\frac{1}{3}$ inch) thick and 6 cm ($2\frac{1}{3}$ inches) long.

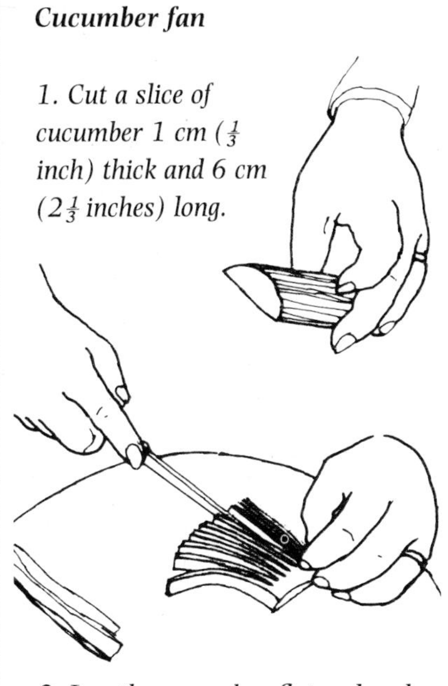

2. Lay the cucumber flat and make regular narrow cuts to within 1 cm ($\frac{1}{3}$ inch) of the end.

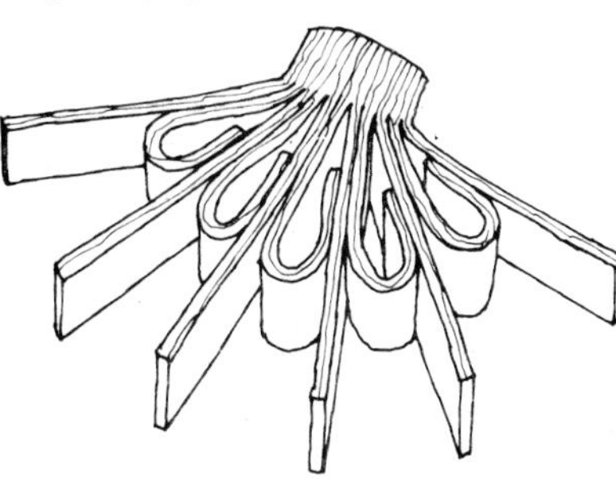

3. Fold in alternate cut strips of cucumber to form a fan.

Chilli flowers

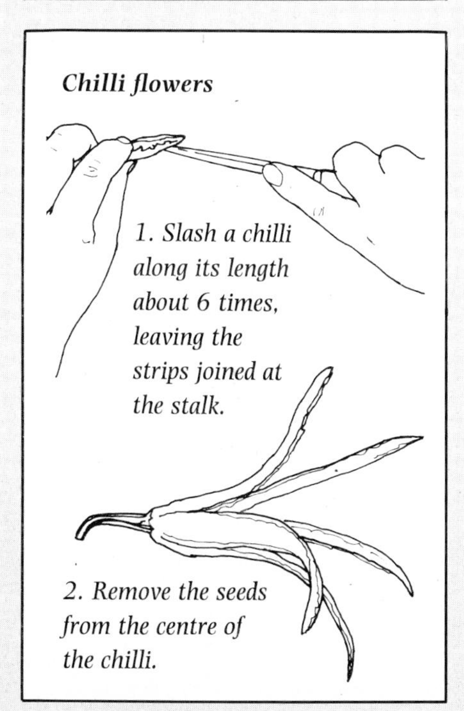

1. Slash a chilli along its length about 6 times, leaving the strips joined at the stalk.

2. Remove the seeds from the centre of the chilli.

Tomato flowers

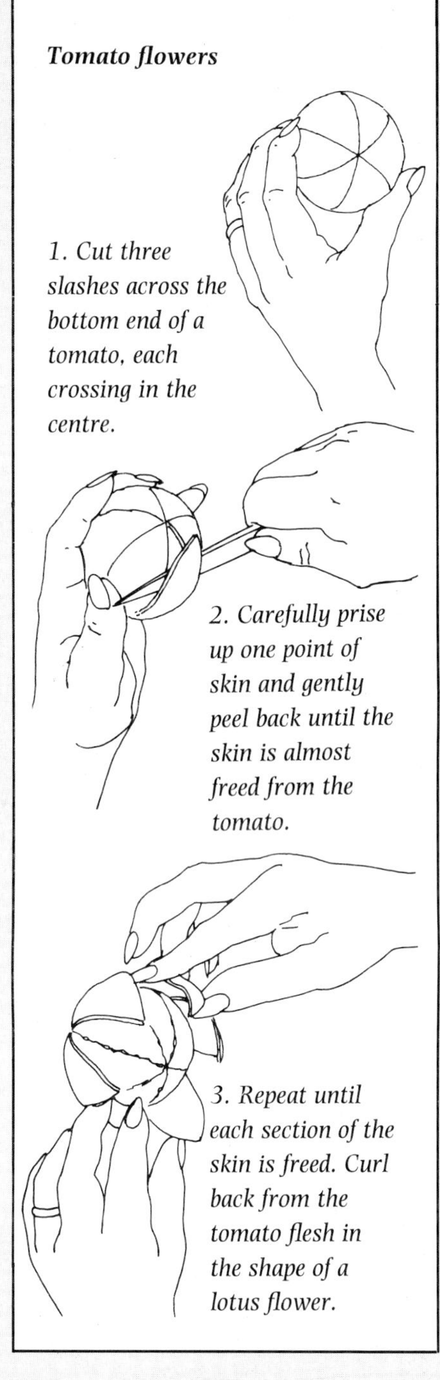

1. Cut three slashes across the bottom end of a tomato, each crossing in the centre.

2. Carefully prise up one point of skin and gently peel back until the skin is almost freed from the tomato.

3. Repeat until each section of the skin is freed. Curl back from the tomato flesh in the shape of a lotus flower.

Turnip or white radish flowers

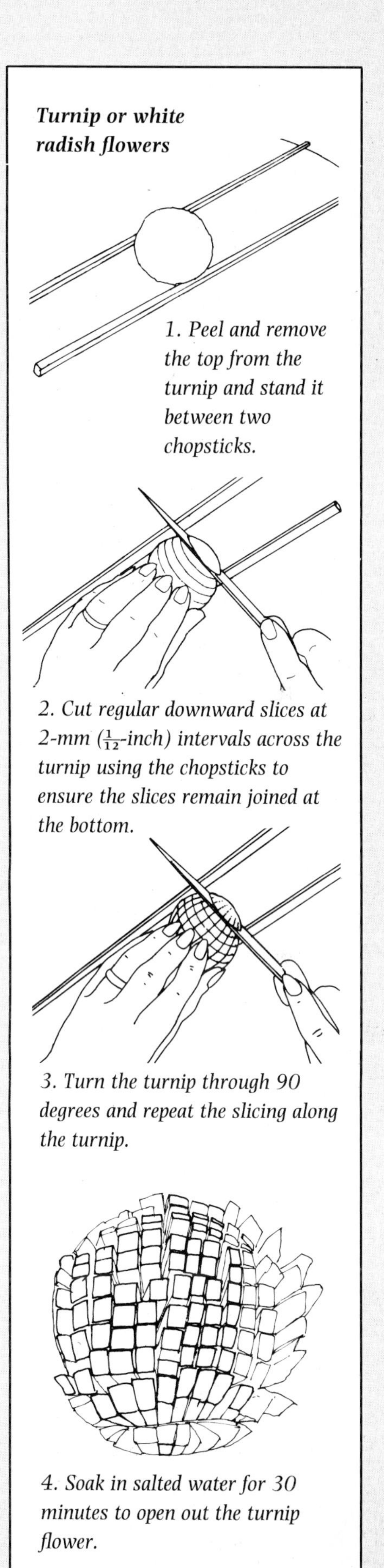

1. Peel and remove the top from the turnip and stand it between two chopsticks.

2. Cut regular downward slices at 2-mm ($\frac{1}{12}$-inch) intervals across the turnip using the chopsticks to ensure the slices remain joined at the bottom.

3. Turn the turnip through 90 degrees and repeat the slicing along the turnip.

4. Soak in salted water for 30 minutes to open out the turnip flower.

CUTTING TECHNIQUES FOR JAPANESE AND CHINESE FOODS

Because no knives are used at table both Chinese and Japanese cuisines lay stress on the way food is cut before it is cooked. 'Knife-work' was one of the central features of Chinese cooking in the seventh century, the time when Chinese cooking had a fundamental influence on Japanese cuisine. Today both the Chinese and the Japanese see the cutting of food as having two purposes; to ensure that the food cooks evenly and efficiently, and to give food an attractive appearance when served. The Japanese in particular believe that the finished look of a dish and its presentation is of prime importance, and for the correct final appearance one must start with the correct preparation, including the cutting of the food. A number of the preparatory cutting techniques used in both China and Japan, together with a few decorative garnishes, are illustrated on pages 38–9.

EQUIPMENT FOR JAPANESE COOKING

No equipment is necessary for cooking Japanese food which cannot, with a little ingenuity, be found in an ordinary Western kitchen. Generally speaking the Japanese use a Western frying-pan for shallow-frying and a saucepan for simmering and stewing. However they have one piece of equipment which can be very helpful in achieving really authentic results – a rolling mat. This gives a professional finish to the rolls of rice, vegetables and egg which feature in many Japanese recipes. It is made of thin strips of wood or bamboo strung together with cotton string into a square of about 23 cm (9 inches) (see illustration on page 116). You can use a closely woven tea-towel folded into three in place of a rolling mat.

BASIC INDONESIAN INGREDIENTS

The special character of almost all Indonesian dishes comes from the spices and seasonings, prepared at the very beginning of the cooking.

They invariably include red onions. You can substitute ordinary onions for red onions, but the latter are milder and sweeter than Western onions and give a rosy tint to any sauce. Grind the onions using a pestle and mortar, or a food processor, or slice them very finely. Ground onions blended in to thicken a sauce while sliced keep their shape and give a thinner final sauce. Garlic, in fairly generous quantities, is usually included with the onions, together with a range of other spices.

The most common are chillis, used fresh in Indonesia. If necessary use either chilli powder (cayenne) or dried chillis instead. Chillis vary in their degrees of hotness; the Indonesians have different names for the various varieties denoting their heat, but generally speaking small chillis are hotter than bigger ones, and green (unripe) chillis are sharper-flavoured than the (ripe) red ones.

Another ingredient commonly used in Indonesian seasoning is *laos*. This looks rather like fresh ginger but has a hotter, sharper flavour with more bite. You can substitute either a pinch of *laos* powder or a slice of ginger for a slice of fresh *laos*.

When you cook Indonesian food there are a few basic ingredients which you will need to prepare before you start on almost any recipe. Perhaps the most important is *santan*, the creamy coconut milk which gives so many Indonesian dishes their characteristic richness. Never cover a pan in which you are cooking *santan* or it will curdle, and always mix it well into any other liquids in the dish. *Santan*, labelled 'coconut milk', can be bought canned in some Far-Eastern stores. It is very thick, with an excellent flavour, and though expensive this does save a lot of time. If you want a thinner *santan* dilute it to half strength with water. You can also make *santan* in the traditional way with fresh coconuts, but unfortunately these are often far from fresh when they reach the shops in the UK.

Santan from fresh coconut

INGREDIENTS

1 coconut
300 ml (1¼ cups, ½ pint) hot water

PREPARATION

Drain the 'coconut milk' from the coconut by piercing two holes in the 'eyes', which are at one end of the nut. You can drink this 'milk', which is not used for cooking. Then crack the coconut and lever out the flesh. If it is discoloured or smells bad, discard the coconut because it will spoil the taste of any dish to which it is added. Cut the flesh, including the brown inner skin, into small squares and put them in a food processor. Reduce to a pulp. Pour in the hot water and run for a further 4 minutes. Squeeze the pulp in the water between your hands before straining it through a cloth or fine sieve. Use as directed.

This makes thick coconut milk; for a thinner milk double the quantity of water and put it through the coconut flesh, twice, using half the water each time.

Santan from desiccated coconut

Another method of making *santan* is to use desiccated coconut. (Frankly it is better to buy a can of *santan* than to make it from desiccated coconut.)

INGREDIENTS

300 g (10 oz) desiccated coconut
300 ml (1¼ cups, ½ pint) boiling water

PREPARATION

Pour the boiling water over the dried coconut and leave for about 20 minutes. Strain through a sieve, squeezing the coconut pulp between your hands to extract as much liquid as possible. Use as required.

This makes thick coconut milk; for a thinner milk add more water and re-squeeze the pulp.

Santan from creamed coconut

It is also possible to buy blocks of creamed, unsweetened coconut from Far-Eastern grocers. This has the advantage that it will keep almost indefinitely in the refrigerator and you do not have to struggle with the coconut, but the quality of the *santan* is not quite as good as that made from a fresh coconut, or of canned coconut milk. However, a lump of creamed coconut can be added in place of thick *santan* in recipes where it is stirred in at the end of the cooking. Do not confuse pure creamed coconut with the sweetened confectionery – coconut cream – sold in Western sweetshops.

INGREDIENTS

90 g ($3\frac{1}{2}$ oz) creamed coconut
300 ml ($1\frac{1}{4}$ cup, $\frac{1}{2}$ pint) hot water

PREPARATION

Break the creamed coconut into small pieces in a bowl and pour in the hot water. Leave for 20 minutes. Mix well and strain. For a thinner milk add an extra 100 ml ($\frac{1}{2}$ cup, 4 fl oz) water.

Tamarind juice

The other initial preparation which you may need for Indonesian recipes is tamarind juice. This can be bought ready-prepared in bottles from Eastern grocers and used diluted with 4 parts water to 1 part tamarind juice. However, tamarind juice can very easily be made from the blocks of tamarind paste sold in Asian stores.

INGREDIENTS

25 g (1 oz) tamarind paste
300 ml ($1\frac{1}{4}$ cups, $\frac{1}{2}$ pint) boiling water

PREPARATION

Soak the paste in the boiling water for 20 minutes. Then remove the seeds from the skin and flesh and strain and rub the remaining pulp through a sieve. Discard any remaining hard fibres and use the juice as directed.

Onion flakes

The Indonesians use thin slices of fried onion as a garnish for many of their dishes. The easiest way to avoid the tedious job of fine-slicing onions is to buy dried onion flakes and deep-fry them.

INGREDIENTS

10 ml (2 teaspoons) dried onion flakes
oil for deep frying

PREPARATION

Shake the dried flakes from the packet into the moderately hot oil. Deep-fry until golden brown (about 1 minute). Lift out with a slotted spoon, drain and use as required.

5

Stir-fries and Deep-fried Dishes

Throughout the Far East and South East Asia food is cut before it is served because knives are never used at table. In China, Japan and Korea food is eaten with chopsticks and the food is cut accordingly into small pieces. In Malaysia and Indonesia they use spoons and forks or sometimes, traditionally, fingers, and the foods are cut correspondingly bigger. Foods that are to be cooked quickly must be cut small, and all dishes look better when the ingredients are of a regular size and shape. Firm vegetables can be cut into matchstick batons or slices for quick cooking, while green vegetables are either cut into short lengths including the stalk or the leaf alone is torn into bite-sized pieces. Some vegetables, such as *bok choi*, may have the stalk and leaf cooked separately.

Over the last twenty years the directions 'stir-fry' have become familiar to us in Western cookbooks, regardless of the origin of the recipe. Yet achieving a perfect Chinese stir-fry is not easy. The cooked foods must be moist and firm while the dish as a whole is dry and not greasy. The success of a stir-fry depends to a large extent on controlling the cooking temperature. Chinese cooks lift and lower the pan over the heat with one hand while they move the food around the pan in a scooping motion with the other hand, thus allowing the food to cook at the highest possible temperature without burning. A little practice will quickly enable you to judge the correct heat for your own cooker and pan.

Throughout the Far East the usual cooking pot is a wide, round-bottomed pan similar to the Chinese wok. With the exception of Japan places as far apart as the north of China, Burma and Java all use such pans, sunk into solid-fuel stoves, for most fried and simmered dishes.

The Japanese at home use a separate deep frying-pan for deep-frying foods, and on the whole we strongly recommend everyone in a Western kitchen to do the same, or to use an electric automatic fryer, and to change to a wok, with or without a flat bottom, or a large frying-pan, for any shallow-frying.

Some of the best-known Korean dishes in the West are the grills and barbecues which the Koreans cook over a charcoal, or nowadays gas, grill at the table. Unfortunately it is dangerous to use an open charcoal grill indoors because of the carbon monoxide fumes given off by burning charcoal, and in restaurants it is now usual to use a gas grill. However, such a grill is almost impossible to obtain in the West, and we have had to compromise with a heavy frying-pan set over a free-standing electric, or gas, ring in the centre of the table. If you can obtain a heavy pan with no handle, such as a Japanese *sukiyaki* pan, so much the better. In the summer, of course, Korean grills make excellent barbecue dishes.

Japanese *tempura* is another Far-Eastern fried food which is becoming increasingly well-known in the West. Vegetables deep-fried in Japanese batter emerge with a crisp and featherlight coating. Batter for *tempura* is never beaten in advance but lightly mixed only moments before it is used. Iced water or ice cubes are used to extend the temperature change when the batter meets the hot oil. The oil itself, to give the best results, should remain at a constant temperature of 180°C (350°F). If the oil is at this temperature the batter will hang midway between the bottom of the pan and the surface of the oil for a few seconds; if it is too cold the batter will sink immediately to the bottom, while if it is too hot it will rise at once to the surface and sizzle furiously.

A thick-bottomed pan or an electric deep-fryer will give the best results in deep-frying. The oil must never be more than half the depth of the pan and should always be twice the depth of any food put into it. Between frying each batch of food, always remove any loose crumbs of batter from the oil, because they may overcook and taint the oil. Filter the warm oil after use and store it in a clean, covered container away from the light. Discard any oil that becomes in the least bit cloudy or discoloured, or you may spoil the flavour of the foods.

This chapter features a wide range of Chinese stir-fried vegetable dishes together with recipes for Japanese *tempura* and other deep-fried dishes, none of which take long to cook. Suggestions are included for other dishes with which these might be served.

QUICK EGG DISHES

All the recipes in this section have the merit of being easy as well as quick to cook, and needing little advance preparation. The quantities given are sufficient for a main dish for 2 people or as one among several dishes for 4 or more people.

Egg fuyung

CHINESE

We like to serve this garlicky egg dish with sweet and sour 'spareribs' (page 95), family aubergines served cold (page 131) and a quickly cooked green vegetable such as stir-fried *choisam* or *bok choi* together with soup (see Chapter 10) and plain boiled rice. If you cannot find Chinese chives, substitute 3 cloves of garlic and 3 more spring onions cut into 3-cm (1-inch) lengths.

INGREDIENTS

50 g (2 oz) bamboo shoots
75 g (3 oz) beansprouts
35 g (2½ oz) Chinese chives
2 spring onions
4 size 4 eggs
3.5 ml (¾ teaspoon) salt
2.5 ml (½ teaspoon) sugar
pinch pepper
5 ml (1 teaspoon) sesame oil
45 ml (3 tablespoons) vegetable oil

PREPARATION

Cut the bamboo shoots into matchstick pieces. Pick over the beansprouts and blanch in boiling water for 1 minute, then dip in cold water before draining well. Wash and cut the Chinese chives into 3-cm (1-inch) lengths. Chop the spring onions finely. Beat the eggs with the salt, sugar, pepper and sesame oil and mix in the bamboo shoots, beansprouts and Chinese chives. Heat the oil in a wok or large frying-pan until very hot and pour in the egg mixture. Stir-fry until the egg is just set and serve at once.

Spiced beancurd omelettes (tahu telur)

SINGAPORE (MALAYSIAN)

Serve these delicious double-textured omelettes in their sour, spicy sauce with a *lodeh* (page 65), braised water-spinach and *sambal tomat*, together with plain boiled rice.

INGREDIENTS
300 g (10 oz) beancurd
SAUCE
15 ml (1 tablespoon) peanuts
4–5 cloves garlic
1 hot chilli
30 ml (2 tablespoons) oil
45 ml (3 tablespoons) light soy sauce
30 ml (2 tablespoons) lime or lemon juice
2 large eggs
45 ml (3 tablespoons) oil
30 ml (2 tablespoons) chopped coriander leaves

PREPARATION
Wrap the beancurd tightly in a clean cloth and leave to drain for about 30 minutes.

Meanwhile make the sauce. Skin the peanuts by dipping them in boiling water. Cut the garlic and de-seeded chilli into thin shreds. Heat the oil in a pan and stir-fry the peanuts, for about 2 minutes; then add the garlic and chilli and continue frying for another 2 minutes. Remove from the heat, leave to cool, then blend in a food processor (or pulverize in a pestle and mortar) together with the soy sauce and lime juice until a smooth cream results. Return this to the pan and add another 45 ml (3 tablespoons) water.

Cut the beancurd into 1-cm ($\frac{1}{3}$-inch) cubes. Beat the eggs and add the beancurd cubes. Make sure they are all well coated with the beaten egg. Heat a clean wok or frying-pan with 45 ml (3 tablespoons) oil and put in about 45 ml (3 tablespoons) of the egg and beancurd. (The mixture will make about 5–6 omelettes in all.) Fry the omelette, turning once, until golden brown on both sides, then lift out on to a heated serving plate and keep warm while frying the remaining omelettes. Add more oil if necessary. When the omelettes are cooked, re-heat the prepared sauce and serve the omelettes with the coriander and sauce poured over them.

NOTE To vary, substitute 10 ml (2 teaspoons) peanut butter for the peanuts in the sauce, but fry only the garlic and chilli, in 15 ml (1 tablespoon) oil.

Tomato and egg omelette

CHINESE

This simple egg dish can be eaten with an elaborate main dish such as deep-fried spinach and beancurd rolls (page 92) or lichi and nut balls (page 97). Since its flavour is bland and natural it can also be served with a hot chilli dish such as Sichuan aubergines (page 62) or with a less strongly flavoured dish such as five-colour 'prawns' (page 51).

INGREDIENTS
300 g (10 oz) tomatoes
3 large eggs
30 ml (2 tablespoons) oil
salt and pepper to taste
30 ml (2 tablespoons) vegetarian stock

PREPARATION
Skin and de-seed the tomatoes. Cut the flesh into big pieces. Beat the eggs. Heat the oil in a wok or large frying-pan and fry the tomatoes for about 2 minutes until soft. Season with salt and pepper and add the stock. Then pour the beaten eggs over the tomatoes and cover the pan. Cook for 1 minute over a high heat, or until the eggs are set. Do not let the eggs overcook. Serve at once.

Stir-fried egg and black fungus

CHINESE

The bright yellow, green and black shreds of this dish make it the perfect foil for Mapo's beancurd (page 80). Serve them with ginger spinach (page 134) as a cold salad, and sesame aubergines (page 48). Steamed bread buns (page 164) and mixed vegetable soup (page 148) would make these a substantial meal.

INGREDIENTS

25 ml (1½ tablespoons) black fungus
3 size 4 eggs
salt
50 g (2 oz) spinach leaves
3 spring onions
2 slices ginger
60 ml (4 tablespoons) oil
15 ml (1 tablespoon) rice wine
5 ml (1 teaspoon) soy sauce
5 ml (1 teaspoon) sesame oil

PREPARATION

Soak the black fungus for 20 minutes in warm water. Rinse well, discard any hard bits and pull into 2-cm (¾-inch) pieces. Beat the eggs with the salt. Tear the spinach leaves into 5-cm (2-inch) pieces and blanch in boiling water for a minute before refreshing in cold water and draining well. Chop the spring onions and ginger finely. Heat 45 ml (3 tablespoons) of the oil in a wok or large frying-pan and stir-fry the onions and ginger for 15 seconds. Add the black fungus and continue stir-frying for another 30 seconds. Then lift out the black fungus and keep on one side. Add the remaining oil to the pan and tip in the beaten egg. Scramble the eggs until just setting, then return the black fungus to the pan with the spinach. Season with the rice wine, soy sauce and salt to taste. Mix well and serve at once sprinkled with sesame oil.

Orak-orak (stir-fried cabbage with eggs)

INDONESIAN

The crisp texture of the cabbage contrasts well with the soft scrambled eggs in this dish. Serve it with a cold salad such as broccoli and black fungus (page 124) and soy-simmered pumpkin (page 70) together with three-colour beancurd soup (page 148) and plenty of rice cooked with coconut. For an Indonesian meal serve *orak-orak* with a curry such as *sayur bening* (page 74) and a salad – perhaps *gado-gado* (page 125) – with the rice.

INGREDIENTS

500 g (1 lb) Chinese leaves
100 g (4 oz) carrot
4 eggs
100 g (4 oz) onions
2 cloves garlic
45 ml (3 tablespoons) vegetable oil
salt and pepper to taste
30 ml (2 tablespoons) fried onion slices to garnish

PREPARATION

Wash the Chinese leaves, pat dry and cut into thin shreds. Peel and cut the carrot into matchstick pieces. Beat the eggs. Slice the onions and garlic finely. Heat the oil in a wok or large frying-pan and stir-fry the onion and garlic for about 5 minutes over a moderate heat. Add the cabbage and carrot shreds and stir-fry over a brisk fire until soft. Season well with salt and pepper and pour in the beaten eggs. Scramble the eggs with the cabbage over a high heat and serve immediately garnished with the fried onion slices.

VEGETABLE DISHES

These quickly cooked vegetable dishes, most of which are Chinese, go well with almost any larger dish from any of the regions. Choose them for colour, shape and texture contrast. It is usual in Chinese meals to include at least one vegetable dish alongside other dishes made with beancurd, eggs or gluten.

Stir-fried green pepper with black beans

CHINESE

INGREDIENTS

250 g (8 oz) green pepper
45 ml (3 tablespoons) oil
45 ml (3 tablespoons) fermented black beans
5 ml (1 teaspoon) rice wine
5 ml (1 teaspoon) sesame oil

PREPARATION

Wash the green pepper, de-seed and cut into 1-cm (½-inch) dice. Heat a frying-pan with the oil and stir-fry the fermented beans for about 30 seconds. Add the green pepper and rice wine and continue stir-frying over a moderate heat until the pepper is cooked (about 4 minutes). Serve sprinkled with sesame oil.

Stir-fried three nuts

CHINESE

INGREDIENTS

50 g (2 oz) bamboo
75 g (3 oz) pepper (preferably red)
1 spring onion
2 slices ginger
oil for deep frying
75 g (3 oz) cashew nuts
75 g (3 oz) pine kernels
15 ml (1 tablespoon) sesame oil
75 g (3 oz) canned ginko nuts
salt to taste
10 ml (2 teaspoons) light soy sauce

PREPARATION

Cut the bamboo into 1-cm (½-inch) cubes. De-seed the pepper and cut it into similar-sized pieces. Chop the spring onion and ginger finely. Heat the oil and deep-fry the cashew nuts and pine kernels, separately, over a moderate heat until golden brown. Drain well. Heat 15 ml (1 tablespoon) oil mixed with 15 ml (1 tablespoon) sesame oil in a wok or large frying-pan and stir-fry the ginger and onion for 15 seconds. Then add the bamboo and after another 30 seconds the pepper and ginko nuts. Continue to stir-fry for another 30 seconds, then tip in the fried nuts. Season with salt and soy sauce, and serve sprinkled with sesame oil.

NOTE You can ring the changes with this recipe by adding or substituting other vegetables as available. Use celery, french beans, or broad beans (par-boiled) instead of or as well as the pepper and bamboo. You can also add peanuts (skinned) or walnuts to the nuts listed. Serve this dish with one based on beancurd, such as crystal beancurd (page 82), a vegetable dish such as sweet and sour 'meat' slices (page 72) and a cold salad dish together with an egg and tomato soup (page 147) and plain rice. Always remember to cook any nuts (deep-frying is usual) before adding them to a dish, or they will taste raw.

Sweet and sour aubergines

CHINESE

An early version of this recipe dates from the ninth century. In it the aubergines, after being dried in the sun, are stir-fried with ginger and basil and afterwards braised in a sweet and sour sauce. A note with the recipe says that the cooked aubergines may be stored in a jar during the winter. The same recipe appeared nearly 900 years later in another Chinese recipe book, but in this version orange peel and cumin had been added to the spices: this is this recipe given below. It is interesting that in northern China today people are still preparing chrysanthemum aubergines for the winter in almost the same manner.

INGREDIENTS

300g (10oz) aubergines
salt
45ml (3 tablespoons) oil
4-cm (1½-inch)-square dried orange peel, soaked and finely sliced
10ml (2 teaspoons) finely chopped ginger
10ml (2 teaspoons) chopped fresh or 5ml (1 teaspoon) dried basil
1.5ml (¼ teaspoon) ground cumin

SEASONING SAUCE

20ml (4 teaspoons) sugar
20ml (4 teaspoons) black vinegar

5ml (1 teaspoon) sesame oil

PREPARATION

Wash and cut the aubergines into wedge-shaped pieces about 3cm (1 inch) long. Put into boiling salted water for 3 minutes, then dip them immediately in cold water and drain well. Heat the oil in a wok or large frying-pan and gently stir-fry the spices for 1 minute. Add the aubergines and continue stir-frying for another 2–3 minutes, turning them over in the oil to make sure they are all well covered. Add the seasoning sauce and boil for 30 seconds before sprinkling with sesame oil. Serve at once.

Sesame aubergines

CHINESE

INGREDIENTS

350g (12oz) aubergines
5ml (1 teaspoon) salt

SEASONING SAUCE

20ml (4 teaspoons) light soy sauce
5ml (1 teaspoon) rice wine
5ml (1 teaspoon) sugar
5ml (1 teaspoon) barbecue sauce
5ml (1 teaspoon) cornflour
15ml (1 tablespoon) water

25g (1oz) sesame seeds
oil for deep frying
15ml (1 tablespoon) finely chopped spring onions
5ml (1 teaspoon) finely chopped ginger
5ml (1 teaspoon) crushed garlic
5ml (1 teaspoon) sesame oil

PREPARATION

Peel and cut the aubergine into batons 3cm (1 inch) long and 1cm (½ inch) thick. Sprinkle with salt and leave for about 20 minutes. Mix the seasoning sauce. Fry the sesame seeds in a dry frying-pan over a moderate heat until they start to dance, then turn out and leave to cool. When the aubergines have drained, rinse well and pat dry. Deep-fry in moderately hot oil until golden brown, then drain well. Heat 30ml (2 tablespoons) oil in a wok or frying-pan and stir-fry the onion, ginger and garlic for about 20 seconds before tipping in the seasoning sauce. Mix well and add the aubergines. Cook for another 2 minutes, then add the sesame seeds and sesame oil. Serve hot.

NOTE The aubergines can be deep-fried and drained in advance of preparing the rest of the dish.

Vegetable basket

CHINESE

INGREDIENTS

50 g (2 oz) carrots
50 g (2 oz) bamboo shoots
8 water chestnuts
2 spring onions
50 g (2 oz) almonds
50 g (2 oz) broccoli spears, or asparagus tips
180 g (6 oz) potato
oil for deep frying
2 slices ginger
15 ml (1 tablespoon) sugar
15 ml (1 tablespoon) light soy sauce
15 ml (1 tablespoon) rice vinegar
8 ginko nuts
2.5 ml (½ teaspoon) cornflour mixed with 5 ml (1 teaspoon) water
salt

PREPARATION

Scrape the carrot and cut into a flower-shape (see page 39) before slicing thinly. Blanch in lightly salted water for 2 minutes, then drain. Slice the bamboo thinly and cut each water chestnut into two rounds. Chop the spring onions finely. Deep-fry the almonds for 3 minutes, until they change colour, then drain well. Blanch the broccoli spears in boiling water for 2 minutes, then refresh in cold water; leave to drain.

Peel the potato and cut into very fine, thin strips about 4 cm (1½ inches) long. Soak in cold water for 5 minutes to remove the starch, then pat dry in a clean cloth. To make the basket you will need a double deep-frying 'basket' (in fact comprising two wire-mesh baskets, shaped like sieves, with long handles) specially designed for the purpose – or it is possible, but difficult, to use two sieves, one slightly larger than the other. Heat the oil until very hot and hold both baskets in the oil until very hot. Lift out the bigger basket and very quickly spread the potato strips around it until it is completely covered by the potato. Press the second basket into the first basket to hold the potatoes in place. Lock the two baskets together. Reduce the temperature of the oil and slowly deep-fry the potato in the baskets until cooked. Lift out and raise the temperature of the oil before returning the potato, still in the baskets, to re-fry until it is golden brown. Turn out the finished potato basket on to a heated serving plate. Keep warm while finishing the filling.

Heat 45 ml (3 tablespoons) oil in a wok or large frying-pan and stir-fry the spring onions and ginger for 15 seconds. Then add the carrot, bamboo shoots and water chestnuts and stir-fry for another 30 seconds. Add the sugar, soy sauce and vinegar. Then add the almonds and ginko nuts and stir in the cornflour paste. Adjust the seasoning and carefully mix in the broccoli spears before spooning the mixture into the prepared potato basket. Serve immediately.

Fried cucumbers

CHINESE

This is a mild, rather soft-textured dish which should ideally be served with a more forceful dish such as Gongbao 'chicken' (page 96) or deep-fried beancurd with sesame sauce (page 85).

INGREDIENTS

200 g (7 oz) cucumber
oil for deep frying
15 ml (1 tablespoon) finely chopped spring onion
5 ml (1 teaspoon) finely chopped ginger
5 ml (1 teaspoon) crushed garlic
2.5 ml (½ teaspoon) cornflour mixed with 60 ml (4 tablespoons) water
salt and pepper to taste
5 ml (1 teaspoon) sesame oil

PREPARATION

Wash and cut the cucumber into batons 5 × 1 cm (2 × ⅓ inch). Heat the oil until hot and deep-fry the cucumber for 2 minutes. Drain well. Heat 30 ml (2 tablespoons) oil in a wok or large frying-pan and stir-fry the onion, ginger and garlic for 15 seconds. Add the cucumber and continue stir-frying for another 30 seconds, then tip in the cornflour and water sauce. Mix well and bring to the boil. Adjust the seasoning with salt and pepper to taste and serve sprinkled with sesame oil.

Chilli mushrooms

CHINESE

INGREDIENTS

200 g (7 oz) fresh small button mushrooms
45 ml (3 tablespoons) oil
5 ml (1 teaspoon) grated ginger
5 ml (1 teaspoon) finely chopped spring onion
2.5 ml (½ teaspoon) sugar
salt and pepper to taste
5 ml (1 teaspoon) chilli oil
5 ml (1 teaspoon) sesame oil

PREPARATION

Wipe the mushrooms and trim the stalk ends. Heat the oil in a wok or large frying-pan and stir-fry the ginger and onion for 15 seconds. Add the mushrooms and continue to stir-fry for another 5–6 minutes, until cooked. Season to taste with sugar, salt and pepper. Just before serving mix in the chilli and sesame oils.

This dish can be eaten either hot or cold.

Marinated mixed mushrooms

CHINESE

INGREDIENTS

3 dried mushrooms
3 pieces black fungus
4 fresh or preserved oyster mushrooms
25 g (1 oz) Western onion
25 g (1 oz) tomato
45 ml (3 tablespoons) oil
8 straw mushrooms

SEASONING SAUCE

15 ml (1 tablespoon) light soy sauce
15 ml (1 tablespoon) rice vinegar
15 ml (1 tablespoon) sesame oil
pinch sugar and black pepper

15 g (½ oz) preserved golden needle mushrooms
lettuce leaves

PREPARATION

Soak the dried mushrooms in warm water for 30 minutes before discarding their hard stalks. Soak the black fungus in warm water separately, then rinse well and cut into small pieces. Rinse and cut each oyster mushroom into four. Chop the onion finely. Skin and de-seed the tomato, then cut the flesh into small pieces. Heat the oil in a wok or large frying-pan and stir-fry the onion and tomato until the onion is soft. Then add the mushrooms and cook for another minute. Pour in the seasoning sauce and finally add the golden needles. Lift from the heat and leave to cool in the seasoning sauce. Serve on a bed of lettuce.

Three-colour shreds

CHINESE

INGREDIENTS

125 g (4 oz) green pepper
125 g (4 oz) red or green pepper
75 g (3 oz) bamboo shoots
25 g (1 oz) Sichuan preserved vegetable
30 ml (2 tablespoons) oil
5 ml (1 teaspoon) soy sauce
salt
5 ml (1 teaspoon) sesame oil

PREPARATION

De-seed and cut the peppers into very fine slices. Cut the bamboo shoots into matchstick shreds. Rinse the Sichuan preserved vegetable and cut into very thin strips. Heat the oil in a wok or large frying-pan and stir-fry the Sichuan preserved vegetable and bamboo shoots for a minute. Add the pepper slices and continue to stir-fry for another 3 minutes. Stir in the soy sauce and adjust the seasoning to taste. (Sichuan preserved vegetable is already salty so you may not need any additional salt.) Sprinkle with sesame oil and serve immediately.

Stir-fried two winters

CHINESE

'Winter' dishes are common in both Chinese and Japanese cooking. In both only seasonal foods are used. So for example in Japan winter dishes feature *yuzu* oranges, which ripen in the winter, while in the Chinese recipe below dried winter mushrooms and the first spring shoots of bamboo are used. This makes it a very expensive dish. However, for a family meal you can use ordinary dried mushrooms and canned bamboo shoots.

INGREDIENTS

10 dried mushrooms
150 g (5 oz) winter bamboo
45 ml (3 tablespoons) oil
1 slice ginger
5 ml (1 teaspoon) soy sauce
pinch salt
2.5 ml (½ teaspoon) sugar
5 ml (1 teaspoon) rice wine
5 ml (1 teaspoon) sesame oil

PREPARATION

Soak the mushrooms in warm water for 30 minutes, then discard the hard stalk and cut the caps into quarters or halves, depending on size. Slice the bamboo shoots into thin slices. Heat a wok or large frying-pan with the oil and stir-fry the ginger and mushrooms for 30 seconds. Add the bamboo shoots and after another 30 seconds season with the soy sauce, salt, sugar and rice wine. Stir-fry for another minute before serving sprinkled with the sesame oil.

Five-colour 'prawns'

CHINESE

This recipe belongs to a tradition of vegetarian cooking in China that embraces both the grandly contrived dishes of temple cooking and these simple fried potato shapes, all of them creating 'mock meat' in place of the real thing.

INGREDIENTS

180 g (6 oz) potato
4 dried mushrooms
25 g (1 oz) french beans
50 g (2 oz) carrots
25 g (1 oz) bamboo shoots
15 ml (1 tablespoon) cornflour
5 ml (1 teaspoon) sesame oil
2.5 ml (½ teaspoon) salt
a good pinch pepper
90 ml (6 tablespoons) potato flour
oil for deep frying

SEASONING SAUCE

10 ml (2 teaspoons) rice wine
5 ml (1 teaspoon) sugar
5 ml (1 teaspoon) red vinegar
90 ml (6 tablespoons) vegetarian stock
5 ml (1 teaspoon cornflour

1.5 ml (¼ teaspoon) freshly ground black pepper
2.5 ml (½ teaspoon) sesame oil

PREPARATION

Steam the potato in its skin until cooked (about 25 minutes). Meanwhile, soak the dried mushrooms in warm water for 20 minutes, then discard the hard stalks and cut the caps into thick slices. Wash and trim the french beans, then cut into 3-cm (1-inch) lengths. Boil in lightly salted water for 3 minutes, then refresh in cold water and leave to drain. Peel and cut the carrot into batons about 3 × 1 cm (1 × ⅓ inch). Boil in lightly salted water for 5 minutes, then drain. Cut the bamboo shoots into similar-sized pieces. When the potato is cooked, skin and mash it with the cornflour, sesame oil, salt and pepper to make a stiff dough. Roll out into a sausage about 1 cm (½ inch) in diameter and cut into 4-cm (1½-inch) lengths. Coat in the dry potato flour and deep-fry in hot oil until golden brown (about 1 minute). Drain well.

Heat 30 ml (2 tablespoons) oil in a wok or large frying-pan and stir-fry the mushrooms for 30 seconds. Add the bamboo shoots, carrots and beans and continue stir-frying for another minute. Pour in the seasoning sauce. Bring to the boil and quickly mix in the potato 'prawns' and black pepper. Serve sprinkled with sesame oil.

NOTE The potato rolls can be prepared well in advance of the meal and deep-fried again for a few seconds in hot oil before being added to the other vegetables.

STIR-FRIED GREEN VEGETABLES

Green leaf vegetables lend themselves particularly well to the Chinese technique of quick stir-frying, which leaves them with a fresh, natural flavour and a firm texture. Serve any of these vegetables with beancurd or a Chinese gluten dish and possibly an egg dish too.

Although these recipes are from China, they are typical of simple vegetable dishes cooked all over South East Asia.

Stir-fried bok choi

CHINESE

INGREDIENTS

350 g (12 oz) bok choi
2 cloves garlic
60 ml (4 tablespoons) oil
2.5 ml (½ teaspoon) salt

PREPARATION

Wash and break up the *bok choi* plants, unless they are very small. Cut each stalk and leaf into 5-cm (2-inch) lengths. Crush the garlic. Heat the oil in a wok or large frying-pan and stir-fry the garlic for 15 seconds. Add the *bok choi* and salt and stir-fry for another minute. Then add about 15 ml (1 tablespoon) water and stir-fry until the water has evaporated and the stalks are cooked but still crisp (about 3 minutes). Adjust the seasoning and serve.

Bok choi with preserved vegetable

CHINESE

This is a Buddhist version of the previous recipe.

INGREDIENTS

250 g (8 oz) bok choi
50 g (2 oz) Sichuan preserved vegetable
45 ml (3 tablespoons) oil

PREPARATION

Wash the *bok choi*, tear the plants into separate leaves and discard any that are wilted. Cut the leaves and stalks into 3-cm (1-inch) lengths. Wash the preserved vegetable and cut into matchsticks. Heat the oil in a wok or large frying-pan and stir-fry the preserved vegetable for about 30 seconds before putting in the *bok choi*. Continue stir-frying for 1 minute, then add about 15 ml (1 tablespoon) water and stir-fry for another 3 minutes. Serve hot.

Stir-fried choisam

CHINESE

INGREDIENTS

350 g (12 oz) choisam
75 ml (5 tablespoons) oil
2 slices ginger
1.5 ml (¼ teaspoon) salt
5 ml (1 teaspoon) sesame oil

PREPARATION

Wash the *choisam* and cut into 5-cm (2-inch) lengths. Heat the oil in a wok or large frying-pan and stir-fry the ginger for 15 seconds before putting in the *choisam*. Continue stir-frying and season with salt. When the *choisam* is cooked (about 3 minutes), serve sprinkled with sesame oil.

Choisam with chilli-bean sauce

CHINESE

INGREDIENTS

350g (12oz) choisam
1 spring onion, very finely chopped
1 slice ginger, very finely chopped
1 clove garlic, very finely chopped
oil for frying
5ml (1 teaspoon) sugar
5ml (1 teaspoon) rice vinegar
5ml (1 teaspoon) soy sauce
5ml (1 teaspoon) chilli-bean sauce
salt and pepper to taste

PREPARATION

Wash the *choisam* and cut into 3-cm (1-inch) lengths. Heat a wok or large frying-pan with 45ml (3 tablespoons) oil and stir-fry the *choisam* until the leaves are soft (about 3 minutes). Lift out and keep on one side while you add another 15ml (1 tablespoon) oil to the pan and stir-fry the chopped onion, ginger and garlic for about 20 seconds. Return the *choisam* to the pan and season with the sugar, soy sauce, vinegar and chilli-bean sauce. Mix well over a low heat. Adjust the seasoning with salt and pepper and serve.

Sweet and sour cabbage

CHINESE

INGREDIENTS

250g (8oz) cabbage (either summer cabbage or spring greens, not a tight-hearted variety)
1 spring onion

SEASONING SAUCE

15ml (1 tablespoon) sugar
15ml (1 tablespoon) black vinegar
15ml (1 tablespoon) water
25ml (1½ tablespoons) soy sauce
1.5ml (¼ teaspoon) black pepper

30ml (2 tablespoons) oil
salt to taste
2.5ml (½ teaspoon) sesame oil

PREPARATION

Wash and cut the cabbage into 5-cm (2-inch) squares. Discard any hard stalks. Finely chop the spring onion. Mix the seasoning sauce. Heat a wok or large frying-pan with the oil and stir-fry the onion for 15 seconds, then add the cabbage and continue stir-frying for another 3 minutes. Pour in the sauce and bring to the boil. Adjust the seasoning with salt to taste and serve sprinkled with sesame oil.

Stir-fried spinach with garlic and sesame

CHINESE

INGREDIENTS

450g (1lb) fresh spinach
1 clove garlic
25ml (1½ tablespoons) sesame oil
7.5ml (1½ teaspoons) oil
5ml (1 teaspoon) salt

PREPARATION

Wash the spinach and tear out the hard centre ribs. Crush the garlic. Heat the sesame oil and cooking oil in a wok or large frying-pan over a moderate heat. Add the garlic and stir-fry for 15 seconds, then add the spinach. Stir-fry over a moderate heat for about 4 minutes until all the spinach leaves are soft. Season to taste with the salt and serve hot.

Stir-fried spinach and mushrooms

CHINESE

INGREDIENTS

4 dried mushrooms
100g (4oz) fresh or preserved oyster mushrooms
200g (7oz) spinach
45ml (3 tablespoons) oil
1 clove garlic, crushed
pinch salt and pepper

PREPARATION

Soak the dried mushrooms for 30 minutes in warm water, then discard the hard stalks and cut the caps into thin slices. Wipe, peel and slice the oyster mushrooms. Wash the spinach, tear out the tough central veins and cut the leaves into 5-cm (2-inch) pieces. Heat the oil in a wok or large frying-pan and stir-fry the garlic for about 15 seconds. Then add the mushroom slices and continue stir-frying for another minute. Put in the spinach leaves and season at once with salt and pepper. Stir-fry until the spinach is soft. Serve at once.

NOTE Take care not to overcook this dish. Ordinary fresh mushrooms can be used instead of oyster mushrooms.

Stir-fried medlar leaves

CHINESE

Medlar leaves come from *Lycium chinense*, a bush which has various names including wolf berry, Chinese medlar, and the Duke of Argyle's tea bush. Its Chinese name is *gouji*. The leaves have a salty, savoury taste which is very refreshing and pleasing. They do not require any additional salt when they are cooked.

INGREDIENTS

250g (8oz) medlar leaves
30ml (2 tablespoons) oil
10ml (2 teaspoons) sugar
30ml (2 tablespoons) soy sauce

PREPARATION

Tear the leaves from the stiff woody stems and rinse them well. Discard the stems and drain the leaves. Heat the oil in a wok or large frying-pan and stir-fry the leaves over a high heat for about 1 minute. Add the sugar. Continue to stir-fry until all the leaves are soft. Lift from the heat and tip in the soy sauce. Mix well and serve.

Stir-fried purslane

CHINESE

Purslane was a traditional herb in early English cooking, often used in salads. In modern times it has disappeared from our kitchens. However, it can now be bought fresh in Chinese grocers during the summer. It has a fresh, slightly dry flavour, very similar to that of spinach.

INGREDIENTS

250g (8oz) purslane
30ml (2 tablespoons) oil
10ml (2 teaspoons) sugar
15ml (1 tablespoon) soy sauce

PREPARATION

Wash the purslane and discard any dead or wilted leaves. Cut the stalks with the leaves into 6-cm ($2\frac{1}{2}$-inch) lengths. Heat the oil in a wok or frying-pan and stir-fry the purslane until the stalks are cooked (about 4 minutes). Season with sugar and soy sauce and serve.

Stir-fried water-spinach

CHINESE

INGREDIENTS

450g (1 lb) water-spinach
30ml (2 tablespoons) oil
salt and pepper to taste

PREPARATION

Wash the water-spinach and discard any wilted or dead leaves. Cut the stalks into 5-cm (2-inch) lengths. Heat the oil in a wok or large frying-pan and stir-fry the spinach for about 2 minutes. Tip in 60ml (4 tablespoons) water and boil gently until the water has almost gone and the stalks are no longer tough (about 4 minutes). Season to taste and serve hot.

KOREAN GRILLS

For almost two thousand years BC the northern half of Korea was ruled by a Chinese noble family, and Korean cookery owes much to this early influence. At this time the Koreans were nomadic herdsmen, dependent on their herds for food, and during this period they established a style of grilling which remains characteristic of their cuisine today. The Koreans remained great meat-eaters, and although after the coming of Buddhism to Korea from China in the fifth century AD many laws were passed forbidding the killing of animals for food, including one in 599 which ordered the confiscation of all fishing tackle, the Koreans clung to their traditional diet. Vegetarianism lost ground in Korea and by the end of the tenth century the killing of animals for food was forbidden only in the fifth and ninth months of the year. Finally, with the invasion of the Mongols – another meat-eating people – in the fourteenth century, all efforts at enforcing vegetarianism were abandoned. In modern Korea, although many people are Buddhists, they expect to eat meat, usually red meat, at every meal, and they use fish sauces and pastes for flavouring their food.

However, Koreans do use the traditional cooking method of grilling for vegetables as well as for meat, and some recipes for grilled vegetables are included below.

Grilled aubergines

KOREAN

INGREDIENTS

350g (12oz) aubergine

SEASONING SAUCE

- *15ml (1 tablespoon) sesame oil*
- *15ml (1 tablespoon) finely chopped spring onion*
- *30ml (2 tablespoons) Japanese soy sauce*
- *5ml (1 teaspoon) sugar*

PREPARATION

Wash and cut the aubergine into slices 1½cm (½ inch) thick. Soak in lightly salted water for 20 minutes, putting a plate over the aubergines to keep them under the water. Meanwhile make the seasoning sauce by heating the sesame oil in a small saucepan over a low heat and stir-frying the spring onion. Add the soy sauce and sugar, remove from the heat and mix well. Dry the aubergine slices on kitchen paper and paint with the prepared sauce. Put under a moderately hot grill until cooked, turning to cook both sides. Serve hot.

Mixed vegetable grill

KOREAN

INGREDIENTS

180g (6oz) Spanish onion
4 large mushrooms
180g (6oz) aubergine
100g (4oz) carrot
250g (8oz) green pepper

DIPPING SAUCE

150ml (⅔ cup, 5 fl oz) Japanese soy sauce
60ml (4 tablespoons) caster sugar
30ml (2 tablespoons) water
15ml (1 tablespoon) rice wine

½ lemon, cut into thin slices
½ tart apple, cut into thin slices
sesame oil

PREPARATION

Prepare the dipping sauce first by boiling the soy, sugar and water together, then adding the rice wine. Lift from the heat. Leave to cool for a few minutes, then add the slices of lemon and apple. Stand for at least an hour in a cool place; before serving discard the apple and lemon slices.

Peel and cut the onion into four thick rings. Spear each ring with a toothpick to hold them together. Soak the dried mushrooms in warm water for 30 minutes, then discard the hard stalks. Cut the aubergine into 1½-cm (½-inch)-thick slices. Soak in lightly salted water for 30 minutes, putting a plate over the aubergines to keep them under the surface of the water, then pat dry. Scrape and cut the carrot into elongated slices. De-seed the pepper and cut into bite-sized pieces. Arrange all the vegetables on a large plate.

Stand a heavy frying-pan on a gas or electric ring in the centre of the table. When all the diners are seated, start to cook the grill. Lightly oil the pan with sesame oil, then put a portion of each vegetable in the pan, moving them round with long wooden chopsticks. When some portions of the vegetables are cooked serve them to the diners, making sure that everyone has a helping of each vegetable. Each diner has his own bowl of the dipping sauce and dips the food into the sauce before eating it.

Alternatively, brush the vegetables with a little sesame oil and grill under a conventional grill in the kitchen. When they are all cooked, arrange on a heated plate and serve with a separate dipping sauce in a small dish.

Grilled winter melon

KOREAN

This is a seventeenth-century Korean recipe in which the main seasoning is vinegar. In those days most families made their own vinegar from rice, which would probably have resembled the modern Chinese red vinegar.

INGREDIENTS

450g (1lb) winter melon
2 cloves garlic
15g (½oz) ginger
15ml (1 tablespoon) sesame oil
30ml (2 tablespoons) Japanese soy sauce
30ml (2 tablespoons) red vinegar

PREPARATION

Peel and de-seed the winter melon, then cut the flesh into 3-cm (1-inch) cubes. Thread on to skewers. Cut the garlic and ginger into hair-fine shreds. Mix the sesame oil and soy sauce together and paint the mixture over the winter melon. Grill until the melon is soft, then take out the skewers and mix the melon cubes with the garlic and ginger. Either pour over the vinegar before serving or serve the vinegar separately as a dip.

DEEP-FRIED DISHES

Deep-fried mushrooms

CHINESE

INGREDIENTS

12 thick, similar-sized dried mushrooms

MARINADE

5 ml (1 teaspoon) ginger juice
5 ml (1 teaspoon) sesame oil
pinch salt and pepper

5 ml (1 teaspoon) potato flour
30 ml (2 tablespoons) cornflour
30 ml (2 tablespoons) plain flour
oil for deep frying
salt-pepper dip (page 24)

PREPARATION

Soak the mushrooms in warm water for 30 minutes, then remove the hard stalks. Marinate the soft mushroom caps for 20 minutes, then steam, with the marinade, in a covered bowl for 10 minutes. Drain well and reserve the cooking liquor. Pat the mushrooms dry and dust with the potato flour. Mix the cornflour and plain flour in a bowl and mix to a thick batter with the reserved cooking liquid, adding more water if necessary. Coat the mushrooms in this batter and deep-fry in hot oil until golden brown. Serve hot with a salt-pepper dip.

Cellophane greens

CHINESE

These delicious, crisp transparent strands of green are aptly named cellophane greens. Serve them with beancurd or eggs together with a more substantial vegetable dish, such as an Indonesian curry or a Japanese mixed-vegetable simmered dish.

INGREDIENTS

250 g (8 oz) fresh spinach
oil for deep frying

DIPPING SAUCE

45 ml (3 tablespoons) red vinegar
45 ml (3 tablespoons) light soy sauce

PREPARATION

Wash the spinach and cut out any tough centre veins. Lay several leaves out flat, one on top of the other, and roll up into a bundle. Slice into 2-mm ($\frac{1}{16}$-inch) shreds. Repeat with all the spinach. Heat the oil until very hot and put in a handful of the shredded spinach. Lift the pan from the heat and continue frying for 20–30 seconds. Lift out on to kitchen paper and drain. Return the pan to the heat and put in another handful of spinach. Repeat the process until all the spinach is fried. The shreds of fried spinach can be re-warmed in the oven if it has been fried in advance of the meal. Serve hot with the dipping sauce.

NOTE To vary, use 30 per cent sesame oil with 70 per cent ordinary vegetable oil instead of all vegetable oil: this gives the spinach a light sesame flavour.

The Chinese also deep-fry a *wakame*-type seaweed; we have tried using the dried Japanese *wakame* available in the UK, finely shredded, but we cannot recommend it.

Sweet potato balls

CHINESE

INGREDIENTS

300g (10oz) sweet potato (white-fleshed variety)
30ml (2 tablespoons) finely chopped spring onion
30ml (2 tablespoons) toasted white sesame seeds (page 36)
30ml (2 tablespoons) beaten egg
5ml (1 teaspoon) soy sauce
30ml (2 tablespoons) potato flour
5ml (1 teaspoon) sesame oil
pinch salt and pepper
oil for deep frying
salt-pepper dip (page 24)

PREPARATION

Peel the potato and cut into pieces. Soak in water for 20 minutes before steaming over a high heat until very soft (about 20 minutes). Mash either in a food processor or with a potato masher and mix in the chopped onion, sesame seeds, beaten egg, soy sauce, potato flour and sesame oil. Add a little more potato flour if the dough seems very soft. Blend very thoroughly and season to taste with salt and pepper. Oil your hands and roll a tablespoonful of the potato mixture at a time into a ball the size of a walnut. Repeat with the remaining sweet potato. Heat the oil and deep-fry over a moderate heat until the potato balls are golden in colour. Serve hot with a salt-pepper dip.

JAPANESE TEMPURA

Japanese *tempura* with its delicate, lace-like coating of batter and fresh-flavoured vegetables is one of the most popular Japanese dishes eaten in the West today. Serve it with a simmered dish, such as the aubergine dish *nasu no misoni* (page 69) or braised beancurd (page 81), and a crisp vinegared salad, together with *miso* soup followed by rice and pickles, either home-made or bought-in. Japanese green tea goes well with the rice.

Tempura is not however as easy as it sounds: it is wise to practise making it once or twice before embarking on it for an important meal. On the whole it is better served and eaten immediately after cooking, so the cook must be prepared to do the deep-frying while the guests are eating. When all the vegetables and sauces are prepared, bring the diners to the table and serve the vinegared salad and hot simmered dish. Then mix the batter very lightly with the iced water. (If making *tempura* for a large number of people, discard the batter and mix a fresh batch halfway through the cooking.) Deep-fry the vegetables in batches, one helping at a time, putting the vegetables into the hot fat in the order of the length of time each takes to cook. It is not the custom to serve second helpings in Japanese meals, so once you have cooked one helping for everybody you can cook your own and eat it.

The recipe below is for *tempura* made with raw vegetables and served with a mildly seasoned, slightly salty dipping sauce. Another recipe for *tempura* made with cooked and seasoned vegetables is given in Chapter 12.

Raw vegetable tempura

JAPANESE

INGREDIENTS

3–4 OF THE FOLLOWING
- *4 fresh flat mushrooms, wiped clean and with central stalks removed*
- *75 g (3 oz) West Indian pumpkin, peeled and cut into 8 bite-sized slices about 1 cm (½ inch) thick*
- *75 g (3 oz) fresh lotus root, washed, peeled and cut into 1-cm (⅓-inch)-thick slices*
- *50 g (2 oz) carrot, scraped and cut into rectangles 3 mm (1/10 inch) thick*
- *50 g (2 oz) sweet potato, preferably orange-fleshed and purple-skinned, thickly peeled and cut into 8 rounds 1 cm (⅓ inch) thick*
- *75 g (3 oz) aubergine, cut lengthways into 8 thin segments (like those of an orange), sprinkled with salt, left to drain for 30 minutes and well rinsed*
- *1 large Western onion, cut into slices about 1 cm (½ inch) thick, each speared with a toothpick*
- *50 g (2 oz) french beans, trimmed to 5-cm (2-inch) lengths*
- *50 g (2 oz) green pepper, de-seeded and cut into rectangles about 3 × 5 cm (1 × 2 inches)*
- *50 g (2 oz) head of calabrese, broken into small florets and well rinsed*
- *4 large sprigs parsley*

DIPPING SAUCE
- *200 ml (7 fl oz)* dashi
- *45 ml (3 tablespoons)* mirin
- *45 ml (3 tablespoons) Japanese soy sauce*

60 ml (4 tablespoons) grated white radish
20 ml (4 tablespoons) grated ginger

BATTER
- *1 egg*
- *200 ml (7 fl oz) iced water*
- *150 g (1 cup, 5 oz) plain flour*

oil for deep frying
sansho *pepper (optional)*

PREPARATION

Prepare your chosen vegetables. Lay out in order of cooking. Make the dipping sauce by mixing the *dashi*, *mirin* and soy sauce in a saucepan and bringing it just to the boil. Keep warm until required. Squeeze the grated white radish dry in a clean tea-towel and divide the pulp between four small plates. Put a small mound of grated ginger on to the plates beside the radish.

When the diners are ready to eat, heat the oil to 180°C (350°F). Beat the egg, stir in the iced water and sift in the flour. Mix lightly. Pat the vegetables dry and dip them one at a time into the batter before dropping into the oil. Coat only the tops of the mushrooms with the batter and just dip the leaves of the parsley in, leaving the stalks uncoated. Hold four or five beans together and dip into the batter in a bundle. Deep-fry only a small quantity of vegetables at a time. Then lift out and drain briefly on kitchen paper.

Serve carefully arranged on individual baskets or dishes together with a plate of grated radish and ginger and a small bowl of warm dipping sauce. Each diner seasons the dipping sauce with the radish and ginger as desired.

Serve *sansho* pepper as an alternative seasoning.

Vegetarian fritters for tempura

Use up the remaining batter by making onion fritters. Prepare 8 spring onions by cutting into 1-cm (½-inch) lengths. Drop into the remaining batter and mix gently. Then drop the batter by the tablespoon into the hot oil to make small onion cakes. Serve with the other *tempura* vegetables.

6 Curries and Braises

The cookery of a country develops and reflects the exchanges its people have with other cultures and cuisines, sometimes importing new foods and seasonings and sometimes adapting locally grown foods to non-indigenous recipes. This is certainly true of Indonesia. Although nothing is known about the indigenous cooking of the people before the second century AD, we do know that the Indians who went as advisers and religious gurus to the aristocratic courts of Java and Bali some 1600 years ago ate rice as their main staple, used yoghurt and ghee in their cooking, and seasoned their foods with black pepper, cumin, turmeric, onions, garlic, ginger, tamarind and possibly coriander. Their kitchens were certainly equipped with pestles and mortars for grinding spices. All these foods and spices are still characteristic of Indian cooking today, and many are commonly used in Indonesian dishes.

As observed in Chapter 1, Indonesia and Malaysia share a cultural inheritance and a common language. Their cuisines bear an obvious resemblance to each other, although there are regional variations, often the result of religious influences.

For example, while many parts of Indonesia and Malaysia were converted to Islam, with varying degrees of success, Bali remained Hindu. Today Indonesian cooking style is very mixed but shows little signs of Buddhist influence. However, many of the Indonesian recipes in this book come from the villages: they represent peasant cooking rather than restaurant or middle-class cuisine. As such they are almost certainly old and traditional forms dating from the earliest Indian, and therefore possibly Buddhist, introductions. These recipes are in strong contrast to those from China and Japan.

Indian Buddhists were strict vegetarians, but as they followed a different interpretation of Buddhist teachings from China and Japan they did not insist upon low levels of seasoning. Some foods were however changed in favour of local products. Coconut milk and coconut oil replaced the yoghurt and ghee of Indian cooking. (Coconut palms are native to Indonesia and are both easier and cheaper to raise than cows.) *Laos*, which resembles ginger, is native to Indonesia and is generally used in its place. Its flavour is more bitter than hot, with an overtone of camphor. Chillis, unknown in Asia until long after the Indian influence on Indonesia had ended, replaced black pepper as the hottest spice in both Indian and Indonesian cuisine during the sixteenth century. Many spices are native to Indonesia – the original Spice Islands – and so, following Indian patterns, even peasant dishes in Indonesia are highly seasoned.

It is a basic rule of Indian and Indonesian cooking that the spices and seasonings – which almost invariably include onions – should be cooked until their flavour is fully matured before any other food is added to the pan. This process of developing flavour by either frying or simmering takes time and cannot be hurried. No thickening is used in Indian or Indonesian cooking: body is given to the sauces by the onions and chillis.

Six hundred years after the Indians visited Java, Moslem Arabs converted the people to Islam. It seems probable that among the dietary changes the Moslems brought was coffee, drunk in the Arab style – sweet, strong and black. Coffee is grown in Indonesia and in the villages unless a family is very poor they drink black coffee, sweetened with plenty of locally grown sugar, with many of their meals. Today Indonesian cookery shows little signs of Buddhist influence. However, many of the Indonesian recipes in this book come from village and peasant cooking rather than restaurant and middle-class cuisine and these are almost certainly old and traditional forms dating from the earliest Indian and therefore possibly Buddhist introductions.

It would be hard to find a greater contrast to Indonesian food than Japanese.

The Japanese, like the Indonesians, experienced an influx of foreign ideas – in this case from Chinese and Korean Buddhist monks who were invited to the Japanese court by the Emperor at about the same time as the Indians went to Java. The monks and the Chinese craftsmen who came with them introduced the Japanese to Buddhist beliefs and dietary laws, including vegetarianism. They brought with them a wide range of Chinese seasonings and foodstuffs such as soy sauce, *miso*, beancurd, vinegar, ginger, white radish and sesame. All are used to this day in Japan.

The Chinese, who until about the seventh century cooked almost all their food either in or over water, or directly over fire, were at that time developing the art of frying in oil, and with it the cutting of foods into sizes suitable for quick cooking. The Japanese learned and still practise these different cutting styles in their cooking. They also developed a simmering technique based on early Chinese cooking styles, in which each seasoning was added in an established order to build up the flavour. The foods are cooked in stocks ranging from a simple *dashi* with a little *sake* to an elaborate and carefully balanced combination of sugar, salt, soy sauce, *miso* and sometimes ginger, added in that order. The Japanese cook many different kinds of vegetables in such a stock, unlike the Chinese, who generally cook their vegetables for a shorter time, reserving slow simmering for dishes that include meat.

CHILLI-HOT DISHES

All the dishes in this section are strongly seasoned with chillis and other spices. Most of them come from Indonesia and Malaysia, whose cuisine is still influenced by early contacts with Indian cookery. The Japanese dislike such strong flavours and the Chinese are divided in their tastes: in the east of China people will not touch dishes which include chillis, while in Sichuan, Yunnan and Hunan in the west a stunning quantity of chillis is used in the cooking and, like the Indonesians, the people eat raw chillis as a side dish.

We suggest you combine a fresh-flavoured or slightly sour salad of lightly cooked or raw vegetables with Indonesian curries. You can vary the texture in the meal by including a crunchy dish of fried nuts in some form to contrast with the curries. For an Indonesian meal any of the first three egg recipes would make an ideal side dish to go with a larger vegetable curry or stew, such as a *lodeh* or *sayur*. You could serve them with a *sambal* and either plain or coconut rice.

Sambal goreng taocoo (eggs in a hot chilli-bean sauce)

JAVANESE

INGREDIENTS

6 eggs
75g (3oz) red onions
2 cloves garlic
2 green chillis
30ml (2 tablespoons) fermented black beans
30ml (2 tablespoons) vegetable oil
1 lime leaf or bay leaf
2 slices ginger
5ml (1 teaspoon) brown sugar
250ml (8fl oz) santan

PREPARATION

Boil the eggs for about 6 minutes, then dip in cold water and shell while still hot. Take care not to tear the white since the yolks are not firmly set. Leave until required. Roughly cut the onion, garlic and de-seeded chillis. Place in a food processor and blend to a smooth paste, or grind with a pestle and mortar. Chop the black beans. Heat the oil and stir-fry the onion paste over a low heat for about 10 minutes, until it smells cooked. Then add the black beans, lime leaf, ginger and sugar and mix well before pouring in the *santan*. Bring to the boil, stirring gently, and allow to simmer for about 15 minutes. Add the hard-boiled eggs and continue cooking, stirring from time to time until the sauce has thickened and small beads of oil start to appear. Serve hot.

Sichuan chilli aubergines

CHINESE

The mixture of garlic, chillis, sugar, vinegar and soy sauce is very common in Sichuan cooking, and is called 'fish-fragrant' although it has nothing to do with fish.

An equivalent Indonesian sour sauce for aubergines is made with 75g (3 oz) red onions, 2 cloves garlic, 2 fresh chillis and a pinch of *laos* powder all beaten to a paste with 300ml (10 fl oz) tamarind water and 20ml (4 teaspoons) brown sugar. Cook the onion paste in the tamarind water for about 10 minutes over a gentle heat, then add the aubergines cut in very thin slices and simmer for another 10 minutes. Adjust the seasoning and garnish with fried onion flakes before serving.

The small Asian aubergines that can be bought in Indian grocers are better for this dish, but not essential.

INGREDIENTS

350g (12oz) aubergines
2 pieces wood ears
8 water chestnuts
oil for deep frying
2 slices ginger
2 spring onions, cut into 1-cm (½-inch) lengths
1 clove garlic, sliced
5–10ml (1–2 teaspoons) chilli-bean sauce, according to strength desired

SEASONING SAUCE

15ml (1 tablespoon) soy sauce
10ml (2 teaspoons) sugar
25ml (1½ tablespoons) red vinegar
45ml (3 tablespoons) water
pinch salt and pepper

5ml (1 teaspoon) cornflour mixed with 10ml (2 teaspoons) water
2.5ml (½ teaspoon) sesame oil

PREPARATION

Slice the aubergine into long, thin slices like the segments of an orange. Soak the wood ears in warm water for 30 minutes, then discard any hard bits and slice finely. Cut the water chestnuts into matchstick pieces. Deep-fry the aubergines until soft (about 2–3 minutes), then drain well. Heat 30ml (2 tablespoons) oil in a wok or frying-pan and stir-fry the onion, ginger and garlic for 15 seconds. Add the wood ears and water chestnuts. After another minute lift the pan from the heat and stir in the chilli-bean sauce. Add the aubergines and seasoning sauce and return to the heat. Bring to the boil and thicken with the cornflour paste. Serve hot, sprinkled with the sesame oil.

Telur bali (eggs cooked in a Balinese style)

INDONESIAN

This recipe is also from Indonesia – more specifically, from Bali. There are many variations, but in this one the eggs are deep-fried after they have been hard-boiled. This is a very usual practice in the Far East. You can of course omit the deep-frying if you prefer. The gherkin is in place of *pete asin* – a sour bean which cannot easily be obtained in the UK, but has rather similar qualities of texture and flavour. The little French gherkins are better than the bigger German or Polish variety for this dish.

INGREDIENTS

6 eggs

oil for deep frying

SAUCE

- *15 ml (1 tablespoon) soy sauce*
- *1 small pickled gherkin*
- *1 slice fresh* laos *or ginger, or a pinch of* laos *powder*
- *1 chilli, de-seeded*
- *25 g (1 oz) red onion*
- *1 clove garlic*
- *2.5 ml (½ teaspoon) brown sugar*
- *salt to taste*

PREPARATION

Boil the eggs for 5 minutes, then dip in cold water and carefully shell while still warm. The yolks will not be set, so take care not to tear the whites. Heat the oil until hot and deep-fry the eggs until golden brown all over (about 3–4 minutes). Lift out and leave to drain. Put all the ingredients for the sauce in a food processor and work into a smooth, wet paste. Add 150 ml (5 fl oz) water and mix well. Pour the sauce into a saucepan and simmer for about 10 minutes. Cut the eggs into halves and add to the sauce. Simmer for another 2 minutes, check the seasoning and serve hot.

Telur kari (curried eggs)

MALAYSIAN

INGREDIENTS

8 eggs

oil for deep frying (optional)

SAUCE

- *75 g (3 oz) red onions*
- *2 cloves garlic*
- *2 fresh chillis*
- *2 slices* laos *or ginger*
- *5 ml (1 teaspoon) ground coriander*
- *2.5 ml (½ teaspoon) turmeric*
- *2.5 ml (½ teaspoon) freshly ground black pepper*
- *1.5 ml (¼ teaspoon) ground cumin*
- *2.5 ml (½ teaspoon) powdered lemon grass*
- *2.5 ml (½ teaspoon) salt*
- *250 ml (1 cup, 8 fl oz)* santan

PREPARATION

Boil the eggs for 5 minutes, then dip in cold water and shell, taking care not to tear the whites around the soft yolks. Heat the oil until very hot and deep-fry the eggs until golden brown all over (about 3–4 minutes). Lift out and leave on one side – or omit the deep-frying altogether and hard-boil the eggs for about 10 minutes before shelling.

Chop the onions, garlic, de-seeded chillis and ginger, then place them in a food-processor and work into a paste. Add the coriander, turmeric, black pepper, cumin and lemon powder. Heat 30 ml (2 tablespoons) oil in a wok or large frying-pan and fry this paste over a low heat for about 10 minutes. Then add the salt and pour in the *santan.* Mix well and leave to simmer for about 10 minutes, stirring from time to time. Slide in the eggs, adjust the seasoning and serve.

Oseng-oseng boncis (braised beans)

JAVANESE

'Oseng-oseng' are the Javanese words expressing the sound food makes while it is frying. In Indonesia this dish is made with long beans, a common variety of bean grown all over the Far East. If you cannot find these, french beans make an excellent substitute. Serve these hot chilli beans or the spicy water-spinach dish which follows in place of a salad with a soupy *sayur* such as *sayur bening* (page 74) or *sayur bobor* (page 75).

INGREDIENTS

500 g (1 lb) long beans or french beans, either fresh or frozen
125 g (4 oz) tomato
125 g (4 oz) red onions
3 cloves garlic
2 chillis
5 ml (1 teaspoon) vegetable oil
15 ml (1 tablespoon) dark soy sauce
1.5 ml (¼ teaspoon) brown sugar, or to taste
1.5 ml (¼ teaspoon) salt, or to taste
1 bay leaf
100 ml (3½ fl oz) water

PREPARATION

If using fresh beans wash, trim and cut them into 5-cm (2-inch) lengths, then boil in lightly salted water for 5 minutes. If using frozen beans put them into lightly salted boiling water, without de-frosting, and bring back to the boil. Drain and set aside until required. Skin and de-seed the tomato and put it with the onions, peeled garlic and de-seeded chillis in a food processor or liquidizer. Work into a coarse paste. (If you do not have a processor use a pestle and mortar to grind the vegetables into a paste.) Oil a wok or frying-pan and fry the onion paste over a low to moderate heat for about 5 minutes, until the onions lose their harsh smell. Stir in the soy sauce, sugar and salt, followed by the beans. Mix well, add the bay leaf and water and bring to the boil. Simmer for about 4 minutes, adjust the seasoning and serve hot.

OPPOSITE *Braised quail eggs and straw mushrooms (page 168): quails' eggs and straw mushrooms simmered in a sauce of soy sauce, rice wine and stock. Stuffed mushrooms (page 107): steamed dried mushrooms filled with sesame-flavoured potato in a sweet and sour sauce. Marinated mixed mushrooms (page 50): five different varieties of mushroom, quickly stir-fried then marinated in soy sauce, rice vinegar and sesame oil; served cold. All three dishes are Chinese.*

OVERLEAF, LEFT *Part of a Korean meal, showing a mixed vegetable grill (page 56) with slices of aubergine, carrot, pepper, mushroom and onion rings being grilled at the table together with cucumber* namuru *(page 130); beansprout salad (page 129), vegetable fritters (page 72), made with thin slices of sweet potato, and plain boiled rice (page 154).*

OVERLEAF, RIGHT *A decorative plate of Chinese cold* hors d'oeuvre *including vegetarian 'ham' (page 100), vegetarian 'chicken' (page 101), smoked vegetarian 'goose' (page 102), garlic peanuts (page 117), pine kernel and* nori *salad (page 114), steamed black mushrooms (page 108), black hair fungus (page 167) and pickled cauliflower (page 117), garnished with tomatoes cut as lotus flowers and cucumber fans (see pages 38–9).*

福祿壽禧

Lodeh

INDONESIAN

Vegetable stews, called *lodeh*, are the principle dish for most rural family meals in Java. Almost every family has its own recipe for these stews, but basically they consist of three or four fresh seasonal vegetables cooked in a spiced stock based on *santan* (coconut milk). In the recipe below you have a choice of different combinations of vegetables, all of which may be cooked in the same simmering stock. Serve with a side dish of eggs or beancurd, a salad, a *sambal* and plenty of rice, either plain boiled or cooked with coconut.

INGREDIENTS

150g (5oz) aubergine
150g (5oz) long beans or string beans
150g (5oz) chayote
4 brazil nuts
75g (3oz) red onions
3 cloves garlic
2 chillis
pinch laos *or 1 slice ginger*
10ml (2 teaspoons) coriander powder
pinch salt
a little oil
1 bay leaf
300ml (1¼ cups, ½ pint) thick santan

PREPARATION

Wash and cut the aubergine into wedge-shaped pieces. String and cut the beans into 3-cm (1-inch) lengths. Wash and slice the chayote. Toast the nuts in the oven or in a dry pan until lightly browned. Crush and place in a food processor with the onion, garlic, chillis, *laos* powder, coriander and salt. Work into a smooth paste. Lightly oil a pan and cook the paste and the bay leaf for about 10 minutes over a gentle heat, stirring from time to time. Then add 450ml (2 cups, ¾ pint) water and the aubergine and chayote. Stir in the *santan* and simmer for 10 minutes. Then add the string beans and continue simmering for another 10 minutes. Check the seasoning and serve.

NOTE Instead of the vegetables listed above, you can substitute 100g (4oz) potatoes, 100g (4oz) carrots, 100g (4oz) Chinese leaves and 100g (4oz) french beans. Peel the potatoes and cut into small chunks. Scrape the carrots and cut into 3-cm (1-inch) lengths. Wash the Chinese leaves and cut into 4-cm (1½-inch) pieces. Make the paste as above but with 600ml (2½ cups, 1 pint) water. Put the carrots and potatoes into the prepared simmering stock to cook for 15 minutes, then add the rest of the vegetables. Cook for a further 10 minutes, then serve.

OPPOSITE *'Buddha leaps over the wall' (page 170): this romantically named Chinese mixed-vegetable soup includes dried mushrooms, yams, winter melon, bamboo shoots, vegetarian 'chicken' and strips of pickled mustard greens. Also shown are stir-fried egg and black fungus (page 46) and family aubergines (page 131), for which aubergines are stir-fried, generally seasoned with soy sauce, sugar and spring onions, and served cold.*

Tomis kangkung (braised water-spinach)

INDONESIAN

INGREDIENTS

250 g (8 oz) water-spinach
25 g (1 oz) red onion
1 clove garlic
50 g (2 oz) tomatoes
2 chillis
15 ml (1 tablespoon) oil
15 ml (1 tablespoon) salted soya beans, crushed
pinch laos *powder, or 1 slice ginger*
1 dried lime leaf, or 1 bay leaf
150 ml (⅔ cup, ¼ pint) tamarind juice (page 42)
15 ml (1 tablespoon) dark soy sauce
1.5 ml (¼ teaspoon) brown sugar
salt to taste

PREPARATION

Pick over the water-spinach and rinse well before cutting into 7-cm (3-inch) lengths. Slice the onion and garlic very finely. Skin and de-seed the tomato before chopping the flesh. De-seed and chop the chillis finely. Heat the oil in a wok or large frying-pan and stir-fry the onions and garlic until lightly browned. Add the chopped tomatoes, crushed soya beans, *laos* powder, chillis and lime leaf. Mix well and add the water-spinach. Tip in the tamarind juice, soy sauce and sugar and bring to the boil. Check the seasoning and simmer for 6 minutes until the water-spinach is just tender. Serve hot.

Setup (chilli-hot braised vegetables)

JAVANESE

The original version of this recipe included shrimp paste (*terasi*) as a flavouring; we have substituted a salty soy sauce. If you wish for a milder dish, de-seed the chillis. *Setup* may be served with a side dish of eggs or beancurd and a vinegared salad.

INGREDIENTS

125 g (4 oz) long beans or french beans
125 g (4 oz) Chinese leaves
75 g (3 oz) carrots
150 g (5 oz) potatoes
100 g (4 oz) red onions
3 cloves garlic
3 fresh chillis
2 tomatoes, skinned
30 ml (2 tablespoons) vegetable oil
1 lime leaf
15 ml (1 tablespoon) light soy sauce
200 ml (1 cup, ⅓ pint) thick santan
salt to taste

PREPARATION

Wash and cut the beans into 5-cm (2-inch) lengths. Wash the Chinese leaves and cut into 4-cm (1½-inch) pieces. Peel the carrot and potato and cut them into batons about 4 cm (1½ inches) long. Par-boil the potatoes, carrots and beans separately in salted water until almost cooked. Leave to drain. Cut the onion and garlic into pieces and put into a food processor to work into a wet paste. Slice the chillis finely and chop the skinned tomatoes. Heat the oil in a wok or large frying-pan and fry the onion paste over a low heat for about 10 minutes, until it no longer smells raw. Then add the chillis, lime leaf, tomato and soy sauce and stir-fry for a few minutes before adding the vegetables. Mix well with the onions and chillis and pour in the *santan*, stirring all the time. Bring gently to the boil and simmer until all the vegetables are cooked (about 7 minutes). Adjust the seasoning and serve.

Sambal goreng kering kentang (fried potatoes in a hot chilli sauce)

INDONESIAN

These fried potatoes with their chillis sauce make a good contrasting dish to go with *sayur bobor*, or try serving with Chinese barbecued 'spareribs'.

INGREDIENTS

500 g (1 lb) waxy potatoes
120 g (4 oz) red onions
3 cloves garlic
3 dried chillis
oil for deep frying
300 ml (1¼ cups, ½ pint) tamarind juice
3 slices laos *or ginger*
1 bay leaf
20 ml (4 teaspoons) brown sugar
salt to taste

PREPARATION

Wash, peel and cut the potatoes as you would for chips. Soak them in lightly salted water for 15 minutes. Blend the onions, garlic and chillis in a food processor or use a pestle and mortar to work into a fine paste. Then heat 5 ml (1 teaspoon) oil in a frying-pan and stir-fry the onion paste over moderate heat until the onions are cooked (about 10 minutes). Put on one side. Heat the oil for the deep frying until very hot. Drain and dry the chips and deep-fry until golden brown. Lift out and drain well on kitchen paper. Put the tamarind juice with the remaining ingredients into a clean pan and bring to the boil. Add the cooked onion paste and mix well. Adjust the seasoning and just before serving mix the fried potatoes into the sauce and bring to the boil. Serve immediately.

MILD DISHES

In contrast to those of the previous section none of the dishes in the remaining sections of this chapter is hot. Their seasonings range from the sour flavours of vinegar and garlic, as in *sayur asam* or braised silk noodles, through the sweet and sour of vinegar and sugar, as in sweet and sour 'meat' rolls, to sweet bean sauces and sesame aubergines with *miso*. They all take time to cook, but once finished they can wait while other dishes are cooked. From the cook's point of view they combine very happily with stir-fried or deep-fried dishes that need last-minute attention.

Most Japanese meals will include one dish cooked in this manner. The Japanese always use different cooking styles for each dish in a meal, so serve a simmered dish with fried beancurd, or a steamed egg dish, a vinegared salad and *miso* soup.

Braised spinach

JAPANESE

INGREDIENTS

300 g (10 oz) spinach
200 ml (1 cup, ⅓ pint) dashi
15 ml (1 tablespoon) mirin
15 ml (1 tablespoon) Japanese soy sauce
pinch salt

PREPARATION

Wash the spinach, remove any tough central veins and blanch the leaves in boiling water for 1 minute. Then refresh in cold water and squeeze dry. Bring the *dashi*, *mirin*, soy sauce and salt to the boil in a saucepan and put in the spinach. Return to the boil, then lift the pan from the heat and leave the spinach in the pan for another minute. Drain and squeeze out the remaining liquid by rolling the spinach in a rolling mat. Cut the firm roll of spinach into 5-cm (2-inch) lengths and serve in four individual dishes.

Braised soya beans

JAPANESE

The *konnyaku* in this recipe is a greyish transparent jelly made in Japan from mountain yams. It needs to be fresh and is always bought ready-made in Japan. It adds an interesting texture to a simmered dish, but must always be blanched in boiling water first to remove the bitter taste.

INGREDIENTS

120g (4oz) dried soya beans
10cm (4 inches) konbu
100g (4oz) konnyaku
50g (2oz) carrot
50g (2oz) fresh or canned lotus root
2.5ml (½ teaspoon) salt
30ml (2 tablespoons) Japanese soy sauce
45ml (3 tablespoons) caster sugar

PREPARATION

Wash the soya beans and leave to soak overnight in 400ml (2 cups, ⅔ pint) water. The next day bring to the boil in this water. When the water boils add 60ml (4 tablespoons) cold water. Bring back to the boil and add 45ml (3 tablespoons) water. Add 45ml (3 tablespoons) water three more times, then cover the pan and cook the beans over a low heat for about 1½ hours. (If necessary add a little more water.)

Meanwhile cut the *konbu* into 1-cm (⅓-inch) squares. Put the *konnyaku* into boiling water and blanch for 1 minute, then drain well and cut into 1-cm (⅓-inch) dice. Peel and cut the carrot and lotus root into similar-sized dice. When the soya beans are soft, add the *konbu, konnyaku,* carrot and lotus root and simmer gently for another 30 minutes. Season with salt, soy sauce and sugar and lift from the heat. Leave to sit for at least 10 minutes before re-heating and serving.

This dish is even better if it is made a day early and left to stand.

Figs with miso sauce

JAPANESE

INGREDIENTS

4 ripe figs

SIMMERING STOCK

300ml (10fl oz) dashi
7.5ml (1½ teaspoons) Japanese or light soy sauce
15ml (1 tablespoon) mirin

MISO SAUCE

40ml (1½ tablespoons) white miso
15ml (1 tablespoon) mirin
30ml (2 tablespoons) sake
5–10ml (1–2 teaspoons) caster sugar to taste

PREPARATION

Dip the figs in boiling water and peel them as you would a tomato. Mix the simmering stock in a clean pan and put in the figs. Bring to a gentle boil and simmer for 10 minutes. Meanwhile in another pan mix the *miso* sauce and cook over a low heat for about 5 minutes, stirring all the time. Arrange the figs in four separate serving bowls with a little of the simmering stock and spoon the *miso* sauce over them. Serve hot.

Aubergines in soy sauce (nasu nimono)

JAPANESE

INGREDIENTS
500g (1 lb) aubergines
10ml (2 teaspoons) salt
1 fresh chilli (optional)
15ml (1 tablespoon) caster sugar
15ml (1 tablespoon) mirin
45ml (3 tablespoons) Japanese or light soy sauce
300ml (½ pint) dashi
oil for deep frying
finely sliced spring onion for garnish

PREPARATION
Cut the aubergines into batons about 3 × 7 cm (1¼ × 7 inches). Lightly score the skin and soak them in 1 litre (1¾ pints) water containing 10ml (2 teaspoons) salt for 30 minutes. De-seed the chilli and chop into small pieces.

Mix the sugar, *mirin*, soy sauce and chilli with the *dashi* in a saucepan and bring to the boil, then leave to simmer over a low heat. Heat the oil and drain and dry the aubergines. Deep-fry until soft, then gently press out the surplus oil before putting them into the sauce to simmer for 2 minutes. Divide between four small plates with a little of the sauce. Garnish with finely sliced spring onion.

Braised bok choi and mushrooms

JAPANESE

INGREDIENTS
100g (4oz) fresh mushrooms
200g (7oz) bok choi
30ml (2 tablespoons) Japanese or light soy sauce
15ml (1 tablespoon) mirin
60ml (4 tablespoons) dashi
1 yuzu *or Seville orange or lemon*

PREPARATION
Wipe the mushrooms and cut into thin slices. Wash and cut the *bok choi* into 3-cm (1-inch) lengths. Put the mushrooms with the soy sauce, *mirin* and *dashi* into a pan and bring to the boil, then simmer gently until the mushrooms are cooked (about 5 minutes). Meanwhile put the *bok choi* into a pan of lightly salted boiling water and boil for 2 minutes before refreshing under cold water and draining well. When the mushrooms are cooked, lift out with a slotted spoon and mix with the *bok choi* in 4 small serving bowls. Add the juice of the *yuzu*, orange or lemon to the sauce and pour over the mixed vegetables. Garnish with threads of *yuzu* or orange or lemon peel.

Aubergines with miso (nasu no misoni)

JAPANESE

INGREDIENTS
50g (1 lb) aubergine
5ml (1 teaspoon) white sesame seeds
SEASONING SAUCE
45ml (3 tablespoons) miso
30ml (2 tablespoons) caster sugar, or more to taste
100ml (3½ fl oz) water
60ml (4 tablespoons) oil
5ml (1 teaspoon) finely chopped ginger
30ml (2 tablespoons) sake

PREPARATION
Cut the aubergines into 1-cm (½-inch) thin slices, then cut each slice in half. Soak the slices in cold water to remove any bitterness, placing a plate over them to keep them under the water. Meanwhile, toast the sesame seeds in a dry frying-pan over a moderate heat until they start to change colour and dance. Tip out on to a plate to cool. Mix the seasoning sauce.

Heat the oil in a frying-pan. Pat the aubergine slices dry and stir-fry with the chopped ginger over a moderate heat until they start to soften (about 5 minutes). Tip in the *sake* and seasoning sauce and continue to stir-fry until the aubergine is cooked and the sauce much reduced. Serve with the sauce in deep individual bowls, garnished with the toasted sesame seeds.

Ginger pumpkin

JAPANESE

Pumpkins grown in the UK (described as Western pumpkins in the recipes) take about 20 minutes to cook in boiling stock of water, after which even the skin can be eaten. They have a delicious, delicate flavour. West Indian pumpkins, with a slightly more robust flavour, take about 7 minutes for the flesh to fall; however, the skin remains hard and cannot be eaten. This recipe can also be used for the small yams called edoes in UK West Indian markets. They take about 20 minutes to cook, and resemble a variety of yam which is available in Japan.

INGREDIENTS

500g (1 lb) Western pumpkin
15ml (1 tablespoon) caster sugar
5ml (1 teaspoon) soy sauce
5ml (1 teaspoon) salt
5ml (1 teaspoon) ginger juice
7.5ml (1½ teaspoons) potato flour mixed with 15ml (1 tablespoon) water

PREPARATION

Wash the pumpkin carefully and scrub the skin clean. Remove the seeds. Cut the pumpkin into 3-cm (1-inch) pieces. Cut a thin rim off the skin around all four sides on each piece. This bevel will help the pumpkin pieces hold their shape. Place in a saucepan with the sugar, soy sauce, salt and sufficient water just to cover. Bring quickly to the boil, then cover the pan and simmer gently until the pumpkin is tender (about 15–20 minutes). Lift out the pumpkin pieces and arrange in four small heated bowls. Add the ginger juice to the remaining liquid in the pan and simmer for about 2 minutes. Thicken with the potato-flour paste. Spoon the sauce over the pumpkins and serve.

Soy-simmered pumpkin

JAPANESE

INGREDIENTS

450g (1 lb) Western pumpkin
SIMMERING STOCK
400ml (⅔ pint) dashi
60ml (4 tablespoons) caster sugar
50ml (3½ tablespoons) Japanese or light soy sauce
15ml (1 tablespoon) sake
45ml (3 tablespoons) sugar, or to taste

PREPARATION

Wash the skin of the pumpkin well before de-seeding it. Cut the flesh with the skin into even-shaped blocks about 3 × 5cm (1 × 2 inches). Place in a pan with the simmering stock and bring to the boil. Reduce the heat and simmer until the pumpkin is tender (about 20–25 minutes). Then stir in the extra sugar to taste and simmer for a further 2 minutes. Serve in four individual deep bowls with the sauce spooned over the pumpkin pieces.
NOTE If you use a West Indian pumpkin the cooking time will be about two-thirds the time stated above. Serve when the pumpkin is soft with about 45ml (3 tablespoons) cooking sauce to each helping.

VEGETABLE FRITTERS

There is a whole range of Chinese recipes in which vegetables are coated in batter and fried before being finally cooked in a piquant sauce. You can prepare and fry the vegetables an hour or so before the meal, then cook the fritters in the sauce just before they are served. As accompaniment, serve a cold salad, a Chinese gluten dish and perhaps a quickly cooked green vegetable, or try including some Chinese fritters in a Western meal with a salad and a bean dish. This section also includes Javanese and Korean recipes that follow similar principles and can be served in a similar context.

Shallow-fried aubergines

CHINESE

INGREDIENTS

200 g (7 oz) aubergines
5 ml (1 teaspoon) salt
1 egg
25 ml (1½ tablespoons) plain flour
60 ml (4 tablespoons) oil
15 ml (1 tablespoon) finely chopped spring onions
5 ml (1 teaspoon) finely chopped ginger
5 ml (1 teaspoon) crushed garlic
75 ml (5 tablespoons) vegetarian stock
5 ml (1 teaspoon) rice wine
salt to taste
10 ml (2 teaspoons) sesame oil

PREPARATION

Slice the aubergines into rounds about 1 cm (½ inch) thick. Sprinkle with the salt and leave to drain for 30 minutes. Then rinse well and pat dry. Beat the egg and flour into a batter and coat each slice of aubergine in it. Heat the oil in a wok or large frying-pan and fry the coated slices until golden brown on both sides (if necessary fry a few at a time). Add the onion, ginger and garlic and stir-fry for a few seconds before pouring in the stock and rice wine. Simmer for 5 minutes. Adjust the seasoning with salt and sprinkle with sesame oil before serving.

NOTE A remarkably similar recipe to the one given above comes from Java; this one includes soy sauce, which suggests that its origin was also Chinese. However, the fat used for the cooking is butter, an ingredient almost unknown in Chinese cooking, and the seasonings are noticeably simpler.

Smoor terong (aubergines in batter)

JAVANESE

INGREDIENTS

200 g (7 oz) aubergines
100 g (4 oz) red onions
1 egg
50 g (2 oz) butter
100 ml (3½ fl oz) vegetarian stock or water
10 ml (2 teaspoons) light soy sauce
1.5 ml (¼ teaspoon) chilli pepper
salt and sugar to taste

PREPARATION

Peel the aubergines and cut into thin slices. Cut the onions into very thin slices. Beat the egg and dip in the aubergine slices one at a time. Fry them in the butter over a moderate heat until golden brown on both sides. Lift out and drain. Fry the onion slices in the remaining butter until lightly browned. Pour in the stock, soy sauce and chilli pepper and bring to the boil. Adjust the seasoning and add the aubergine slices. Simmer until the stock is absorbed by the onions and aubergines; the dish should not be wet.

Sweet and sour 'meat' slices

CHINESE

INGREDIENTS

250 g (8 oz) white radish
2 spring onions
3 slices ginger
1 large clove garlic
15 g ($\frac{1}{2}$ oz) fresh coriander, including stalks

BATTER

45 ml (3 tablespoons) cornflour
25 ml (1$\frac{1}{2}$ tablespoons) water

SEASONING SAUCE

15 ml (1 tablespoon) soy sauce
45 ml (3 tablespoons) sugar
45 ml (3 tablespoons) rice vinegar
45 ml (3 tablespoons) vegetarian stock
5 ml (1 teaspoon) cornflour

oil for deep frying
5 ml (1 teaspoon) sesame oil

PREPARATION

Peel and cut the white radish into oblong slices, $\frac{1}{2} \times 2 \times 6$ cm ($\frac{1}{4} \times \frac{3}{4} \times 2\frac{1}{2}$ inches). Cut the onion, ginger and garlic into thin threads. Wash and cut the coriander into 2-cm ($\frac{3}{4}$-inch) lengths. Mix the batter and seasoning sauce in separate bowls. Put the radish slices into the batter and coat well. Heat the oil until hot and deep-fry the slices, in several batches, for about 1 minute each, stirring to prevent sticking. Lift out and drain. Heat 30 ml (2 tablespoons) oil in a wok or large frying-pan and stir-fry the ginger, onion and garlic threads for 15 seconds. Then add the white radish slices and the coriander and continue stir-frying for another 30 seconds. Pour in the seasoning sauce and bring to the boil. Adjust the seasoning and serve sprinkled with sesame oil.

Korean vegetable fritters

Korean vegetable fritters are very similar to the Chinese fritters described in the previous recipes. You can use a wide range of vegetables to make this dish, such as white radish, carrot or even marrow or cucumber. We particularly like the sweet potato for its contrast with the spicy dipping sauce.

INGREDIENTS

250 g (8 oz) sweet potato (preferably the red-skinned, orange-fleshed variety)
60 ml (4 tablespoons) oil
45 ml (3 tablespoons) plain flour
1 large egg, beaten

DIPPING SAUCE

60 ml (4 tablespoons) Japanese soy sauce
60 ml (4 tablespoons) rice vinegar
15 ml (1 tablespoon) chopped coriander

PREPARATION

Wash and steam the sweet potato for 15–20 minutes, until just soft but not quite cooked. Peel and cut into strips about $\frac{1}{2} \times 3 \times 4$ cm ($\frac{1}{10} \times 1 \times 1\frac{1}{2}$ inches). Heat the oil in a large frying-pan. Dust the potato strips with the dry flour, then dip into the beaten egg. Place in the pan carefully, without overlapping. Cook in several batches. Fry over a moderate to low heat, turning the strips to brown on both sides. Keep warm in the oven while you cook the remaining sweet potato. Serve with the dipping sauce.

Fried persimmons

CHINESE

INGREDIENTS
2 firm persimmons
2 spring onions
2 slices ginger
2 size 4 eggs
75 g (3 oz) plain flour
SAUCE
15 ml (1 tablespoon) black vinegar
10 ml (2 teaspoons) rice wine
25 ml (1½ tablespoons) light soy sauce
1.5 ml (¼ teaspoon) black pepper
75 ml (5 tablespoons) vegetarian stock
5 ml (1 teaspoon) cornflour
45 ml (3 tablespoons) oil

PREPARATION
Cut the persimmons into slices about 1 cm (⅓ inch) thick and cut each slice in half. Cut the spring onions and ginger into thin shreds. Make a batter with the eggs using 50 g (2 oz) of the flour. Mix the sauce. Heat the oil in a wok or large frying-pan. Dust the persimmon slices in the dry flour before dipping them in the batter. Fry them, a few at a time, in the hot oil, turning to brown on both sides. Lift out and put on one side. When the persimmons are cooked, put the spring onions and ginger into the pan and stir-fry for 15 seconds. Then tip in the sauce and bring to the boil. Add the persimmons, adjust the seasoning and serve.

Cherry and peach

CHINESE

The rather fanciful name of this dish comes from the red and gold colour of the white radish when it is served.

INGREDIENTS
350 g (12 oz) white radish
BATTER
2 size 4 eggs
25 g (1 oz) cornflour
25 g (1 oz) plain flour
pinch salt
SEASONING SAUCE
25 ml (1½ tablespoons) tomato paste
10 ml (2 teaspoons) soy sauce
15 ml (1 tablespoon) rice vinegar
7.5 ml (1½ teaspoons) sugar
60 ml (4 tablespoons) stock
5 ml (1 teaspoon) stock
oil for deep frying

PREPARATION
Wash and peel the white radish. Cut into regularly-shaped 3-cm (1-inch) cubes. Put into boiling water and boil gently until just tender (about 15 minutes). Refresh in cold water and leave to drain. Mix the batter and seasoning sauce in separate bowls. Heat the oil until moderately hot in a deep-fat pan. Dry the white radish cubes with kitchen paper and coat in batter. Deep-fry a few at a time, then lift out and drain. When all the white radish cubes are cooked, heat 15 ml (1 tablespoon) oil in a wok or large frying-pan. Pour in the seasoning sauce and bring to the boil. Add the white radish and mix well in the sauce before serving.

Tomato fritters

CHINESE

INGREDIENTS

4 firm medium-sized tomatoes
25 g (1 oz) bamboo shoots
25 g (1 oz) frozen broad beans
2 spring onions
2 slices ginger
2 size 4 eggs
50 g (2 oz) plain flour
45 ml (3 tablespoons) oil
100 ml (3½ fl oz) vegetarian stock
5 ml (1 teaspoon) cornflour mixed with 10 ml (2 teaspoons) water
5 ml (1 teaspoon) sesame oil

PREPARATION

Skin the tomatoes and cut into 1-cm (⅓-inch) slices; it does not matter if the seeds come out. Cut the bamboo shoots into thin slices and de-frost the broad beans. Cut the spring onions and ginger into thin threads. Beat the eggs. Coat both sides of each tomato slice in a little flour, then dip them in the beaten egg. Heat the oil in a wok or large frying-pan and shallow-fry the coated slices on both sides, in batches to avoid overcrowding, until golden brown. When finished return them all to the pan and add the spring onions and ginger. Stir-fry for 15 seconds, then add the bamboo shoots and broad beans. Pour in the stock and bring to the boil. Adjust the seasoning and thicken with the cornflour paste. Serve sprinkled with sesame oil.

INDONESIAN SOUP STEWS (sayurs)

Indonesian *sayurs* are half-way between a soup and stew. As part of a meal, they can be served as a soup and drunk with a spoon. *Sayur bening* is the poor man's *lodeh* in the villages of Java, because it is cooked with water rather than coconut milk. Many families will have *bening* for one meal and a *lodeh* for the other meal of the day. Both are eaten with rice and a *sambal* or chilli relish, and a side dish such as beancurd.

Sayur bening (spinach soup)

INDONESIAN

INGREDIENTS

500 g (1 lb) fresh spinach
8 canned baby corn cobs
1 chayote
25 g (1 oz) onions
1 clove garlic
1 lime leaf
pinch laos *powder or 1 slice ginger*
600 ml (1 pint) vegetarian stock
salt and sugar to taste

PREPARATION

Wash the spinach and discard the tough central veins. Chop the remaining leaves finely. Cut the baby corn cobs into halves. Wash and slice the chayote thinly. Slice the onion and garlic very finely and put them together with the lime leaf, *laos* powder and stock into a pan. Bring to the boil, add the chayote slices and simmer gently until the chayote is cooked (about 15 minutes). Lift out the chayote with a slotted spoon and keep on one side while you cook the spinach in the same stock for about 2–3 minutes. Check the seasoning and return the chayote together with the baby corn cobs. Bring the soup back to the boil and serve hot with rice.

NOTE To vary, use waxy potatoes instead of chayote, cooked as described above.

Sayur asam (vegetable stew)

INDONESIAN

INGREDIENTS

50 g (2 oz) peanuts (preferably jumbo-size)
100 g (4 oz) red onions
2 cloves garlic
1 fresh chilli, de-seeded
2 slices laos *or ginger*
1 small bay leaf
450 ml (2 cups, ¾ pint) vegetarian stock or water
100 g (4 oz) aubergine
100 g (4 oz) french beans
100 g (4 oz) Chinese leaves
300 ml (1¼ cups, ½ pint) tamarind juice
100 ml (½ cup, 3½ fl oz) thick santan, *or 25 g (1 oz) creamed coconut block*
salt and sugar to taste

PREPARATION

Skin the peanuts by dipping in boiling water. Slice the onions and the garlic very finely. Chop the de-seeded chilli into thin shreds. Put the peanuts with the onions, garlic, chilli, *laos* and bay leaf in a pan with the stock and bring to the boil. Cover with a lid and simmer for 10 minutes. Meanwhile cut the aubergine into slices. Top and tail the french beans and cut into 5-cm (2-inch) lengths. Wash and slice the Chinese leaves into thin strips. When the peanuts are cooked add the aubergine and beans to the pan and simmer for another 8–10 minutes. Then add the Chinese leaves and tamarind water and cook, uncovered, for about 3 minutes. Stir in the *santan.* Adjust the seasoning with salt and sugar before serving.

Sayur bobor (spicy braised courgettes)

INDONESIAN

This dish has a light, cool flavour in which the lemon and coriander blend and contrast with the rich, creamy coconut.

INGREDIENTS

500 g (1 lb) courgettes
250 g (8 oz) fresh spinach
75 g (3 oz) red onions
1 clove garlic
pinch laos *powder or 1 slice ginger*
2.5 ml (½ teaspoon) coriander powder
300 ml (½ pint) vegetarian stock
2.5 ml (½ teaspoon) powdered lemon grass or 1 stalk fresh lemon grass
brown sugar to taste
2.5 ml (½ teaspoon) salt
300 ml (½ pint) thick santan *(see page 41)*

PREPARATION

Wash, peel and cut the courgettes into rings. Wash the spinach and tear out the tough central veins. Chop the leaves finely. Blend the onions, garlic, *laos* and coriander powder in a food processor or work to a smooth paste using a pestle and mortar. Mix with the stock in a wok or saucepan, add the lemon grass and bring to the boil. Season with the salt and sugar and simmer for about 5 minutes, until the onions are cooked. Add the courgettes and stir in the *santan.* Leave to simmer until the courgettes are soft (about 5 minutes). Stir in the chopped spinach and continue simmering for another 3–4 minutes. Adjust the seasoning and serve.

NOTE To vary, use vegetable marrow, or one of the silk gourds sold in Chinese grocers, instead of courgettes.

CHINESE BRAISED VEGETABLES

The recipes in this last section of this chapter are all rather domestic in character, using simple and inexpensive ingredients. None of them includes dominating flavours; instead, each relies on natural tastes which blend easily with other dishes. The dishes require little attention during their cooking.

Braised yam bean

CHINESE

INGREDIENTS

250g (8oz) yam bean
oil for deep frying
SEASONING SAUCE
15ml (1 tablespoon) sweet bean sauce
15ml (1 tablespoon) soy sauce (preferably dark)
7.5ml (1½ teaspoons) crystal sugar
5ml (1 teaspoon) rice wine
100ml (3½ fl oz) water
5ml (1 teaspoon) sesame oil

PREPARATION

Peel and cut the yam bean into bite-sized wedges. Deep-fry for about 2 minutes over a moderate heat until they start to change colour. Drain well. Put them with the seasoning sauce into a pan and cook over a moderate heat until the sauce has almost all gone, stirring from time to time. Sprinkle with sesame oil and serve.

NOTE Bamboo shoots may be substituted for the yam bean in this recipe.

Braised konnyaku and mushrooms

CHINESE

INGREDIENTS

100g (4oz) konnyaku
75g (3oz) bamboo shoots
50g (2oz) carrot
100g (4oz) preserved golden needle mushrooms
450ml (2 cups, ¾ pint) stock
30ml (2 tablespoons) frozen green peas (preferably petits pois)
5ml (1 teaspoon) ginger juice
15ml (1 tablespoon (rice wine)
15ml (1 tablespoon) rice vinegar
5ml (1 teaspoon) red vinegar
pinch sugar
5ml (1 teaspoon) potato flour mixed with 5ml (1 teaspoon) water
10ml (2 teaspoons) sesame oil
freshly ground black pepper

This recipe comes from Taiwan, which belonged to Japan from 1896 to 1945. Like many recipes from Taiwan it reflects both Chinese and Japanese influence. *Konnyaku* is a strictly Japanese ingredient, while red vinegar is Chinese. Many Taiwanese dishes, including this one, are almost soups, betraying a Fujian influence in the amount of sauce served – more than is usual in, say, Cantonese cooking (Taiwan was settled by Fujian people before the Japanese took over).

PREPARATION

Cut the *konnyaku* into batons 5mm (¼ inch) across and 3cm (1 inch) long. Blanch in boiling water for a minute, then drain well. Cut the bamboo shoots and carrot into similar-sized batons. Drain the mushrooms. Bring the stock to the boil in a saucepan and put in the *konnyaku*, carrot and bamboo shoots. Simmer gently for 5 minutes, then add the peas and the rice wine, vinegars, sugar and salt. Gently mix in the mushrooms, then thicken the sauce with the potato-flour paste. Serve garnished with the sesame oil and freshly ground pepper.

Braised silk noodles

KOREAN

INGREDIENTS

65 g (2½ oz) silk noodles
4 dried mushrooms
50 g (2 oz) white radish
50 g (2 oz) cucumber
50 g (2 oz) carrots
50 g (2 oz) beansprouts
2 cloves garlic
2 spring onions
25 ml (1½ tablespoons) vegetable oil
25 ml (1½ tablespoons) sesame oil

SEASONING SAUCE

15 ml (1 tablespoon) Japanese soy sauce
5 ml (1 teaspoon) caster sugar
15 ml (1 tablespoon) vegetarian stock
10 ml (2 teaspoons) red vinegar
pinch salt

GARNISH

white and yellow omelettes, cut into strips (see page 37)
30 ml (2 tablespoons) finely chopped coriander
red chilli, cut into hair fine shreds

PREPARATION

Cut the silk noodles into 7-cm (3-inch) lengths, then pour boiling water over them and leave to soak for 15 minutes. Drain. Soak the dried mushrooms in warm water for 30 minutes, then discard the hard stalks and cut the caps into thin slices. Cut the white radish, cucumber and carrot into matchsticks. Par-boil the carrot for 2 minutes, then refresh under cold water and drain well. Pick over, wash and trim the beansprouts. Keep separate from the other vegetables. Chop the garlic and spring onion. Heat the oils in a large frying-pan and stir-fry the onion and garlic for a few seconds. Then add all the vegetables except the beansprouts and stir-fry for about 3 minutes before adding the silk noodles and beansprouts. Pour in the seasoning sauce and continue to stir-fry for another 3 minutes. Serve garnished with egg, coriander and chilli.

Silk gourd with mushrooms

CHINESE

The Far East has a wide range of gourds and melons, many of them with delicate flavours and crisp textures. When cooked, most of them resemble cooked cucumber in texture, though not in taste, and are quite unlike the rather woolly-textured European marrows and courgettes.

INGREDIENTS

1 medium-sized silk gourd (luffa)
250 g (8 oz) fresh button mushrooms
3 spring onions
30 ml (2 tablespoons) oil
100 ml (3½ fl oz) stock
15 ml (1 tablespoon) light soy sauce
5 ml (1 teaspoon) cornflour mixed with 10 ml (2 teaspoons) water
salt

PREPARATION

Wash the silk gourd well and pare off the ridge edges. Cut into 2-cm (¾-inch) wedge-shaped pieces. Wipe and trim the mushrooms, and cut into halves if they are large ones. Chop the spring onions into short lengths. Heat the oil in a wok or large frying-pan and stir-fry the onion for 15 seconds. Add the mushrooms, then the silk gourd and continue stir-frying for another 30 seconds. Tip in the stock and soy sauce, cover with a lid and simmer until the gourd is cooked (about 5 minutes). Thicken with the cornflour paste and adjust the seasoning before serving.

7

Beancurd and Gluten

China has always been and still is pre-eminent in the culinary world of east Asia. Yet the dominance of Chinese cooking is not dependant upon the spread of Chinese restaurants throughout South East Asia. Its appeal knows no national boundaries, and the range of foods it embraces recommends it to millions.

Many Far-Eastern peoples have adopted Chinese techniques and ingredients in their own domestic cooking, and beancurd is a prime example of this takeover.

Beancurd is made from soya beans. These are ground, boiled and strained and the 'milk' so produced is coagulated into a curd: beancurd. Soya beans have 35 per cent protein, of which 61 per cent can be utilized by the body. This compares with 20 per cent protein in red meat, of which 67 per cent can be used by the body. Beancurd itself has 8 per cent protein, of which 65 per cent can be absorbed by the body. A piece of beancurd 125g (4oz) in weight supplies approximately one-tenth of the average daily protein requirements for an adult – about half the protein provided by the same weight of beefsteak. Throughout eastern Asia soya beans have, over the centuries, provided a rich source of cheap vegetable protein for people who had little opportunity to eat animal protein, apart from the occasional fish.

Each culture devised its own methods for processing soya beans for foods other than beancurd. For example, in Indonesia soya beans are made into *tempe* by a process of fermentation induced by bacteria. *Tempe* is unfortunately unobtainable in the UK, although it is widely available in the United States of America. The Japanese ferment boiled soya beans with rice or barley to make *miso*, the bean-paste basis of many Japanese soups. *Miso* was the main source of protein for many generations of Japanese peasant farmers. Other Japanese soya-bean products include *natto* – fermented soya beans – while from beancurd they make *aburage* – fried sheets of beancurd. Soy sauce, also made from soya beans and rich in protein, is common to all South East Asian cultures as well as those of Japan, Korea and China. The Chinese make various other sauces from soya beans, including chilli bean sauce and *hoisin* or barbecue sauce, together with fermented black beans and salted yellow beans. Both China and Japan use dried beancurd skin and dried sticks of beancurd in their cooking. The Japanese use the soya bean residue from making soya milk as a basis for a vegetable dish, while in China this is more usually fed to pigs.

Beancurd comes in two basic varieties – pressed and unpressed. Pressed beancurd (the pressing is part of the manufacturing process) is the most usual and versatile form: it is used for frying, simmering, freezing and drying. Standard beancurd bought ready-made from Chinese grocers is pressed beancurd. In Japan pressed beancurd is called cotton beancurd. When beancurd is listed as a recipe ingredient it is this pressed beancurd that is required. Unpressed beancurd, called silk beancurd or 'silken *tofu*' in Japan, cannot easily be made at home. It can however be bought ready-made in 'long-life' form in packets from Japan, and is sold in Chinese and health-food stores. In silk beancurd the whey and curds hold together in a texture very similar to that of junket, and it requires very delicate handling if the curds are not to break as soon as they are touched. Silk beancurd is used in soups in China and Japan. In Japan it is also eaten cold in the summer with a variety of chilli-flavoured and other sauces.

Each community has been able to adopt basic beancurd to its own schemes of seasoning and cooking while usually retaining beancurd itself in its original state. Names of beancurd in other Asian languages – in Japanese *tofu*, in Korean *doopoo*, in Indonesian *tahu* – are derived from the Chinese *doufu*. Beancurd was invented or perhaps discovered in China some time after AD 200. Soya beans had been cultivated for about a thousand years previously as a grain food, and forms of bean sauce or *miso* had been made since 400 BC. Presumably it was in a region where the water was very alkaline that its effects on boiled soya beans, or soya bean gruel, were first discovered. The first recipe in which beancurd itself appears as an ingredient was published in the seventh century AD. At that time Buddhism was the religion of the imperial court in China, and vegetarian beliefs and practices were widely accepted. Soya beans and beancurd were first introduced to Japan by Buddhist monks, probably during this time. Their progress through South East Asia is less clear, but at some time, and probably earlier rather than later, soya beans and beancurd were absorbed into the indigenous domestic cooking of Indonesia and Malaysia.

BRAISED DISHES USING BEANCURD

Beancurd has little flavour of its own, so it combines well with all kinds of flavours. This section contains a range of recipes offering a wide variety of seasonings. In the first recipe, for winter beancurd, the dry, slightly sour flavour of the pickled bamboo contrasts with the delicate richness of the mushrooms to give the whole dish a refreshing piquancy. Despite the presence of Western onions in the ingredients, this is old-fashioned Chinese cooking: it would be familiar winter fare to May Huang's grandparents.

Winter beancurd

CHINESE

Serve this with a deep-fried dish such as sweet potato balls together with a stir-fried green vegetable and perhaps a gluten dish.

INGREDIENTS

6 dried mushrooms
15 g (½ oz) pickled bamboo shoots
200 g (7 oz) beancurd
50 g (2 oz) green vegetables (e.g. spinach, Chinese broccoli, choisam *or watercress)*
15 g (½ oz) Western onion
30 ml (2 tablespoons) vegetable oil
15 ml (1 tablespoon) light soy sauce
5 ml (1 teaspoon) rice wine
2.5 ml (½ teaspoon) ground Sichuan peppercorns
2.5 ml (½ teaspoon) sugar
salt to taste
5 ml (1 teaspoon) cornflour mixed with 10 ml (2 teaspoons) water

PREPARATION

Soak the dried mushrooms in 200 ml (1 cup, ⅓ pint) warm water for 45 minutes. Then discard the hard stalks and cut the caps into very thin slices. Strain the soaking water and reserve 150 ml (⅔ cup, ¼ pint). Prepare the pickled bamboo shoots as directed on page 000, and cut into 3-cm (1-inch) slices. Cut the beancurd into thin slices. Wash, trim and blanch the green vegetables in boiling water, then refresh in cold water and cut into shreds. Finely slice the onion.

Heat the oil in a wok or frying-pan and stir-fry the onion over a moderate heat for 3 minutes. Add the mushrooms and bamboo and stir-fry for another minute. Tip in the soy sauce and reserved mushroom water. Bring to the boil, season with rice wine, Sichuan pepper, sugar and salt to taste. Finally slide in the beancurd and green vegetables, mix well and stir in the thickening paste. Serve hot.

Mapo's beancurd

CHINESE

INGREDIENTS

300 ml (10 oz) beancurd
25 ml (1½ tablespoons) oil
10 ml (2 teaspoons) fermented black beans, chopped
2 cloves garlic, chopped
5 ml (1 teaspoon) chopped ginger
2 spring onions, finely chopped
5–10 ml (1–2 teaspoons) chilli-bean sauce, to taste

SEASONING SAUCE

15 ml (1 tablespoon) rice wine
25 ml (1½ tablespoons) dark soy sauce
150 ml (¼ pint) water
1.5 ml (¼ teaspoon) chilli powder (optional)
pinch salt

7.5 ml (1½ teaspoons) cornflour mixed with 15 ml (1 tablespoon) water
15 ml (1 tablespoon) finely chopped garlic leaves or green onion

Mapo's beancurd is a well-known Sichuan dish, often cooked with pork as well as beancurd. We prefer this vegetarian version. Its seasoning is more powerful than that of most Indian curries, but you can adjust the quantities of chilli-bean sauce and chilli powder to suit your own tastes. Serve Mapo's beancurd with other Sichuan dishes, such as Sichuan aubergines (page 62); chilli mushrooms or sweet and sour cabbage (pages 50 and 53); an egg *fuyung* (page 44) and hot and sour soup (page 151), together with plain boiled rice and, if you like, a small cold cucumber salad. If you are not sure about having several chilli-hot dishes in one meal serve Mapo's beancurd with other Chinese dishes which are not so highly seasoned.

PREPARATION

Cut the beancurd into 1-cm (½-inch) cubes. Heat a frying-pan and add the oil. Stir-fry the black beans, garlic, ginger and spring onions for 15 seconds. Lift the pan from the heat and add the chilli-bean sauce; mix well before pouring in the seasoning sauce and returning the pan to the heat. Bring to the boil and add the beancurd. Simmer for 5 minutes before thickening with the cornflour paste. Serve very hot with the chopped garlic leaves as a garnish.

Lodeh tahu

INDONESIAN

INGREDIENTS

180 g (6 oz) beancurd
180 g (6 oz) green tomatoes
180 g (6 oz) french beans

SAUCE

75 g (3 oz) red onions
3 cloves garlic
pinch laos *powder*
2 chillis, de-seeded
4 macadamia nuts or brazil nuts
10 ml (2 teaspoons) ground coriander
2.5 ml (½ teaspoon) turmeric
5 ml (1 teaspoon) brown sugar
5 ml (1 teaspoon) salt
10 ml (2 teaspoons) oil
1 lime leaf or bay leaf
300 ml (1¼ cups, ½ pint) thick santan

This is another recipe for the standard Indonesian family dish. Serve it with a salad, and perhaps an egg dish, rice and a chilli *sambal.*

PREPARATION

Cut the beancurd into 4-cm (1½-inch) cubes. Slice the green tomatoes. Trim and cut the french beans into 4-cm (1½-inch) lengths. Put the onion, garlic, *laos* powder, de-seeded chillis, nuts, ground coriander, turmeric, sugar and salt into a food processor, or use a pestle and mortar and work into a fine paste. Lightly oil a wok and cook the paste, with the lime leaf, over a gentle heat for about 10 minutes, stirring from time to time. Then add 600 ml (2½ cups, 1 pint) water and stir in the *santan.* Add the beancurd and vegetables and bring to the boil. Leave to simmer for 20 minutes, then check the seasoning and serve.

Braised beancurd with mixed vegetables

CHINESE

INGREDIENTS

300 g (10 oz) beancurd
oil for deep frying
30 ml (2 tablespoons) black fungus or 2 pieces wood ears
50 g (2 oz) cucumber
40 g (1½ oz) cauliflower
25 g (1 oz) bamboo shoots
2 spring onions, cut into 1-cm (½-inch) lengths
2.5 ml (½ teaspoon) sweet bean sauce

SEASONING SAUCE

15 ml (1 tablespoon) black vinegar
10 ml (2 teaspoons) rice wine
25 ml (1½ tablespoons) light soy sauce
75 ml (5 tablespoons) good vegetarian stock

salt and pepper to taste
5 ml (1 teaspoon) cornflour mixed with 10 ml (2 teaspoons) water
5 ml (1 teaspoon) sesame oil

PREPARATION

Cut the beancurd into 4-cm (1½-inch) squares. Deep-fry for 2 minutes over a moderate heat, then drain well and cut each square in half. Soak the black fungus, or wood ears, in warm water for 30 minutes. Then rinse well, discard any hard bits and cut into ½-cm (¼-inch)-wide strips. Cut the cucumber, unpeeled, into small wedges. Break the cauliflower into small florets and blanch in boiling water for 2 minutes. Then refresh in cold water and drain well. Cut the bamboo shoot into thin slices. Mix the seasoning sauce. Heat 45 ml (3 tablespoons) oil in a wok or large frying-pan and stir-fry the onion and sweet bean sauce for 15 seconds. Add the vegetables and stir-fry for another minute. Slide in the beancurd. Tip in the seasoning sauce and bring to the boil. Adjust the seasoning with salt and pepper and thicken with the cornflour paste. Sprinkle with the sesame oil and serve.

Beancurd and straw mushrooms

CHINESE

This delicate-flavoured beancurd comes from the east of China. If you want to eat in the Chinese style, serve it with a stir-fried green vegetable (pages 52–5), tomato and egg omelette (page 45), chilli mushrooms (page 50) and a soup, together with plain rice.

INGREDIENTS

400 g (14 oz) beancurd
1 can straw mushrooms
3 spring onions
3 slices ginger
45 ml (3 tablespoons) oil
15 ml (1 tablespoon) rice wine
5 ml (1 teaspoon) soy sauce
100 ml (½ cup, 3½ fl oz) vegetarian stock
pinch sugar

PREPARATION

Cut the beancurd into 1-cm (½-inch)-thick slices. Drain the straw mushrooms. Chop the spring onions and ginger finely. Heat the oil in a wok or frying-pan and stir-fry the spring onions and ginger for 15 seconds, then add the rice wine, soy sauce, stock and sugar and bring to the boil. Add the beancurd and straw mushrooms and simmer for 5 minutes, or until the sauce is almost all gone. Check the seasoning and serve hot.

NOTE A variation of this recipe substitutes a luffa (silk gourd) for the straw mushrooms. Remove the hard-ridged edges of the silk gourd and cut into 1-cm (½-inch) wedges. Stir-fry it (after the onion and ginger) for about 30 seconds, then pour in the rice wine, soy sauce, stock and sugar. Bring to the boil and add the beancurd. Simmer until the silk gourd is soft and most of the stock has gone (about 5 minutes). Check the seasoning and serve.

Beancurd and mushroom pot

KOREAN

INGREDIENTS
750g (1½lb) beancurd
250g (8oz) fresh button mushrooms
DIPPING SAUCE
5 spring onions, finely chopped
4 cloves garlic, grated
60ml (4 tablespoons) coriander, finely chopped
45ml (3 tablespoons) sesame seeds, toasted
45ml (3 tablespoons) Japanese soy sauce
45ml (3 tablespoons) sesame oil
chilli oil to taste
1200ml (5 cups, 2 pints) stock
salt and pepper

This pot can be served with rice as a basic meal, or as the central dish in a full-scale Korean dinner.

PREPARATION
Cut the beancurd into 12 equal-sized squares. Wipe and trim the mushrooms. Mix the dipping sauce and add the chilli oil to taste. Divide the sauce between four small bowls. Bring the stock to the boil and add the beancurd and mushrooms. Adjust the seasoning with salt and pepper and simmer for about 4 minutes until the beancurd is heated through. Ladle the beancurd, mushrooms and stock into a large heated serving bowl, taking care not to break the beancurd squares. Serve hot, giving each diner a small bowl of the dipping sauce. Diners eat the beancurd and mushroom first, seasoning them in the dipping sauce, and then drink the stock as a soup.

Crystal beancurd

CHINESE

INGREDIENTS
300ml (1¼ cups, ½ pint) well seasoned vegetarian stock
300g (10oz) beancurd
DIPPING SAUCE
1.5ml (¼ teaspoon) chilli oil
1 clove garlic
10ml (2 teaspoons) grated ginger
30ml (2 tablespoons) dark soy sauce
2 spring onions, finely chopped

PREPARATION
Bring the stock to the boil and slide in the beancurd squares. Simmer gently for about 5 minutes. Lift out carefully, using a slotted spoon, and serve hot with the dipping sauce.

FRIED BEANCURD

Dishes of fried beancurd in various forms are common in both restaurant and domestic cooking in South East Asia as well as China and Japan. The recipes that follow include both traditional Japanese and modern Chinese as well as dishes typically served in small restaurants in Indonesia and Malaysia. The fresh lime juice in the Indonesian recipe is a common ingredient in South East Asian cookery, while the mainland Chinese traditionally use vinegar. Although the grated white radish in the Japanese recipe can be found in early Chinese cooking, it is not generally used in this form in China today. It is however often used in Japanese dishes and is known as 'autumn leaves'.

Basic fried beancurd

CHINESE

INGREDIENTS
beancurd
potato or plain flour
oil for deep frying

PREPARATION
Wrap the beancurd in a tea-towel and press between two boards for an hour. Then cut into the sizes required by the recipe and dust with the dry flour. Heat the oil until moderately hot and deep-fry the beancurd for 4–5 minutes until golden brown. Lift out and drain. Use as required.

Fried beancurd can be kept in the refrigerator for several days.

Fried summer beancurd

JAPANESE

The Japanese vary the sauces they serve with fried beancurd according to the season – a pepper-hot sauce served cold for summer, and a heavier sauce served hot for winter. The recipe below is a summer dish in Japan, so serve it with a cooling salad of white radish and carrot together with simmered aubergines and *miso* sauce and a clear soup with egg slices followed by rice and pickles.

INGREDIENTS
250g (8oz) fried beancurd, cut into 3 × 5-cm (1 × 2-inch) pieces before frying
SAUCE
100ml (½ cup, 3½ fl oz) dashi
5ml (1 teaspoon) mirin
30ml (2 tablespoons) Japanese soy sauce
GARNISH ('AUTUMN LEAVES')
40g (1½ oz) white radish
1 dried chilli

PREPARATION
Prepare the fried beancurd as directed in the previous recipe. Mix the sauce ingredients in a small pan and bring to the boil. Then remove from the heat and leave to cool. Meanwhile make the 'autumn leaves'. Peel the white radish and make a hole through its centre with a chopstick. Insert the chilli and grate both the white radish and chilli together. Squeeze the pulp dry in a clean cloth. Serve the hot fried beancurd pieces arranged on individual plates with a small mound of white radish and chilli beside them. Sprinkle the beancurd with chilli pepper and serve the sauce in small bowls as a dip.

Tahu masak bali (Bali beancurd)

INDONESIAN

INGREDIENTS
300g (10oz) beancurd
oil for deep frying
SAUCE
15ml (1 tablespoon) soy sauce
1 small pickled gherkin
pinch laos *powder*
1 chilli, de-seeded
25g (1oz) red onion
1 clove garlic
2.5ml (½ teaspoon) brown sugar
pinch salt

PREPARATION
Cut the beancurd into 4-cm (1½-inch) squares and deep-fry in hot oil until golden brown. Lift out and drain. Put the sauce ingredients in a food processor or liquidizer and work into a smooth paste, then add 150ml (¼ pint) water and mix well. Pour the sauce into a pan and simmer for about 5 minutes, then add the fried beancurd. Continue simmering for another 2 minutes, check the seasoning and serve hot.

NOTE We have substituted a French pickled gherkin for a *pete*, a pickled bean – not obtainable in the UK – which is used in Indonesian cookery. Its flavour and texture are not too dissimilar from those of gherkins.

Fried beancurd with vegetables (tahu goreng dengan sayur)

INDONESIAN

Serve this delicious Indonesian-style fried beancurd with a soupy stew such as *sayur bobor* (page 75), quickly fried cabbage and egg (*orak-orak*, page 46) and a chilli-hot *sambal* (*sambal jenggot*, page 137), together with plain boiled rice.

INGREDIENTS

350g (12oz) beancurd
45ml (3 tablespoons) cornflour
oil for deep frying
100g (4oz) beansprouts
180g (6oz) cucumber
15ml (1 tablespoon) salt

SAUCE

1 small hot chilli, de-seeded and cut into pieces
2 cloves garlic, sliced
10ml (2 teaspoons) finely chopped red onion
15ml (1 tablespoon) lime or lemon juice
30ml (2 tablespoons) dark soy sauce
sugar to taste

15ml (1 tablespoon) fried onion flakes (page 42)

PREPARATION

Cut the beancurd into cubes about 4 × 5cm ($1\frac{1}{2}$ × 2 inches) and roll in dry cornflour. Deep-fry over a moderate heat for about 4 minutes until golden brown, lift out and drain. Pick over the beansprouts and rinse well before blanching in boiling water for 1 minute. Immediately refresh in cold water, then drain. Rub the cucumber all over with the salt and leave for 20 minutes. Then rinse and cut into thin batons about 1 cm ($\frac{1}{3}$ inch) wide and 5cm (2 inches) long.

Make the sauce by blending the sauce ingredients in a food processor or liquidizer until smooth. Adjust the sugar to taste.

Arrange the beancurd in the centre of a plate with the beansprouts and cucumber batons around them. Pour the sauce over the beancurd and garnish with the fried onion flakes.

Tahu campur (peanut sauce for beancurd)

MALAYSIAN

This is an alternative sauce for the beancurd in the preceding recipe, fried beancurd with vegetables.

INGREDIENTS

100g (4oz) peanuts, skinned and deep-fried, or 45ml (3 tablespoons) peanut butter
2 chillis, de-seeded, or 1.5ml ($\frac{1}{4}$ teaspoon) chilli powder (or to taste)
2 cloves garlic, crushed
15ml (1 tablespoon) light soy sauce
45ml (3 tablespoons) barbecue sauce
juice of 1 lemon

PREPARATION

If using peanuts and chillis put them with the garlic in a food processor and grind to a smooth paste. Mix all the ingredients except the lemon juice in a pan with 60ml (4 tablespoons) water and bring to the boil over a low heat, stirring all the time. Add the lemon juice and spoon over the fried beancurd arranged on a serving plate. Garnish with fried onion flakes and chopped coriander.

Sweet and sour beancurd with cashew nuts

CHINESE

This spicy sweet and sour goes well with an egg dish, such as egg and black fungus (page 46).

INGREDIENTS

250g (8oz) beancurd
100g (4oz) cucumber
1 spring onion
oil for deep frying
50g (2oz) cashew nuts
15ml (1 tablespoon) fermented black beans
12g (½oz) ginger
3 cloves garlic

SAUCE

- *15ml (1 tablespoon) sugar*
- *15ml (1 tablespoon) red vinegar*
- *60ml (4 tablespoons) light soy sauce*
- *5ml (1 teaspoon) chilli oil*

15ml (1 tablespoon) sesame oil

PREPARATION

Wrap the beancurd in a clean cloth and leave to drain for 30 minutes. Cut into 1-cm (⅓-inch) cubes. Cut the cucumber into similar-sized cubes. Chop the onion very finely. Heat the oil until hot, then deep-fry the cashew nuts over a low heat for about 4 minutes until golden brown. Leave on one side to drain. Chop the fermented beans, ginger and garlic very finely. Mix the seasoning sauce.

Heat a wok or frying-pan with the sesame oil over a moderate heat and stir-fry the beans, ginger and garlic for 30 seconds. Add the seasoning sauce and mix well. Bring just to the boil, then remove from the heat and keep warm. Heat the oil and deep-fry the beancurd for 2 minutes. Drain quickly and put the cubes on a heated plate with the cucumber and cashew nuts. Pour over the warm sauce and mix quickly. Serve at once garnished with chopped spring onion.

Deep-fried beancurd with sesame sauce

CHINESE

The crunchy nut sauce is a marvellous foil to the fried beancurd in this dish. We like to serve it with lichi and walnut 'meat' balls, and a cold salad.

INGREDIENTS

300g (10oz) beancurd
2 spring onions
100g (4oz) cucumber

SEASONING SAUCE

- *30ml (2 tablespoons) sesame paste*
- *45ml (3 tablespoons) sesame oil*
- *45ml (3 tablespoons) light soy sauce*
- *15ml (1 tablespoon) sugar*
- *15ml (1 tablespoon) rice vinegar*
- *2.5ml (½ teaspoon) chilli oil*

oil for deep frying
50g (2oz) salted peanuts

PREPARATION

Wrap the beancurd tightly in a clean cloth and leave to drain for 30 minutes. Cut into 2-cm (¾-inch) cubes. Cut the cucumber into similar-sized cubes and chop the spring onions finely. Mix the seasoning sauce carefully. Heat the oil until hot and deep-fry the beancurd until golden brown (about 1½ minutes). Have ready a warmed serving dish. Drain the beancurd quickly and arrange on the serving dish with the cucumber and peanuts. Spoon over the sauce and serve at once garnished with the spring onions.

Hirouzu (beancurd balls)

JAPANESE

These beancurd balls can be served with simmered yams (see page 176) and braised spinach (page 67). Drain the beancurd balls and yams and quickly arrange them with a little spinach in four separate serving bowls. Serve hot.

INGREDIENTS
400g (14oz) beancurd
8 lotus petals
15ml (1 tablespoon) sake
1 egg
10ml (2 teaspoons) grated yam
15ml (1 tablespoon) black fungus
50g (2oz) carrot
30ml (2 tablespoons) poppy seeds, toasted
8 ginko nuts
400ml (2 cups, ⅔ pint) dashi
15ml (1 tablespoon) Japanese soy sauce
pinch salt
oil for deep frying

PREPARATION
Press the beancurd for an hour under a weight. Then wrap in a cloth and squeeze out any extra water. Meanwhile poach the lotus petals in the *sake* with a little water until soft but still firm. Lift out and leave to drain. Put the beancurd in a food processor and work into a smooth paste. Add the egg and grated yam and continue beating for another minute. Put on one side to rest while the vegetables are prepared. Soak the black fungus in warm water for 20 minutes, rinse well, discard any hard bits and pat dry. Cut into needle-fine shreds. Scrape and cut the carrot into similarly fine shreds – if using an electric grater use the finest cutting surface.

Mix the beancurd paste with the black fungus, carrot and poppy seeds and divide into 8 equal portions. Coat your hands generously with warmed oil, preferably at about 90°C (200°F), which feels hot but not uncomfortable to the hands. Take one portion of beancurd and stuff one lotus petal and a ginko nut into it. Shape into a ball, throwing it from one hand to the other until smooth and round. Stand it on an oiled plate while you make the remaining 7 balls in the same way. Deep-fry the balls, in oil heated to only 100°C (220°F), for 5 minutes over a low heat. Then lift out and drain. Re-heat the oil to 180°C (350°F) and re-fry the balls until golden brown (about 2 minutes). Lift out and drain. Bring the *dashi*, soy and salt to the boil in a saucepan, add the beancurd balls and simmer for 5 minutes.

Beancurd and simmered vegetables

JAPANESE

This is a traditional Japanese recipe for beancurd, but the recipe for beancurd 'steak' that follows it is an example of a new style of recipe in the East which imitates Western modes. The beancurd 'steak' could easily be served as a main dish in a Western-style meal. In China there are continual moves to shift the people's eating habits away from the traditional – such as a move in 1983 to encourage consumption of factory-sliced bread, and a recent suggestion that people might take to eating with knives and forks. In Japan, American hamburger chains vie with traditional noodle houses for customers wanting quick lunches.

You could serve beancurd and simmered vegetables in a traditional Japanese meal with steamed egg *tofu*, a salad and a *miso* soup. Beancurd 'steak' could however also be served in a Western-style meal with mounds of puréed potatoes, carrots and green beans.

INGREDIENTS

300 g (10 oz) Japanese cotton beancurd
oil for deep frying
2 dried mushrooms
40 g (1½ oz) carrot
25 g (1 oz) french beans
2 spring onions, very finely sliced
200 ml (⅓ pint) dashi
15 ml (1 tablespoon) caster sugar
40 ml (2½ tablespoons) Japanese or light soy sauce
15 ml (1 tablespoon) sake
10 ml (2 teaspoons) potato flour mixed with 15 ml (1 tablespoon) water
5 ml (1 teaspoon) grated ginger
hair-like shreds of lemon peel for garnish

PREPARATION

Wrap the beancurd tightly in a clean tea-towel and leave to drain for 30 minutes. Cut into 8 equal cubes. Deep-fry over a moderate heat until a light golden brown. Lift out and drain well. Soak the dried mushrooms in warm water for 30 minutes, then discard the hard stems and cut the caps into thin slices. Peel and cut the carrot into flower-shapes (see illustration on page 39), and par-boil in lightly salted water for 5 minutes. Drain well. Top and tail the beans and cut into 3-cm (1-inch) lengths. Par-boil for 5 minutes in fresh water.

Put the *dashi*, sugar, soy and *sake* into a saucepan and bring to the boil. Add the carrots and mushrooms and simmer for 4 minutes before adding the french beans, grated ginger and potato-flour paste. Stir well while the sauce thickens, then leave on one side. Re-heat the oil and re-fry the beancurd for another 2 minutes. Lift out and place on four serving plates. Arrange the mixed vegetables in small piles beside the beancurd and spoon over the sauce. Serve hot, garnished with a few fine shreds of lemon peel.

Beancurd 'steak'

JAPANESE

INGREDIENTS

450 g (1 lb) Japanese cotton beancurd
100 g (4 oz) Western onions
30 ml (2 tablespoons) oil
30 ml (2 tablespoons) Japanese or light soy sauce
15 ml (1 tablespoon) sake
100 ml (½ cup, 3½ fl oz) dashi
15 ml (1 tablespoon) ginger juice
salt to taste
4 spring onions, finely sliced into rings
watercress for garnish

PREPARATION

Press the beancurd between two plates for an hour, then cut into four equal rectangles. Grate or put the onion through the food processor. Heat the oil in a wok or large frying-pan and fry the beancurd pieces over a low to moderate heat until brown on both sides. Lift out and keep warm in the oven. Stir-fry the onion in the remaining oil until light brown (about 5 minutes). Pour in the soy sauce, *sake* and *dashi* and bring to the boil. Add the ginger juice and adjust the seasoning with salt. Arrange the beancurd pieces on four separate plates and spoon over the sauce. Garnish with the spring onion rings and watercress. Serve hot.

DRIED BEANCURD

Dried beancurd is often used in Chinese family cooking as a meat substitute; since its texture and colour are considered to resemble those of meat. Commercially-made dried beancurd in China will keep for several weeks; the home-made variety described below can be kept in a cool place for several days.

Basic dried beancurd

CHINESE

INGREDIENTS
300 g (10 oz) beancurd
STOCK
1.2 litres (5 cups, 2 pints) water
10 ml (2 teaspoons) cloves
10 ml (2 teaspoons) fennel seeds
10-cm (4-inch) stick of cinnamon
5 square cm (2 square inches) dried orange peel
10 ml (2 teaspoons) Sichuan peppercorns

PREPARATION
Wrap the beancurd tightly in a clean cloth and press it under a weight for an hour. Then re-wrap yet more tightly and press for a further 5 hours. Meanwhile make the seasoning stock by gently boiling all the spices in the water for 1 hour. Strain the stock and when the beancurd has finished pressing cut it into 7-cm (3-inch) squares and put into the prepared stock. Bring to the boil; boil for 1 minute, then leave the beancurd overnight to marinate in the stock. Use as directed in the recipe below.

Dried beancurd and Chinese chives

CHINESE

INGREDIENTS
2 squares dried beancurd (see above)
25 g (1 oz) flowering heads of Chinese chives
10 ml (2 teaspoons) light soy sauce
pinch salt
5 ml (1 teaspoon) sesame oil

PREPARATION
Cut the dried beancurd into matchstick strips. Wash and cut the Chinese chives into 3-cm (1-inch) lengths. Heat the oil in a wok or large frying-pan and add the beancurd. Stir-fry for about a minute, then add the soy sauce. Stir-fry for a few seconds, then add the Chinese chives. Continue stir-frying and season to taste with the salt. When the chives are cooked (about 2–3 minutes), serve sprinkled with sesame oil.

Spiced beancurd (baceman tahu)

INDONESIAN

This recipe, which comes from Java, follows the same basic principles as Chinese dried beancurd (page 88), but it is spiced entirely according to Indonesian custom; it is not used as a substitute for meat.

INGREDIENTS
300 g (10 oz) beancurd
1 green chilli
2 cloves garlic
40 g (1½ oz) red onion
5 ml (1 teaspoon) ground coriander
pinch laos powder *or 2 slices ginger*
5 ml (1 teaspoon) brown sugar
2.5 ml (½ teaspoon) salt
milk from one coconut made up to 300 ml (1¼ cups, ½ pint) with water
45 ml (3 tablespoons) vegetable oil

PREPARATION
Wrap the beancurd in a clean cloth and press between two plates for at least 2 hours. Then cut the beancurd into 6 equal pieces. De-seed the chilli and slice it with the garlic and onion. Put them with the coriander, *laos*, brown sugar and salt into a wok or large frying-pan with the coconut 'milk' and water mixture. Slide in the beancurd and bring to the boil. Boil gently for 30 minutes, taking care not to boil dry. Then lift out the beancurd and leave to drain. Heat the oil in a clean wok or frying-pan. Shallow-fry the beancurd over a low to moderate heat until lightly browned on both sides. Serve hot.
NOTE The coconut 'milk' in this recipe is the liquid inside a coconut (not *santan*, which is made from the flesh of a coconut). Another version of this dish can be made using tamarind juice in place of the coconut 'milk'.

FREEZE-DRIED BEANCURD

Beancurd used to have one problem as a domestic food: it would not keep. This was overcome to some extent by drying it, but the Chinese also discovered fairly early that beancurd could be frozen in the winter. This gave it an interesting spongy texture and prolonged its life during the winter frosts. However, in the thirteenth century Japanese monks in the Koyo monastery near Kyoto developed a method of freezing the beancurd at night then thawing and drying it in the sun during the day and re-freezing it. This treatment produced light, dry cakes of beancurd that could be stored and easily transported, in addition to being good to eat. Freeze-dried cakes of beancurd are still produced in Japan today, and can be bought in Japanese grocers in the West. They keep well and have all the nutritional value of fresh beancurd. We have developed our own recipe for home-made freeze-dried beancurd, which needs to be stored in a freezer.

Frozen and freeze-dried beancurd

PREPARATION

Pat the beancurd dry and cut into 8-cm (3-inch) squares. Freeze overnight. The next day thaw the beancurd and squeeze out as much water as possible. Return to the freezer and re-freeze. Use when required.

Simmered mixed vegetables and frozen beancurd

JAPANESE

INGREDIENTS

4 squares frozen beancurd (see previous recipe)
4 dried mushrooms
8 snow peas or french beans
75 g (3 oz) carrot
75 g (3 oz) canned lotus root

SIMMERING STOCK

300 ml ($1\frac{1}{4}$ cups, $\frac{1}{2}$ pint) dashi
25 g (1 oz) caster sugar
7.5 ml ($1\frac{1}{2}$ teaspoons) Japanese soy sauce
7.5 ml ($1\frac{1}{2}$ tablespoons) mirin
pinch salt

3 cm (1 inch) konbu
shreds yuzu *orange peel or lemon peel*

PREPARATION

De-frost the beancurd and squeeze out any remaining water. Soak the dried mushrooms in warm water for 30 minutes, then discard the hard stalks. Trim the snow peas and cut diagonally into halves. Scrape the carrot and cut into flower-shaped pieces (see page 39). Cut the lotus root into thin slices. Cook the snow peas and carrot in lightly salted boiling water until just tender, then rinse in cold water and drain well. Put the simmering stock and the *konbu* into a saucepan and bring almost to the boil. Add the beancurd, mushrooms and lotus root and simmer for about 5 minutes, without a lid. Take care the stock does not actually boil. Lift out the *konbu* and add the snow peas and carrot. Simmer for another minute, then cut each square of beancurd into four with a sharp knife. Serve with the vegetables in four separate deep bowls garnished with a few shreds of *yuzu* orange peel.

This dish tastes much better if it can be made a little while in advance and allowed to cool down and stand for an hour or so. Then re-heat and serve.

Frozen beancurd with Chinese leaves

CHINESE

INGREDIENTS

300g (10oz) frozen beancurd
450g (1 lb) Chinese leaves
15g (½ oz) ginger
45ml (3 tablespoons) oil
30ml (2 tablespoons) rice wine
salt
5ml (1 teaspoon) sesame oil

PREPARATION

Cut the beancurd into 3-cm (1-inch) cubes. Wash and cut the Chinese leaves into 3-cm (1-inch) squares. Cut the ginger into very fine shreds. Heat the oil in a casserole or heavy saucepan and stir-fry the ginger for 15 seconds. Then add the Chinese leaves and quickly stir-fry. When all coated in the oil, lay the beancurd squares on top of the Chinese leaves. Add the rice wine, cover the pan with a lid and simmer over a very low heat for 1 hour. Season to taste with salt and sprinkle over the sesame oil before serving.

BEANCURD STUFFINGS AND FILLINGS

There are numerous recipes for stuffed vegetables, featuring a range of fillings. A few are given below, but other vegetables such as aubergines, dried mushrooms, cabbage or omelettes are all possible candidates for treating in the same way. Cut the aubergines into 'open-mouth' slices and dust inside with dry cornflour before filling and dipping in the batter described for green peppers. Deep-fry and serve. Replace the fresh mushrooms in the recipe below with soaked dried mushrooms, well drained. Make small egg omelettes, as directed on page 37, and fill them with the stuffing described for soft egg packets. Roll up into cigar-shaped parcels and steam for 10 minutes before serving hot, cut into slices, with a dipping sauce of 15ml (1 tablespoon) red vinegar and 45ml (3 tablespoons) soy sauce. Alternatively, leave the filled egg rolls to cool, then serve cold cut into slices.

Japanese stuffed mushrooms

INGREDIENTS

12 fresh flat mushrooms

FILLING

180g (6oz) beancurd
25ml (1oz) potato flour
15g (½ oz) carrot
12 frozen broad beans
5ml (1 teaspoon) poppy seeds or black sesame seeds
pinch salt

cornflour for dusting
60ml (4 tablespoons) sake
60ml (4 tablespoons) dashi
7.5ml (1½ teaspoons) caster sugar
15ml (1 tablespoon) Japanese or light soy sauce
seven-spice pepper

PREPARATION

Wipe the mushrooms clean and remove their central stalks without breaking the caps. Make the filling by mashing the beancurd with the potato flour. Scrape the carrot, cut into slices and par-boil for 2 minutes. Also par-boil the broad beans (separately) for 2 minutes and remove their tough outer skins. Chop the carrot and broad beans into minute pieces about the size of rice grains. Mix, with the poppy seeds, into the beancurd, and season to taste with salt.

Dust the insides of the mushroom caps lightly with the cornflour and fill each cap with a spoonful of the beancurd mixture. Smooth over the tops with a damp spoon. Place, filling-side up, in a large frying-pan, without overlapping. Pour in the *sake* and cook over a moderate heat until the *sake* begins to steam. Then add the *dashi*, sugar and soy sauce. Cover the pan and simmer over a low heat for 8–10 minutes, spooning a little of the sauce over the beancurd from time to time. Check the seasoning and serve hot in individual bowls with the remaining sauce poured over the mushrooms. Garnish with a light sprinkling of seven-spice pepper.

Stuffed green peppers

CHINESE

INGREDIENTS

2 medium-sized green peppers

STUFFING

- *4 dried mushrooms*
- *50g (2oz) bamboo shoots*
- *100g (4oz) beancurd*
- *pinch five-spice powder*
- *5ml (1 teaspoon) grated ginger*
- *15ml (1 tablespoon) finely chopped spring onion*
- *5ml (1 teaspoon) sesame oil*
- *pepper and salt to taste*

30ml (2 tablespoons) dry cornflour
1 egg
45ml (3 tablespoons) water
60ml (4 tablespoons) plain flour
60ml (4 tablespoons) cornflour
5ml (1 teaspoon) vegetable oil
oil for deep frying

PREPARATION

Cut the green peppers into halves and de-seed. Cut each again into halves, across, and trim into 2 ovals, making 8 in all. To make the stuffing, soak the dried mushrooms in warm water for 30 minutes, discard the hard stalks and chop the caps very finely. Chop the bamboo shoots very finely. Mash the beancurd and mix in the chopped bamboo and mushrooms. Season with the remaining stuffing ingredients and mix well. Dust the insides of the pepper pieces with the dry cornflour and fill with the stuffing. Smooth over the tops with the back of a wet spoon. Beat the egg and water very well in a clean bowl, then lightly stir in the sifted cornflour and plain flour together with 5ml (1 teaspoon) oil. Heat the deep fat until very hot. Dip the stuffed green peppers in the batter and deep-fry over a moderate heat until golden brown. Serve immediately with a salt-pepper dip (page 24).

Alternatively, if you prefer a hot dipping sauce, use 15ml (1 tablespoon) soy sauce, 5ml (1 teaspoon) chilli-bean sauce, 5ml (1 teaspoon) sesame oil and 5ml (1 teaspoon) rice vinegar.

Soft egg packets

CHINESE

These can be made in advance and cooked in the stock when required.

INGREDIENTS

4 size 3 eggs
20ml (4 teaspoons) cornflour
60ml (4 tablespoons) water
2.5ml (½ teaspoon) salt
pinch sugar

FILLING

- *180g (6oz) beancurd*
- *15ml (1 tablespoon) black fungus*
- *2 slices Sichuan preserved vegetable*
- *5ml (1 teaspoon) sesame oil*
- *5ml (1 teaspoon) ginger juice*
- *salt to taste*

60ml (4 tablespoons) oil
200ml (1 cup, ⅓ pint) well-seasoned vegetarian stock
5ml (1 teaspoon) cornflour mixed with 10ml (2 teaspoons) water
15ml (1 tablespoon) finely chopped chives, or tops of spring onions

PREPARATION

Beat the eggs with the cornflour and water and season with the salt and sugar. Leave on one side while you make the filling. Wrap the beancurd in a clean cloth and leave to drain. Soak the black fungus in warm water for 20 minutes, then rinse well and discard any hard parts. Chop finely. Rinse the Sichuan preserved vegetable and chop finely. Mash the beancurd in a bowl and beat in the chopped black fungus and Sichuan vegetable, together with the sesame oil and ginger juice. Add a little salt to taste (Sichuan vegetable is quite salty so this may not be necessary).

Heat a little oil in a 10-cm (4-inch) frying-pan over a high heat and put in 25ml (1½ tablespoons) of the egg mixture. Allow to set at the bottom, then lift from the heat and put one portion of the beancurd filling on the egg. Fold over half the egg skin to cover the filling. Press round the edge to seal and return to the heat for another 15 seconds. Lift out on to a plate. Repeat with the remaining 11 portions.

Just before serving the egg packets boil the stock in a large frying-pan and thicken with the cornflour-and-water paste. Slide in the egg packets very gently and simmer for 2 minutes. Serve garnished with the finely chopped chives or spring onions.

Spinach and beancurd rolls

CHINESE

Choose simple dishes to cook with these, such as sweet and sour aubergines, braised yam bean, an avocado salad and three-colour egg soup.

INGREDIENTS

180 g (6 oz) beancurd
3 spring onions, finely chopped
3 slices ginger, finely chopped
2.5 ml ($\frac{1}{2}$ teaspoon) sesame oil
pinch salt and pepper
500 g (1 lb) large-leaved spinach

SEASONING SAUCE

100 ml ($\frac{1}{2}$ cup, $3\frac{1}{2}$ fl oz) vegetarian stock
15 ml (1 tablespoon) soy sauce
10 ml (2 teaspoons) rice wine
1.5 ml ($\frac{1}{4}$ teaspoon) black pepper
pinch sugar
5 ml (1 teaspoon) cornflour

1 large egg
30 ml (2 tablespoons) plain flour
oil for deep frying

PREPARATION

Mash the beancurd with the spring onion, ginger and sesame oil. Season to taste with salt and pepper. Wash and select the largest spinach leaves and tear out the stalks and thick veins, keeping the leaves as whole as possible. Bring a large pan of water to the boil, remove from the heat and plunge in the spinach leaves. Leave for 1 minute, then lift out and drain. Pat dry and spread the leaves out flat. Arrange to make 16 sheets, each about $15 \times 7\frac{1}{2}$ cm (6×3 inches). Where necessary use 2–3 leaves to cover any holes or tears. Put a spoonful of mashed beancurd across the bottom of one spinach leaf, leaving a space of approximately 1 cm ($\frac{1}{2}$ inch) on both sides. Fold over the sides and roll the leaf tightly round the beancurd into a package about 5 cm (2 inches) long × 1 cm ($\frac{1}{2}$ inch) across. Repeat with the remaining leaves and beancurd. Mix the seasoning sauce.

Make a batter with the egg and flour. Heat the oil in a deep-fat pan. Coat the spinach rolls in the batter and deep-fry for about 2 minutes. Lift out and drain. Bring the seasoning sauce to the boil in a wok or large frying-pan and adjust the seasoning. Slide in the rolls, simmer for 1 minute, then serve.

GLUTEN OR FLOUR PROTEIN

The protein in flour develops into gluten when it is mixed with water. Its elastic-like threads form the spongy structure in bread. Washing flour separates the gluten from the starch. Strong flour (bread flour) has a greater percentage of protein than plain flour, but we have found the gluten from plain flour better for making 'mock meats'. Plain-flour gluten is stiffer and firmer than strong-flour gluten, which is softer and less able to hold a shape.

Although it seems that the Chinese knew that gluten could be made from flour about 700 years ago, for some reason it did not spread through Asia, and even today it is hardly known or made outside China. In China itself it is only in the last hundred years that chefs, working mainly in the east, have developed into a highly skilled art the making of mock, or representational,

Washing gluten

1. Flour and water dough ready for washing.

2. Half-washed gluten: still white with a smooth texture.

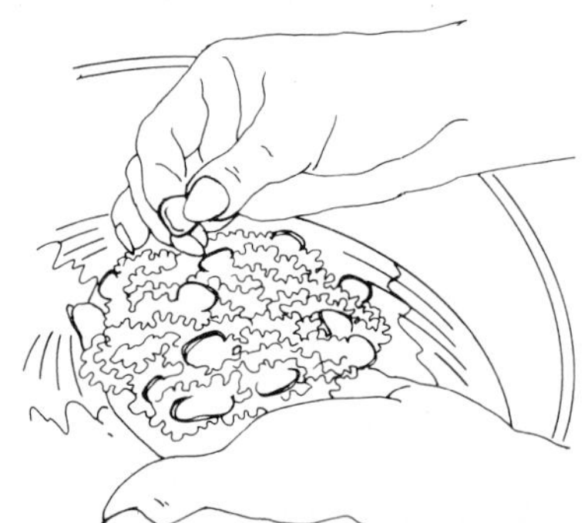

3. Almost finished: the gluten now a ball of grey elastic threads with the remaining starch showing as white flakes.

meats from flour protein. More traditional forms of meat substitute were made with beancurd skins (some recipes for these appear in Chapter 8), but below are a few examples of the 'false-meat' dishes which can be made with gluten. These are protein-rich dishes. Serve them either with other Chinese dishes or in a Western vegetarian meal: for instance, lichi and walnut balls go well with a green salad and a bean dish.

Gluten

INGREDIENTS

450g (3½ cups, 1 lb) plain flour
250ml (1¼ cups, 9 fl oz) warm water

PREPARATION

Mix the water and flour together into a stiff dough and cover with a damp cloth or clingwrap. Leave to rest for 30 minutes. Then put the dough into a large, clean bowl filled with warm water and gently start to wash the dough as if you were washing a jersey. Rub and squeeze between your hands until the water is milky white and quite opaque while the dough has turned a light greyish brown and is full of elastic-like threads. Transfer to another bowl of clean water, straining out the loose crumbs of gluten from the first batch of water. Now work on removing any white flakes still lying in the mass of rubbery threads, for these are the remaining bits of starch. As the gluten becomes free of the starch it becomes more and more cohesive; when finished it can be all rolled together as one lump. Always store it under water until it is cooked, because if the threads dry unevenly this will spoil the texture of the finished gluten. The yield from 450g (3½ cups, 1 lb) plain flour is 150g (5oz) uncooked gluten.

NOTE For deep-fried gluten balls it is better to make gluten from strong flour, because this gives them a looser texture. Substitute strong flour where plain flour is mentioned in the recipe above. The yield from 450g (1 lb) strong flour is 200g (7oz) raw gluten.

Mushrooms and 'vegetarian meat' in a spicy sauce

CHINESE

INGREDIENTS

150g (5 oz) uncooked plain-flour gluten
plain flour for dusting
oil for deep frying
5 dried mushrooms
75g (3oz) bamboo shoots
20 canned ginko nuts
15 snow peas
2 slices ginger
1 petal star anise
45ml (3 tablespoons) dark soy sauce
30ml (2 tablespoons) crystal sugar
5ml (1 teaspoon) sesame oil

PREPARATION

Shape the gluten into a strip about 5cm (2 inches) wide and 1cm (½ inch) thick. Boil a pan of water and put in the gluten. Boil for 20 minutes, then lift out and leave to drain and cool. When it is cool enough to handle, pat dry and cut into thick slices about 3cm (1 inch) long. Dust the gluten slices with the dry flour and deep-fry in hot oil for about 1 minute until golden brown. Lift out and drain. Meanwhile soak the dried mushrooms in 250ml (8fl oz) warm water for 45 minutes, then discard the hard stalks and cut the caps into thick slices. Strain and reserve the soaking water. Cut the bamboo shoots into slices. Trim the snow peas and blanch in boiling water for 1 minute; refresh in cold water and drain well.

Heat 30ml (2 tablespoons) oil in a wok or frying-pan and stir-fry the ginger and mushrooms. Add the bamboo shoots, ginko nuts and gluten and stir-fry for another minute, then pour in the reserved mushroom water. Add the star anise, soy sauce and sugar and simmer for about 10 minutes. Mix in the snow peas and sprinkle with sesame oil before serving.

Spring in two winters

CHINESE

This rather romantic name comes from the mixing of two dried or preserved vegetables, mushrooms and bamboo shoots, which are winter foods, with a fresh new food, gluten (representing spring). Everything up to the point of cooking the seasonings and vegetables may be done well in advance of the meal.

INGREDIENTS
5 dried mushrooms
150 g (5 oz) uncooked plain-flour gluten, (page 93)
25 g (1 oz) picked bamboo shoots
2 spring onions
2 slices ginger
MARINADE
30 ml (2 tablespoons) egg white
40 ml (2½ tablespoons) cornflour
7.5 ml (1½ teaspoons) rice wine
7.5 ml (1½ teaspoons) dark soy sauce
pinch salt
oil for deep frying
5 ml (1 teaspoon) rice wine
salt and sugar to taste
5 ml (1 teaspoon) cornflour mixed with 10 ml (2 teaspoons) water
2.5 ml (½ teaspoon) sesame oil

PREPARATION
Soak the dried mushrooms in warm water for 45 minutes, then discard the hard stalks and cut the caps into thick slices. Strain and reserve 90 ml (6 tablespoons) of the soaking water. Press the washed, but uncooked, gluten into a flat sheet about 0.75 cm (¼ inch) thick, then place in a pan of boiling water and boil for 20 minutes. Lift out, drain and leave to cool. Prepare the pickled bamboo according to the directions on page 14. Then cut into strips 3 cm (1 inch) long and 1 cm (⅓ inch) wide. Chop the onions and ginger finely. Mix the marinade. Pat the gluten dry and cut into thin shreds. Marinate for 20 minutes. Afterwards heat the oil until hot and deep-fry the gluten for about 1 minute, making sure that the strips are well separated (if necessary, fry in two batches). Then drain well.

Heat 30 ml (2 tablespoons) oil in a wok or large frying-pan and stir-fry the onion and ginger for about 30 seconds. Add the mushrooms and cook for another 30 seconds, then pour in the reserved stock and rice wine. Add the bamboo shoots and gluten and bring to the boil. Thicken the sauce with the cornflour paste and adjust the seasoning. Serve sprinkled with sesame oil.

Deep-fried 'spareribs'

CHINESE

This dish is extremely realistic when finished, as well as being good to eat. It was devised in this form by a chef called Han Yuming, one of a family of chefs, who lives and works in Shenyang in northern China and has specialized in vegetarian foods for many years.

INGREDIENTS
150 g (5 oz) uncooked plain-flour gluten (page 93)
MARINADE
15 ml (1 tablespoon) soy sauce
15 ml (1 tablespoon) sweet bean sauce
50 g (2 oz) bamboo shoots
45 ml (3 tablespoons) cornflour
45 ml (3 tablespoons) water
oil for deep frying
salt-pepper dip (page 24)

PREPARATION
Divide the gluten into 3 portions and pull each out into a thin strip. Wind each strip round two wooden chopsticks. Bring a large pan of water to the boil and put in the three pairs of coated chopsticks. Boil the gluten for 20 minutes, then lift out and leave to cool. When cool enough to handle, slide out the chopsticks and cut the rolls of gluten into 3-cm (1-inch) lengths. Mix the marinade in a bowl and coat the gluten rolls in the mixture. Leave for 30 minutes. Meanwhile, cut the bamboo shoots into flat strips – to represent rib bones – about 1 cm (⅓ inch) wide and 4 cm (1⅓ inches) long. Mix the cornflour and water into a wet paste in another bowl. When the gluten has finished marinating thread a piece of bamboo through the centre of each

roll. Heat the deep fat until very hot and after dipping the rolls in the cornflour paste deep-fry, a few at a time, in the hot oil for about 1 minute. Lift out and drain, then serve very hot with a dip of spicy salt.

Sweet and sour 'spareribs'

CHINESE

This is another dish for which much of the work may be done in advance, up to the point where the seasonings and vegetables are stir-fried.

INGREDIENTS

150 g (5 oz) uncooked plain-flour gluten (page 93)
30 ml (2 tablespoons) light soy sauce
1 spring onion
1 slice ginger
1 small clove garlic
150 g (5 oz) green pepper
4 water chestnuts
25 g (1 oz) carrots
50 g (2 oz) bamboo shoots

SEASONING SAUCE

15 ml (1 tablespoon) soy sauce
30 ml (2 tablespoons) sugar
25 ml (1½ tablespoons) rice vinegar
60 ml (4 tablespoons) water
7.5 ml (1½ teaspoons) cornflour
pinch salt

COATING BATTER

45 ml (3 tablespoons) cornflour
45 ml (3 tablespoons) water

oil for deep frying
5 ml (1 teaspoon) sesame oil

PREPARATION

Divide the prepared gluten into three and pull each piece out into a flat ribbon. Wind each ribbon round two wooden chopsticks. Bring a large pan of water to the boil and put in the three pairs of coated chopsticks. Boil the gluten for 20 minutes, then lift out and leave to cool. When cold enough to handle, slide out the chopsticks and cut the rolls of gluten into 3-cm (1-inch) lengths. Soak these rolls in the soy sauce for 30 minutes. Meanwhile, finely chop the onion, ginger and garlic. De-seed and cut the pepper into bite-sized pieces. Slice the water chestnuts and carrots. Par-boil the carrot slices in lightly salted water for 3 minutes, then refresh in cold water and leave to drain. Cut the bamboo shoots into flat strips about 1 cm (⅓ inch) wide and 4 cm (1⅓ inches) long, to represent the 'bones' in the spareribs. Mix the seasoning sauce and coating batter in separate bowls.

Thread one piece of bamboo through the centre of each roll of gluten. Heat the oil until hot, dip the rolls in the coating batter and deep-fry, a few at a time, for about 1 minute. Lift out and drain. Afterwards deep-fry the green pepper for 30 seconds then drain well.

Heat 30 ml (2 tablespoons) oil in a wok or large frying-pan and stir-fry the onion, ginger and garlic for 15 seconds. Add the par-boiled carrot, green pepper and water chestnuts and continue stir-frying for another minute. Add the gluten rolls and the seasoning sauce. Bring to the boil, taking care that the rolls are well coated in the sauce. Adjust the seasoning and serve sprinkled with the sesame oil.

Gongbao 'chicken'

CHINESE

This dish is the vegetarian imitation of a famous western Chinese dish made with chillis and chicken. It belongs to the new-style meatless cooking in China, rather than to any form of Buddhist or traditional cooking. The original dish was said to have been a favourite of an Imperial minister during the nineteenth century, but since a very similar dish was also claimed to be Mao Zedong's favourite the probability is that everyone likes hot western Chinese food. Everything up to the point of frying the seasonings and mashed beans may be done in advance. Note, too, that you can reduce the number of chillis to suit your own taste, but as gluten absorbs and dulls flavouring it is necessary to season with a fairly heavy hand. Take the chillis out before serving.

INGREDIENTS

150g (5oz) uncooked plain-flour gluten (page 93)
plain flour for dusting
oil for deep frying
75g (3oz) cashew nuts
6–10 dried chillis
3 spring onions, finely chopped
3 slices ginger, finely chopped
1 clove garlic
10ml (2 teaspoons) mashed yellow beans

SEASONING SAUCE

10ml (2 teaspoons) sugar
60ml (4 tablespoons) vegetarian stock
15ml (1 tablespoon) red vinegar
25 ml (1½ tablespoons) soy sauce
5ml (1 teaspoon) cornflour

PREPARATION

Shape the gluten into a strip about 4cm (1½ inches) wide and 1cm (½ inch) thick. Boil a large pan of water and drop in the gluten. Boil for 20 minutes, then lift out and leave to drain. When cool enough to handle, cut into thin slices. Pat dry and dust with plain flour. Heat the oil until hot and deep-fry the gluten for 30 seconds, in several batches. Lift out and leave to drain. Deep-fry the cashew nuts in hot oil over a low to moderate heat until they start to colour (about 3 minutes). Lift out and drain.

Put 30ml (2 tablespoons) oil in a wok or large frying-pan and fry the chillis over a moderate heat for 30 seconds. Add the onion, ginger, garlic and mashed beans. Stir-fry for another 30 seconds, then mix in the gluten and cashew nuts. Pour in the seasoning sauce and bring to the boil, stirring all the time. Serve hot.

OPPOSITE *A Japanese meal, showing a place setting for one person, consisting of* miso *soup (page 143); vegetarian* tempura *(page 59), deep-fried vegetables coated in a lace-like batter; soy-simmered pumpkin (page 70), pumpkin wedges simmered in soy sauce, sweet wine and stock; okra and* natto *salad (page 115); plain boiled rice (page 154) and pickles.*

OVERLEAF, LEFT *A basket of vegetables (Chinese, page 49), a crisp basket made from deep-fried potato straws filled with lightly stir-fried broccoli spears, bamboo shoot, carrot, water chestnuts and almonds, with silver wood ears and straw mushroom soup (Chinese, page 150): two kinds of fungi in a clear vegetable consommé.*

OVERLEAF, RIGHT *Beancurd frying in a wok, and a plate of deep-fried beancurd with sesame sauce (Chinese, page 85), this crunchy sweet and sour sauce makes an ideal foil for beancurd.*

Lichi and walnut balls

CHINESE

INGREDIENTS

150g (5 oz) uncooked plain-flour gluten (page 93)

50g (2 oz) walnuts, deep-fried for 3 minutes

MARINADE

5 ml (1 teaspoon) soy sauce

5 ml (1 teaspoon) rice wine

1.5 ml (¼ teaspoon) salt

pinch ground Sichuan pepper

45 ml (3 tablespoons) cornflour

45 ml (3 tablespoons) egg white

180g (6 oz) green pepper

75 ml (3 oz) canned lichis, drained

3 spring onions

2 slices ginger

SEASONING SAUCE

30 ml (2 tablespoons) sugar

30 ml (2 tablespoons) white rice vinegar

10 ml (2 teaspoons) tomato paste

75 ml (5 tablespoons) water

5 ml (1 teaspoon) soy sauce

5 ml (1 teaspoon) cornflour

oil for deep frying

2.5 ml (½ teaspoon) sesame oil

PREPARATION

Divide the gluten into four and press each piece out into a strip about 3 cm (1 inch) wide and 1 cm (⅓ inch) thick (it is easier to do this on a damp surface). Cut each strip into slices about ½ cm (¼ inch) wide and wrap each slice round a piece of walnut. Pinch the edges to seal well. Bring a large pan of water to the boil and drop in the gluten balls. Simmer for 5 minutes, then lift out and leave to drain and cool. Meanwhile, mix the marinade. When the gluten balls are cold, pat dry and drop into the marinade. Leave for 30 minutes.

De-seed the peppers and cut into bite-sized pieces. Drain the lichis. Chop the spring onion and ginger finely. Mix the seasoning sauce. Heat the oil until hot and deep-fry the gluten balls for about 1 minute, in several batches. Drain well. When they have all been fried, heat 15 ml (1 tablespoon) oil in a wok or large frying-pan and stir-fry the onion and ginger for 15 seconds. Add the green peppers and continue stir-frying for another 2 minutes. Add the lichis and pour in the seasoning sauce. Bring to the boil over a moderate heat. Re-heat the deep-frying oil and drop in the gluten balls. Re-fry for 20 seconds, then lift out quickly, drain for a moment and drop into the seasoning sauce. Mix quickly and serve sprinkled with sesame oil.

OPPOSITE Telur kari *(Indonesian, page 63): deep-fried eggs served in a rich coconut sauce lightly flavoured with curry spices; silver and gold (Chinese and Indonesian, page 154): mixed rice and corn kernels; and* sayur bening *(Indonesian, page 74): spinach, baby corn and chayote, lightly seasoned and cooked in a vegetarian stock.*

Satay-style grilled gluten

This is an entirely invented recipe: the only one in this book not from a vernacular source. The Indonesians do not use gluten as a meat substitute and the Chinese do not have *satays*. However, since everyone likes eating *satays* it seemed a shame not to try to marry the two cultural styles.

INGREDIENTS

150g (5oz) uncooked plain-flour gluten (page 93)
15ml (1 tablespoon) dark soy sauce
pinch five-spice powder
1 clove garlic, crushed

DIPPING SAUCE

15ml (1 tablespoon) crunchy peanut butter
15g (½oz) red onion
1 clove garlic
1 chilli, de-seeded and finely chopped
pinch salt
juice of half a lemon
1.5ml (¼ teaspoon) ground coriander
60ml (4 tablespoons) water
45ml (3 tablespoons) thick canned santan

MARINADE

15ml (1 tablespoon) dark soy sauce
15ml (1 tablespoon) clear honey

oil for deep frying

PREPARATION

Divide the gluten into four and roll each portion into a roll about 2cm (¾ inch) in diameter. Cut one roll into four equal slices and fold each slice over into an oval-shaped ball. Repeat with the remaining rolls of gluten. Bring a large pan of water to the boil and drop in the gluten balls. Boil for 5 minutes, then lift out and leave to drain for a few minutes before mixing with the dark soy sauce, crushed garlic and five-spice powder. Leave to marinate in this mixture for 30 minutes while making the dipping sauce. Put the peanut butter, onion, garlic, chilli, salt, lemon juice and coriander into a food processor and blend to a smooth paste. Add the water and pour into a pan. Simmer over a low heat until the onion and garlic are cooked (about 10 minutes), if necessary adding a little more water. Then leave on one side until the gluten is finished. Heat the oil until hot and deep-fry the gluten for 30 seconds. Drain well, then coat the gluten balls with the marinade of soy sauce and honey. Push them on to four *satay* skewers and place under a hot grill for about 4 minutes. After 2 minutes, re-paint with the remaining marinade and turn to brown on the other side. At the same time warm up the dipping sauce and stir in the *santan*. Adjust the seasoning and serve hot in a separate dish.

Barbecued 'spareribs'

CHINESE

INGREDIENTS

150 g (5 oz) uncooked plain-flour gluten (page 93)
30ml (2 tablespoons) soy sauce
50g (2oz) bamboo shoots
4 cloves garlic

SEASONING SAUCE

25ml (1½ tablespoons) soy sauce
25ml (1½ tablespoons) rice wine
25ml (1½ tablespoons) hoisin *sauce*
30ml (2 tablespoons) sugar
75ml (5 tablespoons) water
2.5ml (½ teaspoon) salt
pinch five-spice powder

COATING BATTER

45ml (3 tablespoons) cornflour
45ml (3 tablespoons) water

oil for deep frying

PREPARATION

Divide the gluten into three and work each piece into a flat strip. Wind each of the three strips round a pair of wooden chopsticks held together. Bring a large pan of water to the boil and put in the three pairs of coated chopsticks so that the gluten is immersed in the boiling water. Boil for 20 minutes, then lift out and allow to cool. When cool enough to handle, pull out the chopsticks and cut the rolls of gluten into 3-cm (1-inch) lengths. Marinate in the soy sauce for 30 minutes. Meanwhile, cut the bamboo shoots into flat strips about 1 cm (⅓ inch) wide and 4cm (1½ inches) long, to represent the 'bones' of the spareribs. Crush the garlic and mix the seasoning sauce and coating batter in separate bowls.

Thread the bamboo strips through the centre of the gluten rolls, so that a piece of bamboo sticks out at each end. Heat the oil until hot, dip the rolls in the coating batter and deep-fry a few at a time for about 1 minute. Drain well. Put the seasoning sauce and garlic into a wok or large frying-pan and bring to the boil. Add the gluten rolls and simmer for 5 minutes, turning the rolls from time to time to ensure all are well coated in the sauce. Serve hot.

8

Cooking in Steam

The Chinese have cooked in steam over boiling water for over two and a half thousand years, and they still use it for many different kinds of dishes, ranging from meat, fish and beancurd to most of their breads and buns. The Japanese use steam for cooking traditional recipes, especially vegetarian foods. Steaming is one of the styles of cooking which is always represented in a big Korean or Japanese meal, along with raw food, simmered, grilled and deep-fried foods. Indonesia, however, has no tradition of steamed foods.

In Chinese cuisine, dishes are steamed to preserve the shape and appearance of the foods which might otherwise be lost in more vigorous cooking methods. Foods being steamed do not move about and therefore do not break up. It is normal in China to put foods in bowls or on plates to be steamed so that their juices are retained and the natural flavour of the food is strengthened.

A Chinese steamer is a circular wooden box or tray with a lattice-work bottom. Several tiers can be cooked at one time, each fitting firmly on to the one below and covered on top by a domed lid. This means that a number of different dishes can all be cooked together, saving both space and fuel. The steamer stands in a wok filled with water. The Japanese at home use a Western metal steamer. These work perfectly well, although heat loss through the metal sides is faster and they cannot hold as much food as a stack of Chinese bamboo steamers. Another method of steaming a small quantity of food is to stand it on a rack either in a covered wok or large saucepan of boiling water, making sure that the water level is at least 1 cm (½ inch) below the top of the rack.

The length of time any steaming dish can take to cook varies wildly according to the equipment used and the strength of heat from the cooker when it is full on. We have therefore stated the longer cooking times which we found necessary, as rough guides only. You may find that your equipment will cook the foods in less time than has been specified.

There is a wide range of different styles of steamed dish in Chinese cuisine, including soups and the various representational meats created from beancurd skins. Often the Chinese use steam where we in the West would use an oven, for domestic kitchens in China have no ovens.

MOCK MEATS FROM DRIED BEANCURD SKINS

Beancurd skin is made from the skin that forms on the top of boiling soya-bean milk, which is lifted off sheet by sheet as it forms and laid out to dry. In China and Japan it is possible to buy freshly-made beancurd skin, but in the West we have to make do with a coarser dried beancurd skin imported from China. Unfortunately it is very brittle and by the time it reaches the consumer the sheets are often cracked and broken, and they cannot be repaired. This means that where in a recipe a sheet of beancurd skin is mentioned you may find that you have to use several parts of sheets laid one on another to form a whole sheet. This cannot be helped, and will not spoil the dish as a whole, but it does make it a little harder to handle. However, as you become more familiar with handling beancurd skins they will become much easier to use and produce really satisfactory results. Beancurd skin needs to be softened in warm water before it is used. It is both delicate and tough: it needs very long cooking to prevent it being leathery in texture.

Beancurd skin is the traditional ingredient used by Buddhist chefs to make 'mock meats'. The skins, seasoned with soy sauce and sesame oil, are arranged and then tied together so that their layers simulate the texture of different meats. Skilled chefs can shape them into whole chickens and ducks, or even mould stuffed beancurd into fish with scales. Though no such heights of artistry are required in the recipes that follow, basic 'ham', 'chicken', 'goose' and 'fish' recipes are included so that you can explore fully this intriguing sidelight on vegetarian cookery.

Vegetarian 'ham'

CHINESE

INGREDIENTS

150 g (5 oz) dried beancurd skins

SEASONING SAUCE

- *15 ml (1 tablespoon) light soy sauce*
- *2.5 ml (½ teaspoon) sugar*
- *pinch five-spice powder*
- *15 ml (1 tablespoon) rice wine (preferably* shaoxing*)*
- *5 ml (1 teaspoon) ginger juice*
- *200 ml (1 cup, ⅓ pint) mushroom soaking water, strained (page 141)*

15 ml (1 tablespoon) sesame oil

PREPARATION

Tear the beancurd skins into little bits and simmer very gently in the seasoning sauce until the beancurd is very soft and the sauce has almost all evaporated (about 30 minutes). Mix in the sesame oil. Spread out a clean cloth and lay the beancurd on it. Roll up the cloth around the beancurd very tightly, shaping it into a sausage. Use plenty of string to tie it into this shape. (If not tied tightly the cooked 'ham' will fall to pieces when sliced.) Steam over fast-boiling water for 2 hours, taking care not to let the pan boil dry. Leave for several hours to cool, then unroll the cloth and use as directed.

Serve cold, cut into slices and garnished with chopped chives and coriander, or use as an ingredient in other dishes. This 'ham' can be kept covered in the refrigerator for up to a week.

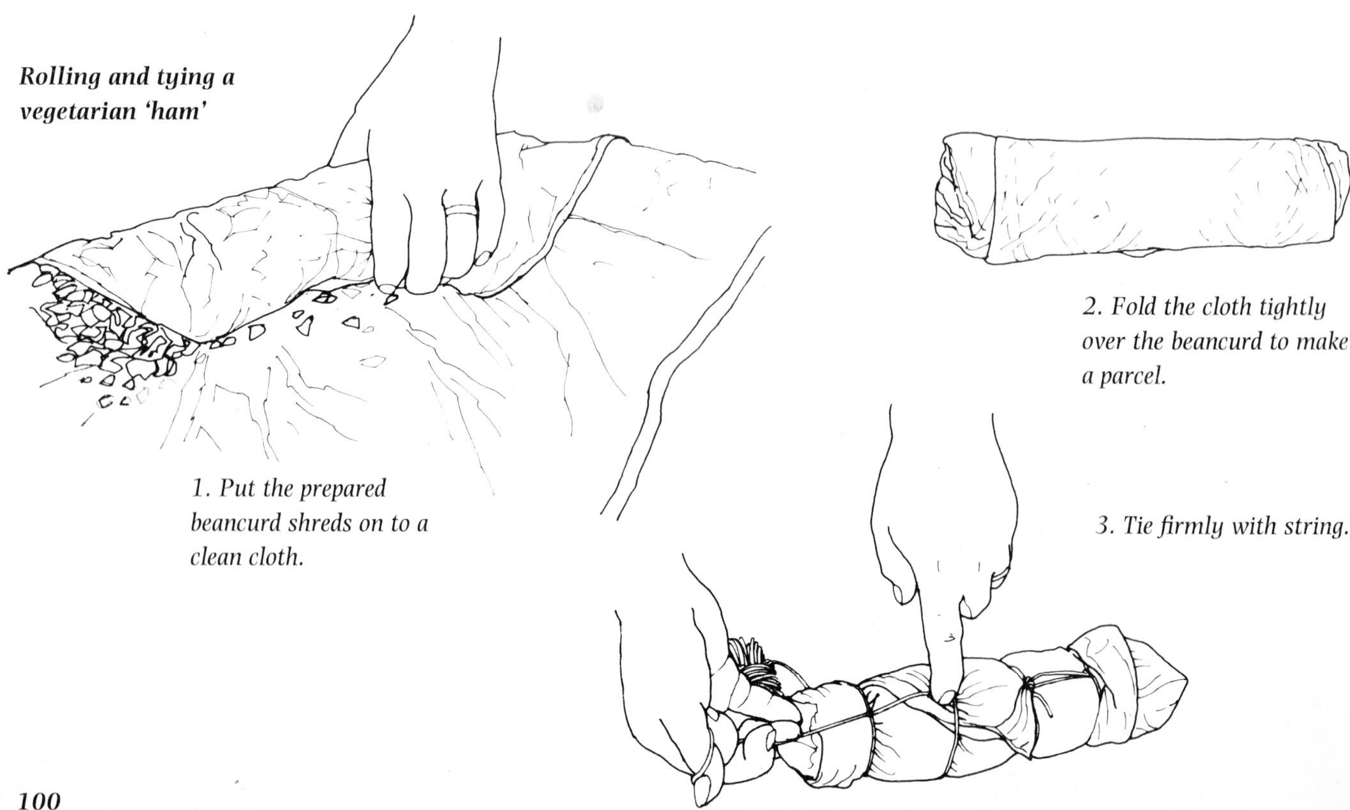

Rolling and tying a vegetarian 'ham'

1. Put the prepared beancurd shreds on to a clean cloth.

2. Fold the cloth tightly over the beancurd to make a parcel.

3. Tie firmly with string.

Vegetarian 'chicken'

CHINESE

INGREDIENTS
8 sheets dried beancurd skin
SAUCE
30 ml (2 tablespoons) dark soy sauce
1.5 ml (¼ teaspoon) salt
7.5 ml (½ tablespoon) sugar
7.5 ml (½ tablespoon) sesame oil
oil for deep frying

PREPARATION
Soak the beancurd skins in hot water just long enough to soften (about 3 minutes), then pat dry and cut off any hard edges with a pair of scissors. Bring the sauce ingredients to the boil in a small pan, then leave to cool. Spread a sheet of beancurd skin on a clean cloth laid on a flat surface.

Paint all over with the prepared sauce. Lay another sheet on top of the first and brush over with the sauce. Repeat until all the sheets are piled up and coated in the sauce. Roll up tightly and tie firmly in the cloth to make a sausage about 6 cm (2½ inches) in diameter. Steam over a high heat for 2 hours. Allow to cool, then unwrap. Heat the oil and deep-fry the beancurd roll over a moderate heat until golden brown (about 2–3 minutes). Serve hot, cut into slices and garnished with a sprig of coriander, or use as an ingredient in another dish.

Spiced vegetarian 'chicken'

CHINESE

INGREDIENTS
vegetarian 'chicken' (made as above)
SEASONING SAUCE
200 ml (1 cup, ⅓ pint) stock
15 ml (1 tablespoon) soy sauce
15 ml (1 tablespoon) rice wine
2.5 ml (½ teaspoon) ginger juice
5 ml (½ teaspoon) sugar
pinch five-spice powder
salt to taste
5 ml (1 teaspoon) sesame oil

PREPARATION
Leave the vegetarian 'chicken' unsliced. Put the seasoning sauce in a pan and bring to the boil. Slide in the 'chicken' and simmer for 5 minutes, basting all the time. Then lift out and slice. Serve hot with the sauce and the sesame oil poured over.

NOTE Another version of this beancurd roll can be made by substituting a sheet of *nori* for one of the sheets of dried beancurd skin. Season, roll and cook as directed for vegetarian 'chicken'. Serve cold, cut into slices, as a starter, either on its own or as part of a plate of mixed cold foods (see page 117).

Steamed 'chicken'

CHINESE

INGREDIENTS
8 dried red dates
15 g (½ oz) silver wood ears
200 g (7 oz) vegetarian chicken
45 ml (3 tablespoons) Chinese medlars (optional)
800 ml (3½ cups, 1⅓ pints) stock
salt and freshly ground pepper to taste
pinch sugar

PREPARATION
Soak the red dates for 3 hours, then rinse well. Soak the silver wood ears for 30 minutes in warm water, then rinse well, discard any hard bits and tear into separate leaves. Cut the chicken into 1-cm (⅓-inch)-thick slices. Put the chicken, dates, silver wood ears and Chinese medlars into a bowl and pour in the stock. Steam over a high heat for an hour. Before serving, season to taste with salt, pepper and sugar.

Smoked vegetarian 'goose'

CHINESE

INGREDIENTS

8 sheets dried beancurd skin
20 ml (4 teaspoons) sesame oil
20 ml (4 teaspoons) dark soy sauce

SMOKING MIXTURE

45 ml (3 tablespoons) used tea leaves, drained and dried
45 ml (3 tablespoons) rice
45 ml (3 tablespoons) brown sugar

PREPARATION

Soak the beancurd sheets in warm water for 3 minutes, then pat dry. Paint each sheet with a mixture of the sesame oil and soy sauce. Select the 3 most complete sheets and lay them on top of each other on a clean cloth. Cut or tear the other sheets into fine shreds and pile on to the 3 whole sheets. Roll the beancurd skins very tightly round the shreds and tie firmly in the cloth to make a roll about 5 cm (2 inches) in diameter. Steam over a high heat for 2 hours. Then leave to cool still tied in the cloth. When completely cold, unwrap and lay the beancurd roll on an oiled rack. Heat the oven to 230°C, 450°F, Gas 8 and line the bottom of a roasting tin with tinfoil. Put the tea, sugar and rice on the tinfoil, cover with the lid and place in the oven for 15–20 minutes, until the mixture is smoking vigorously. Then put the rack with the beancurd roll over the smoking mixture, cover with the lid again and return to the oven. Turn off the heat and smoke for 5 minutes. Lift out and leave to cool. Serve cut into slices as part of a cold plate (see page 117).

Smoked pine-kernel rolls

CHINESE

INGREDIENTS

75 g (3 oz) pine kernels
oil for deep frying
200 g (7 oz) sweet potato (preferably white-fleshed)
2.5 ml (½ teaspoon) sugar
5 ml (1 teaspoon) ginger juice
salt and pepper to taste
10 ml (2 teaspoons) sesame oil
4 sheets dried beancurd skin

SMOKING MIXTURE

45 ml (3 tablespoons) rice
45 ml (3 tablespoons) used tea leaves, drained and dried, or fresh tea leaves
45 ml (3 tablespoons) brown sugar

PREPARATION

Deep-fry the pine kernels in hot oil over a moderate heat for about 3 minutes, until golden brown. Lift out and drain. Wash the sweet potato and steam, without peeling, until soft (about 30 minutes, depending on size). Then peel and mash. Blend in the pine kernels, ginger juice and sesame oil. Season to taste with salt and pepper. Soak the beancurd skins in warm water for about 3 minutes to soften. Then pat dry, lay out flat and paint with a little oil. Put one-quarter of the mashed potato mixture on the bottom quarter of one skin and roll up into a neat package about 3 cm (1 inch) in diameter. Repeat with the remaining potato and sheets of beancurd. Put the rolls in a steamer and steam for 1 hour over a moderate heat. Lift out and leave to cool. Pre-heat the oven to 230°C, 450°F, Gas 8. Line a roasting tin with tinfoil and spread the rice, tea and sugar over the bottom. Cover with the lid and put into the oven for 15–20 minutes. When the mixture is smoking vigorously, place the beancurd packets on an oiled rack over the smoking mixture in the tin, cover again with the lid and return to the oven. Turn off the heat and smoke the rolls for 5 minutes. Lift out and serve hot cut into 5-cm (2-inch) slices sprinkled with sesame oil. Alternatively, serve cold cut into 1-cm (⅓-inch) diagonal slices as a whole dish, or serve these cold slices as part of a cold plate for a starter (see page 117).

STEAMED SAVOURY CUSTARDS

Various styles of savoury custards are represented in the cuisines of China, Korea and Japan. In Japan they are served as a steamed dish among other dishes cooked by different methods. The Chinese also have hot savoury custards which are eaten with a spoon, but the Chinese recipe given here is for a cold dish in which the custard is cut into slices and eaten with chopsticks. These dishes can all be served as a protein dish among other vegetable dishes, or even as a side dish with an Indonesian curry.

Japanese egg 'tofu'

JAPANESE

INGREDIENTS

4 size 2 eggs
300 ml ($1\frac{1}{4}$ cups, $\frac{1}{2}$ pint) dashi *(of equal volume to the eggs)*
3.5 ml ($\frac{3}{4}$ teaspoon) salt
7.5 ml ($1\frac{1}{2}$ teaspoons) mirin

SAUCE

150 ml ($\frac{2}{3}$ cup, $\frac{1}{4}$ pint) dashi
15 ml (1 tablespoon) Japanese soy sauce
salt to taste
10 ml (2 teaspoons) mirin
3 square cm (1 square inch) lime or lemon peel or wasabi *mustard*

PREPARATION

Carefully line a 500-g (1-lb) loaf-tin with tinfoil (so that you can lift out the cooked egg custard without breaking it). Beat the eggs with the *dashi*, salt and *mirin*, using a fork to avoid creating bubbles. Strain the beaten egg into the lined tin and remove any bubbles which appear on the surface. Steam over a high heat for 2 minutes only, then reduce the heat and steam over a low heat until the egg is completely set (about 25 minutes). Lift the tin from the steamer and leave to cool. Meanwhile, make the sauce by bringing the *dashi* to the boil with the soy sauce, salt and *mirin*, then leaving on one side to cool. Cut the lime peel into hair-like shreds. When the egg is cold, lift carefully from the tin and cut into four equal slices. Arrange in four serving bowls and spoon over the sauce. Garnish with threads of lime peel, or a tiny cone of *wasabi* mustard.

Three-coloured eggs

CHINESE

INGREDIENTS

1 salted egg
1 preserved egg
3 size 4 eggs
45 ml (3 tablespoons) water
2.5 ml ($\frac{1}{2}$ teaspoon) salt
pinch pepper
15 ml (1 tablespoon) sesame oil
15 ml (1 tablespoon) chopped coriander or chives

PREPARATION

Wash the soot coating from the salted egg and boil the egg for 5 minutes. Cool in cold water and shell. Cut the hard-boiled egg into 1-cm ($\frac{1}{3}$-inch) dice. Shell the preserved egg and cut into similar-sized dice. Beat the ordinary eggs with the water and season with the salt, pepper and sesame oil. Mix in the diced eggs. Carefully line a 500-g (1-lb) loaf-tin with tinfoil so that the cooked egg custard can be lifted out without breaking. Lightly oil the tinfoil lining and pour in the egg mixture. Steam over a moderate to low heat until the egg is set (about 15 minutes). Lift out and leave to cool in the tin, then remove and cut into $1\frac{1}{2}$-cm ($\frac{1}{2}$-inch)-thick slices. Serve cold with chopped coriander or chives as a garnish.

'A thousand grasses' steamed custard

JAPANESE

INGREDIENTS
50g (2oz) snow peas
3 dried mushrooms
40g (1½ oz) carrot
40g (1½ oz) bamboo shoots
SIMMERING STOCK
45ml (3 tablespoons) sake
15ml (1 tablespoon) Japanese soy sauce
15ml (1 tablespoon) mirin
1.5ml (¼ teaspoon) salt
300ml (1¼ cups, ½ pint) dashi, *plus a little extra*
2 eggs, beaten
SAUCE
120ml (4 fl oz) cold seasoned dashi
5ml (1 teaspoon) Japanese soy sauce
3.5ml (¾ teaspoon) kudzu *or potato flour mixed with 7.5ml (1½ teaspoons) water*
shreds of yuzu, *bitter orange or lemon peel for garnish*

PREPARATION
Wash and trim the snow peas. Cut lengthways into very thin strips. Soak the dried mushrooms in warm water for 30 minutes, then discard the hard stalks and cut the caps into thin slices. Scrape and cut the carrot into thin matchstick pieces and the bamboo shoots into similar-sized strips. Mix the simmering stock in a small saucepan and bring to the boil. Pour in the *dashi*, and when it returns to the boil add the vegetables. Cover the pan and simmer for 5 minutes over a very low heat. Lift the pan from the cooker and cool immediately by standing the pan in a bowl of cold water. When cold, drain off the liquid and make it up again to 300ml (1¼ cups, ½ pint) with the extra *dashi*. Add to the beaten eggs and stir in the cold mixed vegetables. Divide the egg and vegetable mixture between four deep, mug-shaped bowls or cups and stand them in a steamer. Cover and cook for 15 minutes over boiling water. Meanwhile bring the sauce ingredients to the boil in a small saucepan, stirring all the time. After 15 minutes test with a skewer to make sure the custard is set. Spoon the prepared sauce over the custards and serve in the bowls in which they were cooked, garnished with a few shreds of *yuzu*, bitter orange or lemon peel.

Beancurd 'fish' balls

CHINESE

INGREDIENTS
350g (12oz) beancurd
5g (¼ oz) black hair fungus
25g (1oz) water chestnuts
25g (1oz) carrot
25g (1oz) canned pickled mustard greens
2.5ml (½ teaspoon) salt
sugar to taste

PREPARATION
Wrap the beancurd in a towel and press for 1 hour. Soak the black hair fungus in warm water for 30 minutes, then squeeze as dry as possible and cut into 3-cm (1-inch) lengths. Dry the water chestnuts and chop with the carrot very finely. Soak the mustard greens in water for 1 minute, then dry very thoroughly and chop finely. Blend the beancurd with the water chestnuts, carrot and mustard greens to a smooth paste, then mix in the black hair fungus. Season to taste with salt and sugar. Shape into small balls the size of walnuts and stand on a plate. Steam over a high heat for 10 minutes. Serve hot or cold on their own or use for a soup (see page 150).

STUFFED VEGETABLES

Chinese cuisine is particularly rich in stuffed-food dishes – beancurd, pastry skins and buns as well as vegetables. These dishes make a good contrast to stir-fried or simmered vegetable dishes, as well as having the advantage that they can all be prepared well in advance of the meal and need no last-minute attention. They also blend in well with many Western meals, since although the ingredients may be unfamiliar none of the dishes is highly or distinctively seasoned.

Stuffed cabbage

JAPANESE

INGREDIENTS

300 g (10 oz) cotton beancurd
4 good-sized cabbage leaves
2 dried mushrooms
25 g (1 oz) bamboo shoots
5 ml (1 teaspoon) grated ginger
15 ml (1 tablespoon) chopped onion
10 ml (2 teaspoons) rice wine
5 ml (1 teaspoon) sesame oil
15 ml (1 tablespoon) toasted sesame seeds (page 36)
300 ml (1¼ cups, ½ pint) dashi
10 ml (2 teaspoons) kudzu *or potato flour mixed with 15 ml (1 tablespoon) cold water*
salt and pepper to taste

PREPARATION

Wrap the beancurd tightly in a cloth and leave to drain for 1 hour. Wash the cabbage leaves and tear away the hard central stalk. Blanch in boiling water for 1 minute, then immediately refresh in cold water. Drain well. Soak the mushrooms in warm water, then discard the hard stalks and chop the caps finely. Chop the bamboo shoots finely. Mash the beancurd and beat in the mushrooms, bamboo shoots, ginger, onion, rice wine, sesame oil and sesame seeds. Blend very well. Divide the mixture into four. Put one portion on a cabbage leaf and roll up into a packet. Fasten with a toothpick. Repeat with the remaining cabbage leaves. Put the packets into a large bowl and pour in the *dashi*. Season to taste and steam over a high heat for 20 minutes.

Arrange the packets in four heated serving bowls. Pour the stock into a small pan and stir in the *kudzu* paste. Bring to the boil, stirring all the time, adjust the seasoning and divide between the serving bowls. Garnish with lime or lemon triangles.

Stuffed cucumber

CHINESE

INGREDIENTS

100 g (4 oz) beancurd
4 dried mushrooms
1 long cucumber
50 g (2 oz) bamboo shoots
1 egg white, beaten
5 ml (1 teaspoon) ginger juice
2 spring onions, very finely chopped
5 ml (1 teaspoon) sesame oil
pinch salt and pepper
1 good-sized cucumber

PREPARATION

Press the beancurd between two plates for 1 hour. Soak the mushrooms in warm water for 30 minutes, then discard the hard stalks and chop the caps into minute pieces. Chop the bamboo shoots into pieces the size of a grain of rice. Mash the pressed beancurd in a bowl and blend in the bamboo shoots and mushrooms together with the beaten egg, ginger juice, spring onions and sesame oil. Season to taste with salt and pepper. Wash the cucumber and cut in half lengthways. Cut each half into 4-cm (1½-inch) lengths and scoop out the seeds. Fill with the beancurd mixture and steam for 12 minutes over a high heat. Serve hot.

Stuffed cucumber rings

CHINESE

This dish is different in both appearance and texture from the preceding one.

INGREDIENTS

1 long, thin cucumber
2 sheets dried beancurd skin
3 small dried mushrooms
20 g (¾ oz) carrot
20 g (¾ oz) vegetarian 'ham' (page 100)
well-seasoned stock
5 ml (1 teaspoon) crystal sugar

PREPARATION

Peel the cucumber and cut into quarters. Scoop out all the seeds, to leave 4 hollow tubes of cucumber. Soak the beancurd skin for 3 minutes in warm water, then cut each sheet across into half. Soak the mushrooms in warm water for 30 minutes, then discard the hard stalks and cut the caps into thin shreds. Scrape and cut the carrot into thin shreds. Cut the vegetarian 'ham' into thin batons. Wrap one-quarter of the mixed shreds in each half sheet of beancurd into a thin roll and push the roll through the centre of each length of cucumber. Using a sharp knife, cut the cucumber into 3-cm (1-inch) lengths and trim off the extra beancurd at the ends. Stand the rounds of cucumber, cut face up, in a shallow dish and pour in just sufficient stock to cover them. Add the sugar and steam over a high heat for 1 hour. Serve hot.

Stuffed cucumber with a corn sauce

CHINESE

This recipe is quite unlike traditional Chinese recipes, and belongs to the new style of Chinese cooking which owes much to Western and particularly to American fashion. More suited to a dinner-party than to an ordinary domestic meal, it can be served as part of either a Western or a Chinese meal.

INGREDIENTS

750 g (1½ lb) cucumber (about 2 large cucumbers)
125 g (4½ oz) yam
2 dried mushrooms
20 ginko nuts
100 g (4 oz) canned unsweetened chestnut purée
15 ml (1 tablespoon) chopped coriander
15 ml (1 tablespoon) light soy sauce
15 ml (1 tablespoon) rice wine
5 ml (1 teaspoon) sugar
pinch salt and pepper
1 300-g (10-oz) can creamed corn
150 ml (½ cup, ¼ pint) well-seasoned stock

PREPARATION

Peel the cucumber and cut into 3-cm (1-inch) slices. Scoop out the seeds. Peel the yam and cut into wedges. Steam over a high heat for about 25 minutes, until very soft. Meanwhile soak the dried mushrooms in warm water for 30 minutes, then discard the hard stalks and chop the caps finely. Chop the ginko nuts. Mash the cooked yam with the chestnut purée and blend in, using a food processor if available, the chopped mushrooms, ginko nuts and coriander. Season with the soy sauce, rice and sugar. Add salt and pepper to taste.

Fill the cucumber rounds with the stuffing, piling it up to cover the top of each slice. Arrange in a steamer without allowing them to touch, and steam for 20 minutes over a high heat. Meanwhile, mix the creamed corn and the stock in a saucepan and bring to the boil. Have ready a large, heated serving dish and pour in the corn sauce. As soon as the cucumber rings are cooked, arrange on the dish in the sauce and serve. Do not allow to stand.

Stuffed mushrooms

CHINESE

INGREDIENTS

12 evenly-sized large dried mushrooms

FILLING

- *180 g (6 oz) potatoes*
- *2.5 ml (½ teaspoon) salt*
- *15 ml (1 tablespoon) sesame oil*
- *15 ml (1 tablespoon) cornflour*
- *pepper to taste*

SAUCE

- *200 ml (1 cup, ⅓ pint) stock*
- *15 ml (1 tablespoon) soy sauce*
- *25 ml (1½ tablespoons) sugar*
- *25 ml (1½ tablespoons) rice vinegar*
- *5 ml (1 teaspoon) cornflour*

cornflour for dusting

15 ml (1 tablespoon) finely chopped spring onion or coriander

PREPARATION

Soak the dried mushrooms in warm water for 30 minutes. Meanwhile prepare the filling. Wash the potatoes and steam in their skins for 20–25 minutes, depending on size. When soft, peel and mash in a bowl with the salt, sesame oil and cornflour. Cut the hard stalks from the softened mushrooms, taking care not to tear the caps. Discard the stalks. Pat the caps dry and dust inside with the dry cornflour. Put a spoonful of the mashed potato into each cap and smooth over the top with the back of a damp spoon. Lay the finished mushrooms on a plate in a steamer and steam for 10 minutes. Meanwhile, make the sauce by bringing the sauce ingredients to the boil in a small saucepan. When the mushrooms are cooked pour over the sauce and garnish with the chopped spring onion or coriander.

Stuffed winter melon

CHINESE

This dish stands or falls by the quality of its stock. Neither winter melon nor beancurd has a strong flavour of its own, but both are delicate and clear in taste so they must be cooked with a carefully flavoured and seasoned stock.

INGREDIENTS

650 g (21 oz) winter melon

STUFFING

- *100 g (4 oz) beancurd*
- *1 dried mushroom*
- *15 g (½ oz) bamboo shoots*
- *5 ml (1 teaspoon) ginger juice*
- *2.5 ml (½ teaspoon) sesame oil*
- *pinch salt*

200 ml (1 cup, ⅓ pint) stock

5 ml (1 teaspoon) cornflour mixed with 5 ml (1 teaspoon) water

5 ml (1 teaspoon) sesame oil

PREPARATION

Peel the winter melon and remove any seeds. Cut into 5-cm (2-inch)-thick wedges about 5 cm (2 inches) wide. Place in a pan with sufficient water to cover and bring to the boil. Simmer for 10 minutes, then drain and soak in fresh cold water for a further 20 minutes. Wrap the beancurd tightly in a towel to drain for an hour. Soak the dried mushroom for 30 minutes in warm water, then discard the hard stalks and chop the cap finely. Chop the bamboo into minute pieces. Mash the beancurd and mix in the mushroom and bamboo shoots together with the ginger juice, sesame oil and salt. Cut each slice of winter melon almost in half, leaving them joined only at one side. Sandwich a portion of the beancurd stuffing between the two halves. Arrange the filled winter melon wedges in a bowl. Pour over the stock and steam for 15–20 minutes until the melon is very tender. Lift out the wedges carefully on to a serving plate and keep warm. Meanwhile re-boil the stock. Check the seasoning and thicken with the cornflour paste, then pour over the winter melon wedges. Sprinkle with sesame oil and serve hot.

STEAMED VEGETABLE DISHES

The aubergine recipe that follows is unique in Chinese cooking in that it is steamed not as a dish but as a plain vegetable. The two succeeding recipes are much more typical, and represent a very delicate method of cooking vegetables which allows them to keep their shape and develop a rich gravy from their natural juices.

Steamed aubergines

CHINESE

INGREDIENTS

250g (8 oz) aubergine
5 ml (1 teaspoon) salt

SEASONING SAUCE

25 ml (1½ tablespoons) light soy sauce
15 ml (1 tablespoon) sesame oil
10 ml (2 teaspoons) red vinegar
salt to taste

PREPARATION

Bleed the aubergine by cutting off strips of skin lengthwise and sprinkling it with salt. Leave to stand for 1 hour, then rinse well and squeeze out as much juice as possible. Steam, whole, for 20 minutes over fast-boiling water. Afterwards leave to cool, then tear into shreds with the fingers. Mix the seasoning sauce and pour over the aubergine.

If preferred, cut the steamed aubergine into rounds, or mash with a fork into a cream before adding the sauce.

Alternative sauces can be made with the addition of 1 clove crushed garlic to the sauce described above or 15 ml (1 tablespoon) sesame oil, 15 ml (1 tablespoon) sesame paste, 1 clove garlic, crushed, and 15 ml (1 tablespoon) finely chopped coriander leaves.

Steamed black mushrooms

CHINESE

INGREDIENTS

25 g (1 oz) dried mushrooms
5 ml (1 teaspoon) rice wine
10 ml (2 teaspoons) dark soy sauce
pinch sugar to taste
2.5 ml (½ teaspoon) sesame oil

PREPARATION

Wash the mushrooms carefully and soak in 300 ml (1¼ cups, ½ pint) warm water for 45 minutes. Strain and reserve the soaking water. Cut off the hard stalks and discard, taking care not to tear the mushroom caps. Place the mushroom caps with the rice wine, soy sauce, sugar, sesame oil and reserved soaking water in a small bowl and steam over a moderate heat for 30 minutes. Leave the mushrooms in the stock to cool, then serve as part of a cold plate (see page 117).

Steamed white radish

CHINESE

To make this a more elaborate dish, suitable for a large-scale dinner, you can use 450g (1lb) white radish and cut it into small balls using a melon scoop.

INGREDIENTS

300ml (10oz) white radish
rice water (see below)
4 dried mushrooms
25g (1oz) bamboo shoots
100ml (½ cup, 3½ fl oz) stock
5ml (1 teaspoon) rice wine
1 slice ginger
1 spring onion
15ml (1 tablespoon) chopped mitsuba *or coriander leaves*
15ml (1 tablespoon) sesame oil

PREPARATION

Peel and cut the white radish into 1-cm (½-inch) dice. Soak the mushrooms in warm water for 30 minutes, then discard the hard stalks and cut the caps into quarters. Cut the bamboo shoots into small slices. Put the white radish into the rice washing water and bring to the boil. Boil for 2 minutes, then discard the water and rinse the white radish. Put the white radish, mushrooms and bamboo shoots into a serving bowl with the stock, rice wine, ginger and onion. Steam over a high heat for 20 minutes. Then remove the ginger and onion and add the chopped *mitsuba* or coriander and sesame oil. Serve hot.

RICE WATER Rinse the rice quickly in cold water to rid it of any sand and dirt, then wash very thoroughly in a bowl of clean, cold water to remove the loose starch. The water will become quite cloudy. Strain the rice and cook as usual, but reserve the cloudy water in which the rice was washed. If white radish is boiled for a short time in rice water it will lose its rather bitter flavour while retaining its white colour. However, the water must be changed after boiling for 5 minutes.

Steamed winter-melon soup

CHINESE

INGREDIENTS

4 dried mushrooms
2 pieces black fungus
100g (4oz) beancurd
50g (2oz) bamboo shoots
15 snow peas
1½–2kg (3–4lb) winter melon
2 slices ginger
15ml (1 tablespoon) rice wine
450ml (2 cups, ¾ pint) boiling stock
salt to taste

PREPARATION

Soak the dried mushrooms and black fungus separately in warm water for 30 minutes. Discard the hard mushroom stalks and cut the caps into slices. Rinse the black fungus well, discard any hard bits and cut the rest into thin strips. Cut the beancurd into slices, about 3cm (1 inch) long and ½cm (¼ inch) thick. Cut the bamboo shoots into pieces 1cm (⅓ inch) wide and 4cm (1½ inches) long. Top and tail the snow peas. Wash the winter melon and cut off the top. Scoop out the seeds and some of the flesh to make a hollow in the melon. Stand the melon in a bowl. Put all the prepared vegetables, except the snow peas, into the melon together with the ginger and rice wine. Pour in sufficient boiling stock to come to about 1½cm (½ inch) below the rim of the melon.

To cook the melon soup, either stand the bowl and melon in a steamer and steam over a high heat for 50 minutes. Then add the snow peas and continue steaming until the melon is very soft and almost jelly-like. Serve in the bowl in which it was cooked. Alternatively, pre-heat the oven to 180°C, 350°F, Gas 4 and stand the bowl with the melon in a pan of boiling water, cover completely with tinfoil and cook for 1¼ hours. Add the snow peas and adjust the seasoning. Raise the oven temperature to 190°C, 375°F, Gas 5 and cook for a further 20–30 minutes. Serve as above.

Steamed bean-flower soup

CHINESE

INGREDIENTS

5 g (⅕ oz) black hair fungus
10 straw mushrooms
25 g (1 oz) vegetarian 'chicken' (page 101) (optional)
1 packet silk beancurd
25 g (1 oz) almond flakes
15 ml (1 tablespoon) potato flour
500 ml (2 cups, 17 fl oz) stock
2.5 ml (½ teaspoon) sugar
5 ml (1 teaspoon) salt
15 ml (1 tablespoon) sesame oil
1 sprig mitsuba *or coriander and 45 ml (3 tablespoons) either, finely chopped*
15 ml (1 tablespoon) freshly ground white pepper

Bean flowers are curded soya-bean milk before it has been drained and pressed into beancurd. It cannot be bought in the West, but this thick cream soup can be made using a packet of silk beancurd.

PREPARATION

Soak the black hair in warm water for 30 minutes, then rinse well. Cut the straw mushrooms into halves and slice the vegetarian 'chicken' thinly. Put the beancurd, almonds, vegetarian chicken and straw mushrooms into a big serving bowl which will fit into your steamer. Mix the potato flour with the stock, sugar and salt and stir gently into the beancurd. Spread the black hair over the top. Then tie a double sheet of greaseproof paper over the top of the bowl to seal. Steam over a high heat for 35 minutes. Just before serving remove the paper, add the sesame oil and garnish with the sprig of *mitsuba* or coriander. Serve the chopped *mitsuba* or coriander and white pepper in small dishes at the side.

Steamed mushroom soup

CHINESE

INGREDIENTS

8 dried mushrooms
150 g (5 oz) vegetarian 'ham' or 'chicken'
100 g (4 oz) white radish
a few fresh basil or mint leaves
900 ml (3½ cups, 1½ pints) stock
5 ml (1 teaspoon) crystal sugar
5 ml (1 teaspoon) salt

PREPARATION

Soak the dried mushrooms in warm water for 30 minutes, then discard the hard stalks leaving the caps whole. Cut the vegetarian 'ham' or 'chicken' into 1-cm (⅓-inch)-thick slices. Peel and cut the white radish into slices. Arrange the 'ham' or 'chicken', basil and white radish rounds in a large bowl. Put the mushrooms on top and pour in the stock. Add the sugar and steam over a high heat for 1 hour. Adjust the seasoning with the salt and serve.

Silver wood-ears soup with rice crust

CHINESE

INGREDIENTS

25 g (1 oz) silver wood ears
50 g (2 oz) rice crust (pages 153–4)
500 ml (2¼ cups, 1 pint) well-seasoned stock
oil for deep frying

PREPARATION

Soak the silver wood ears in warm water for 30 minutes, then discard the hard, discoloured bits and tear into separate leaves. Bring the stock just to the boil, then put it with the silver wood ears into a bowl in a steamer. Steam for 1¼ hours, taking care that the steamer does not boil dry. Check the seasoning. Just before serving, deep-fry the rice crust in hot oil until golden brown (about 3 minutes). Drain for a few seconds, then put the rice into a heated soup tureen. Immediately place both the soup tureen and the bowl of hot soup on the table and pour the soup over the rice in front of the diners (it will go 'snap, crackle, and pop').

9

Salads, Cold Dishes and Pickles

Salads made with raw lettuce and other vegetables as we know them in the West are almost unknown in the Far East, partly because of the dangers inherent in a countryside traditionally fertilized with human excreta. The southern Chinese in particular claim never to eat uncooked foods, although pickling with salt or vinegar is sometimes considered to be equivalent to cooking in the preparation of vegetables. However, salads of cooked vegetables served cold with some form of dressing are traditional and quite central to Eastern meal planning. Over a thousand years ago the Chinese made a beansprout 'salad' dressed with sesame oil, soy sauce, sugar and pepper. This is very similar to the simple salads eaten in Japanese family meals today, and, moreover, is an example of how over the centuries prestigious dishes move down-market. Most modern small salads in China include vinegar in their dressing, but in Japan, as well as vinegar, a wide range of ingredients such as *miso*, sesame or other nuts, egg yolks and beancurd are all used to make creams and dressings for salads, while in Indonesia and Malaysia peanuts are a base for many salad dressings. Every Japanese meal includes a salad of some kind, usually a simply dressed salad for a family meal but for more formal meals more elaborately dressed salads are served. Nowadays raw fruits such as tomatoes, avocados and cucumbers are included in modern Chinese salads, while in South East Asia pineapples, paw-paw and mangoes are frequently mixed with vegetables in a salad. Such mixtures are increasingly common, no doubt in part following contemporary American fashions.

However, in Japan, unlike the rest of the Far East, there is a strong tradition of eating raw foods. This comes from the teaching of the Zen Buddhists, which since the twelfth century has been influential in all aspects of Japanese life. The Zen Buddhists introduced the tea ceremony and a whole school of tea-ceremony cooking, which many believe to be the origin of today's Japanese *haute cuisine*. They taught that there are five ways of cooking foods, including serving it raw, together with five natural flavours and five colours suitable for foods. They believed that food prepared in accord with these harmonies increased the diner's harmony with the outside world. From this teaching came not only *sashimi* (raw fish) but also raw vegetable salads. Alongside the salads, and almost as important in the whole spectrum of Japanese food, are the foods prepared for picnics or cold lunch-box dishes sold in small restaurants. Long before Japan became industrialized and packed lunches for factory-workers, schoolchildren and railway-travellers became standard, Zen Buddhist beliefs encouraged people to carry meals out into the countryside to eat them surrounded by natural scenery in an atmosphere of natural harmony and balance. From this has come a whole range of picnic recipes for outdoor eating to be enjoyed while admiring the cherry blossom, the chrysanthemums or other natural scenes. Some of these dishes belong to a continuum of small *hors d'oeuvre* which run through to cold luncheon dishes.

Vinegared rice, *sushi*, is the basis of many of these dishes, but others are made from plain rice or beans. *Sushi* itself is said to have been invented during the seventeenth and eighteenth centuries in Edo, now modern Tokyo, at the same time as the method for processing *nori* seaweed, so often used with *sushi*. At that time a whole area of the city, called rather romantically the 'floating world', was set aside for entertainment – theatres, brothels, tea-houses and wine-bars. The tiny *sushi* bars that can now be found in most districts of central Tokyo and other Japanese cities are the direct descendants of the 'floating world'. Small *sushi* are associated with fun eating and entertainment. Even today small *sushi* bars are an almost exclusively male preserve; *sushi* bars are where men go after work to drink, eat *sushi* and relax with their male friends, and women are not usually welcomed as customers.

The Chinese do not have the same continuing tradition of picnics as the Japanese, although they too may sit outside, in a courtyard or terrace, eating and drinking to celebrate a festival, such as the autumn moon. But there is no special group of foods particularly associated with eating outdoors in Chinese cuisine. However, they often serve one cold dish among the hot dishes; provided that the food has originally been cooked there is no special need to serve all dishes piping hot.

For convenience this chapter has been divided into sections suggesting at what stage of the meal the different kinds of salads may be served (see below), but there are no hard and fast rules.

SALADS FOR STARTERS

Everyone likes starters made with vegetables, and the cuisines of the Far East are particularly rich in such dishes. It is customary in formal meals, in both northern China and Japan, to serve small dishes of raw or cooked vegetables with a vinegar dressing at the beginning of a meal as an appetizer before the 'serious' eating starts.

There is no very clear distinction in Far-Eastern meals between drinks before the meal and the beginning of the meal itself. Diners gather round the table at the very beginning of the meal drinking rice wine and using their chopsticks to eat the little salads. Probably the fact that little *hors d'oeuvre* are found in both northern China and Japan marks them as a very old style of dish, going back to the time in the seventh century when many Chinese food habits were introduced to Japan, although most of the recipes now used are modern. The southern style of cooking in China belongs to a different tradition and such small vinegared dishes at the start of a meal are virtually unknown in Cantonese cuisine. You can serve any of these cold vegetable dishes as an *hors d'oeuvre* to any style of meal, but it is wise to avoid serving a dish containing chilli before more blandly flavoured foods; if you wish to serve a hot *hors d'oeuvre* follow it with other strong-flavoured dishes.

Avocado salad

CHINESE

This salad from Taiwan is a very new recipe. Avocados are not a Chinese fruit, and only in the last ten years have the Chinese made any real attempt to incorporate them into their cuisine, influenced by their increasing popularity in the West. Avocados are however very much suited to Chinese flavours.

INGREDIENTS

SEASONING SAUCE

30 ml (2 tablespoons) light soy sauce
30 ml (2 tablespoons) rice vinegar
15 ml (1 tablespoon) sesame oil
1 clove garlic, crushed

2 avocados

PREPARATION

Mix the seasoning sauce. Just before the meal peel and stone the avocado and cut the flesh into cubes. Mix with the dressing. Serve in one dish for people to help themselves.

Avocado and wakame salad

JAPANESE

Nowadays many Far-Eastern salad recipes are no longer traditional, but use new ingredients and sometimes quite Western concepts to produce modern and 'smart' dishes. This recipe, for example, includes fruit, which is not usually eaten raw as part of a meal in Japan.

INGREDIENTS

5 g ($\frac{1}{5}$ oz) wakame *seaweed*
1 grapefruit
30 ml (2 tablespoons) lime, bitter orange or lemon juice
75 ml (5 tablespoons) raw vegetable oil
5 ml (1 teaspoon) Japanese soy sauce
2.5 ml ($\frac{1}{2}$ teaspoon) salt
pinch freshly ground pepper and sugar
2 avocados

PREPARATION

Prepare the *wakame* as directed on page 36, then cut into lozenge-shaped pieces. Peel the grapefruit and divide into segments. At the last minute before serving mix a dressing of lime juice, oil, soy sauce, salt, pepper and sugar and toss the *wakame* and grapefruit in half the dressing. Cut the avocados into halves and remove the stones. Fill with the dressed grapefruit and *wakame* and pour the remaining dressing over. Serve with spoons.

Carrot and coriander salad

CHINESE

This salad appears to have mixed origins. The seasonings of coriander, red vinegar and sesame oil are all typically Chinese, but the treatment of the carrot is in the style of a Japanese salad while carrots themselves are Western in origin.

INGREDIENTS

200 g (7 oz) carrot
10 ml (2 teaspoons) salt
10 g ($\frac{1}{3}$ oz) coriander leaves

DRESSING

5 ml (1 teaspoon) chilli oil
30 ml (2 tablespoons) red vinegar
30 ml (2 tablespoons) sugar
5 ml (1 teaspoon) sesame oil
pinch salt

PREPARATION

Scrape and cut the carrot into matchstick pieces. Sprinkle with salt and leave to marinate for 30 minutes. Rinse thoroughly and drain well. Wash and roughly chop the coriander leaves. Mix the carrot with the coriander and pour over the dressing. Chill for an hour before serving.

Hot and sour cucumbers

CHINESE

INGREDIENTS
200g (7oz) cucumber
2.5ml (½ teaspoon) salt
1–2 chillis, to taste
1 slice ginger
25ml (1½ tablespoons) oil
30ml (2 tablespoons) rice vinegar
45ml (3 tablespoons) sugar

PREPARATION
Wash the cucumber and cut into wedge-shaped pieces about 3cm (1 inch) thick. Sprinkle with salt and leave for 2 hours. Rinse and drain well. De-seed and slice the chillis finely. Cut the ginger into hair-like threads. Heat the oil in a wok or frying-pan and stir-fry the chillis over a moderate heat for about 1 minute. Tip out the oil and chillis into a bowl and leave to cool. Then stir in the sugar, vinegar and ginger threads. Mix with the cucumber wedges and leave to marinate for at least 30 minutes before serving.
NOTE You can use the same dressing for beansprouts. Wash and pick over the beansprouts, then blanch in boiling water for 1 minute. Refresh immediately in cold water and drain well before mixing with the sauce. A quicker version of the dressing can be made substituting 5ml (1 teaspoon) chilli oil and 15ml (1 tablespoon) vegetable oil for the chillis and oil.

Asinan (vegetable pickle)

INDONESIAN

INGREDIENTS
100g (4oz) cucumber
100g (4oz) beansprouts
100g (4oz) Chinese leaves
50g (2oz) carrots
30ml (2 tablespoons) sugar
45ml (3 tablespoons) white rice vinegar
1.5ml (¼ teaspoon) chilli powder
salt to taste
fried peanuts, crushed, to garnish (optional)

This recipe, from Indonesia, has a similar hot and sour sauce, but in the Indonesian recipe the emphasis is on the sour. The name means 'salty pickles', and it features a selection of vegetables, not just cucumber. The oil is omitted and chilli powder takes the place of fresh chillis. It may be served either as an appetizer, or as an accompaniment to the main dishes, or as a salad to finish a meal.

PREPARATION
Wash the cucumber and cut into thin batons. Wash, pick over and blanch the beansprouts. Drain well. Cut the Chinese leaves into thin shreds. Scrape and cut the carrots into matchsticks. Mix the sugar, vinegar, chilli powder and salt and pour over the vegetables. Mix well and leave for at least an hour before serving.

Pine kernel and nori salad

CHINESE

INGREDIENTS
1 sheet nori *seaweed*
100g (3½ oz) pine kernels
oil for deep frying
15ml (1 tablespoon) toasted sesame seeds (page 36)
5ml (1 teaspoon) salt

PREPARATION
Toast the *nori* over a gas flame or electric ring for about 10 seconds until it changes from purple to green. Then cut into fine shreds with a pair of scissors. Heat the oil until hot and deep-fry the nuts over a moderate heat until golden brown. Lift out and drain well. Mix the fried pine kernels with the salt, sesame seeds and *nori* shreds. Serve cold as a starter.

Chrysanthemum leaf salad

KOREAN

INGREDIENTS
200 g (7 oz) chrysanthemum leaves
1 fresh chilli
3 spring onions
SEASONING SAUCE
60 ml (4 tablespoons) Japanese soy sauce
5 ml (1 teaspoon) grated garlic
30 ml (2 tablespoons) sesame oil
2.5 ml (½ teaspoon) chilli powder
5 ml (1 teaspoon) toasted sesame seeds

PREPARATION
Wash and trim the chrysanthemum leaves. Blanch in boiling water for 1 minute before refreshing in cold water. Squeeze dry. De-seed the chilli and cut it with the spring onions into very fine shreds. Mix into the seasoning sauce. Pour the sauce over the chrysanthemum leaves and mix well. Serve with the toasted sesame seeds sprinkled over as a garnish.

Okra and natto salad

JAPANESE

Natto, fermented soya beans, is a Japanese delicacy which people either like or hate. Said to date from the eighth century, it has a slightly putrid taste and is particularly popular in the east of Japan.

INGREDIENTS
20 okra pods
1 packet natto
10 ml (2 teaspoons) Japanese soy sauce

PREPARATION
Scrape the okra lightly to remove the bloom, but leave each pod whole. Cook in lightly salted boiling water for 5 minutes, then refresh in cold water. Drain well and cut off the stalk ends. Slice the pods very thinly and mix with the *natto*. Serve in small individual dishes with a little soy sauce poured over.

Seaweed salad

CHINESE

INGREDIENTS
25 g (1 oz) dried kelp, preferably Chinese (page 37)
1 small clove garlic
1 fresh chilli
1 slice ginger
15 ml (1 tablespoon) sesame oil
SEASONING SAUCE
10 ml (2 teaspoons) soy sauce
15 ml (1 tablespoon) red vinegar
pinch black pepper and salt
2.5 ml (½ teaspoon) sugar

PREPARATION
Boil the seaweed for 10 minutes in fresh water, then wash thoroughly in cold water until no longer sticky. Drain well and dry in a clean cloth. Cut into very thin strips. Cut the garlic, chilli and ginger into very thin shreds and stir-fry in the sesame oil for 1 minute over a moderate heat. Add the seaweed and the seasoning sauce to the pan and mix well over the heat. Turn out on to a serving plate and leave to cool before serving.

Red and white salad

JAPANESE

This is a New Year dish in Japan, where the red and white colours are considered lucky. The red stands for blood and life and the white for purity and God – so this dish represents God and man in harmony.

INGREDIENTS

120g (4oz) white radish
25g (1oz) carrot
5ml (1 tablespoon) salt

DRESSING

45ml (3 tablespoons) rice vinegar
7.5ml (½ tablespoon) dashi
25ml (1½ tablespoons) caster sugar
pinch salt

finely pared peel of half a lime or lemon

PREPARATION

Wash and peel the white radish and carrot. Cut both into matchstick pieces. Mix with the salt and leave to marinate for 30 minutes. Rinse and drain well. Put the ingredients for the dressing in a small pan and bring to the boil; then set aside to cool. Cut the peel into hair-like shreds. Mix the cooled dressing with the white radish, carrot and lime or lemon shreds and leave to marinate for 3 hours in the refrigerator before serving.

Spinach and nori rolls

JAPANESE

INGREDIENTS

350g (12oz) spinach
7.5ml (1½ teaspoons) Japanese soy sauce
2 large sheets of nori *seaweed*

DIPPING SAUCE

25ml (1½ tablespoons) Japanese soy sauce
10ml (2 tablespoons) lemon juice

PREPARATION

Wash and tear the central tough ribs from the spinach. Cook in lightly salted boiling water for 4 minutes. Refresh immediately under cold water and squeeze as dry as possible. Then sprinkle with the soy sauce. Toast the shiny side of the *nori* sheets over a high heat for about 3 seconds until they change from green to purple. Cut the sheets into halves. Lay one half-sheet on a rolling mat and place a quarter of the spinach leaves on top. Roll up tightly into a cylinder about 3cm (1 inch) across. Cut the roll slantwise into 4 unequal lengths. Repeat with the remaining sheets of *nori*. Serve arranged on small dishes with a tiny bowl of the dipping sauce at the side.

NOTE The original Japanese recipe uses 500g (1lb) chrysanthemum leaves instead of spinach, which gives the dish a more piquant flavour. Chrysanthemum leaves can now be bought fresh from some Chinese grocers. Preparation is the same as described above for the spinach.

Spinach and* nori *rolls

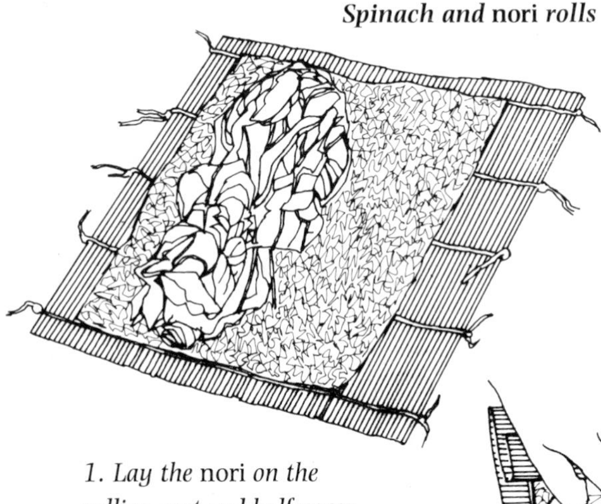

1. Lay the nori *on the rolling mat and half-cover with par-boiled spinach.*

2. Using both hands, draw up the mat to roll the nori *around the spinach.*

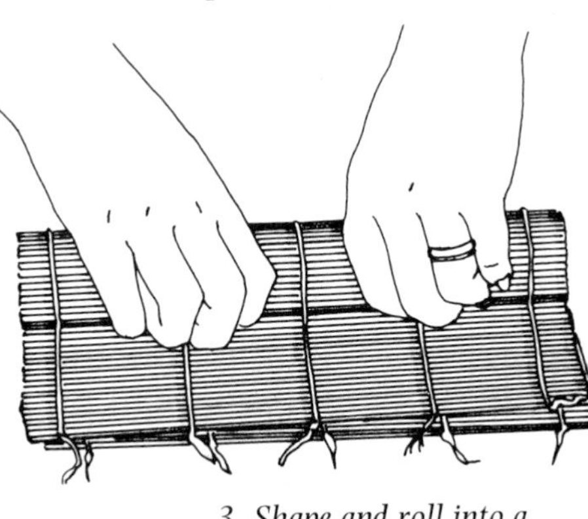

3. Shape and roll into a tight cylinder.

Cold mixed hors d'oeuvre plate

CHINESE

A plate of different cold meats and substitute meats is often served at the beginning of a big formal meal as an *hors d'oeuvre* in China. Such a dish is often arranged in an elaborate and complicated design, for example, to resemble a creature such as a phoenix or as a dragon. The individual elements can be served as cold starters for simpler family-style meals.

Spicy vegetarian 'ham'

INGREDIENTS

SAUCE

15 ml (1 tablespoon) soy sauce
10 ml (2 teaspoons) barbecue sauce
tiny pinch five-spice powder
200 ml (1 cup, $\frac{1}{3}$ pint) vegetarian stock
15 ml (1 tablespoon) rice wine

150 g (5 oz) vegetarian 'ham' (page 100)

PREPARATION

Bring the sauce to the boil in a pan and add the 'ham'. Reduce the heat and simmer for 5 minutes, basting the ham all the time with the sauce. Lift out and cut into slices about $\frac{1}{2}$ cm ($\frac{1}{4}$ inch) thick. Serve cold.

Garlic peanuts

INGREDIENTS

1 clove garlic
150 g (5 oz) salted peanuts

PREPARATION

Crush the garlic and mix it with the peanuts in a saucepan. Cover the pan with a lid and cook for 5 minutes, shaking the pan frequently. Turn out and leave to cool.

Pickled cauliflower

INGREDIENTS

200 g (7 oz) cauliflower
200 ml (1 cup, 7 fl oz) rice vinegar
150 g (5 oz) caster sugar
15 ml (1 tablespoon) sesame oil
1 chilli, de-seeded

PREPARATION

Wash and cut the cauliflower into small florets. Put into lightly salted boiling water for 2 minutes. Then drain well. Shred the chilli. Heat the vinegar in a small pan with the sugar and sesame oil. Bring to the boil stirring all the time to dissolve the sugar. Lift from the heat and allow to cool. Put the cauliflower and chilli shreds in a bowl and pour over the sweetened vinegar. Leave to marinate overnight before serving.

Arrange all these items on one plate and serve together as an *hors d'oeuvre.*
NOTE Other cold foods such as cold sliced vegetarian 'ham' or smoked 'duck', steamed black mushrooms or sliced fried beancurd can all be used to make up a plate of cold mixed *hors d'oeuvre.*

SUSHI

Sushi means vinegared rice, but in the West we have come to associate all *sushi* with the eye-catching and delicately shaped mouthfuls of rice and raw fish so elegantly presented in Japanese *sushi* bars. The recipe below is for small vegetarian *sushi* which can, with a little practice, be achieved at home. *Sushi* in Japan are always presented in the most attractive way, often in lacquer boxes and looking almost too good to eat. Each little *sushi* should be as neat and as carefully finished as possible. Lay them out in lines or circles according to your serving plates. In Japan it is not usual for housewives to make small *sushi* for themselves; more often they buy them ready-made from professional *sushi*-makers. *Sushi* can be eaten as an *hors d'oeuvre*, as a lunch on their own, or as canapés with drinks. They are very delicately flavoured and should not really be mixed with strongly seasoned foods. This section also includes other *sushi* recipes together with some cold dishes that can be served for lunch.

Basic sushi

JAPANESE

INGREDIENTS
300g (2 cups, 10oz) short-grained rice (American Rose, not *pudding rice)*
20ml (4 teaspoons) caster sugar
5ml (1 teaspoon) salt
45ml (3 tablespoons) rice vinegar
400ml (1⅔ cups, 14 fl oz) water
1 square konbu *7 × 7cm (2½ × 2½ inches)*
20ml (1½ tablespoons) mirin

MAKES 40

PREPARATION
Wash the rice very well in several lots of cold water. (The Japanese use a bamboo egg-beater to whisk free the loose starch from the rice grains.) Drain and leave for an hour. Meanwhile make the vinegar dressing by dissolving the sugar and salt in the vinegar over a low heat, then leaving it to return to room temperature. Put the rice in a heavy-bottomed saucepan with the measured water. Wipe the *konbu* and slash it several times, then lay it on top of the rice. Cover the pan and bring to the boil over a moderate heat. Then discard the *konbu* and add the *mirin*. Boil over a high heat for 2 minutes, then reduce the heat and boil very gently for 5 minutes. Reduce the heat once more to its lowest point and simmer for another 10 minutes. Finally, wrap a towel over the pan lid and leave away from the heat to cook in its own steam for a further 10 minutes.

When the rice is ready, tip into a wide bowl. Using a wooden spatula, make figure-of-eight cutting strokes to toss the rice as you sprinkle in the prepared vinegar dressing. While you work with the spatula in one hand fan the rice vigorously with the other hand (failing a fan, use a stiff sheet of folded paper: this is to cool the rice (alternatively, use a hand-held hair-dryer set to cold). This process takes about 10 minutes and its purpose is to coat all the rice with the dressing as it cools so that it becomes shiny. Ideally, get someone to help, either fanning or tipping in the dressing. When all the dressing has been mixed into the rice and it is cool, cover with a damp cloth until you are ready to shape it into individual *sushi*.

Mix 15ml (1 tablespoon) vinegar with 45ml (3 tablespoons) water in a small bowl and use this mixture to dampen your hands before you start to handle the rice. (This prevents the rice from sticking to your hands.)

NOTE For a larger quantity of *sushi* increase the quantities stated by half as much again, to yield 60 individual *sushi*.

Avocado nigiri

JAPANESE

INGREDIENTS

sushi *rice (see above)*
15 ml (1 tablespoon) wasabi *mustard*
1–2 avocados, depending on size
2 sheets nori

PREPARATION

Dampen your hands in a vinegar-and-water mixture, then pick up about 20 ml (1 heaped tablespoon) of the prepared rice. Shape into a block $1\frac{1}{2} \times 3 \times 3$ cm ($\frac{1}{2} \times 1\frac{1}{4} \times 1\frac{1}{4}$ inches). Spread a little *wasabi* on top of the rice and lay a thin slice of freshly cut avocado on the *wasabi*. Cut a strip of *nori* about $\frac{1}{2}$ cm ($\frac{1}{4}$ inch) wide and wrap over the avocado and around the rice. Repeat for as many avocado *sushi* as you require.

Kappamaki

JAPANESE

INGREDIENTS

250 g (8 oz) cucumber
2 sheets nori
sushi *rice (see above)*
15 ml (1 tablespoon) wasabi *mustard*

PREPARATION

Cut the cucumber lengthways into quarters and remove the seeds. Cut the flesh into batons about $\frac{1}{2}$ cm ($\frac{1}{5}$ inch) thick and 15 cm (6 inches) long. Toast the *nori* over a high heat until it turns purple (about 3 seconds), then cut each sheet in half. Have ready a vinegar-and-water mixture to dampen your hands. Lay one half-sheet of *nori* over the rolling mat, then add a layer of *sushi* rice about $\frac{1}{2}$ cm ($\frac{1}{4}$ inch) thick. Leave 1 cm ($\frac{1}{2}$ inch) clear at the top and bottom. Smear a line of *wasabi* mustard along the centre of the rice and put a quarter of the cucumber batons along the line of mustard. Roll up the *nori* and rice around the cucumber, using the rolling mat as illustrated to make a roll about 3 cm (1 inch) in diameter. Cut into 4-cm ($1\frac{1}{2}$-inch) lengths. Repeat with remaining *nori* sheets.

Serve with a dip of soy sauce.

NOTE As an alternative, use dried melon strips (cooked as described for *norimaki*, overleaf) instead of the cucumber batons, and omit the *wasabi* mustard.

Kappamaki

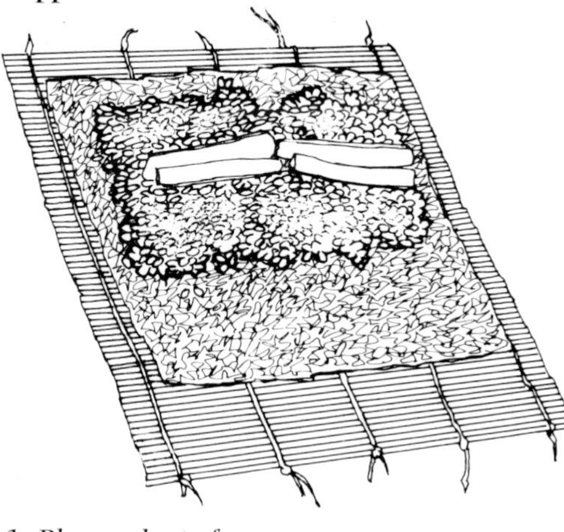

1. Place a sheet of nori *on the rolling mat. Cover two-thirds of the* nori *with the* sushi *rice. Lay the cucumber strips along the centre.*

2. With both hands use the mat to draw the nori *and rice around the cucumber.*

3. Shape and roll into a tight cylinder.

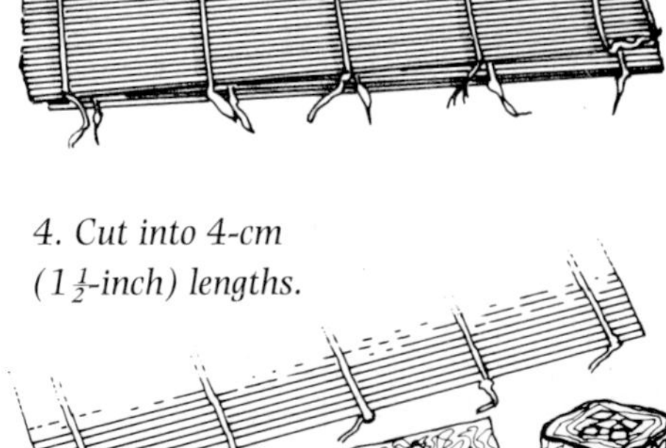

4. Cut into 4-cm ($1\frac{1}{2}$-inch) lengths.

Norimaki

JAPANESE

INGREDIENTS
5 dried mushrooms
STOCK FOR DRIED MUSHROOMS
100 ml (3½ fl oz) dashi
45 ml (3 tablespoons) Japanese soy sauce
15 ml (1 tablespoon) caster sugar
15 ml (1 tablespoon) mirin
10 g (½ oz) Japanese dried melon strips
5 ml (1 teaspoon) salt
STOCK FOR MELON STRIPS
200 ml (1 cup, 7 fl oz) dashi
30 ml (2 tablespoons) caster sugar
30 ml (2 tablespoons) mirin
30 ml (2 tablespoons) Japanese soy sauce
100 g (4 oz) lightly boiled chrysanthemum leaves or spinach
4 sheets nori
3 size 4 eggs, made into omelettes (page 37)
sushi *rice (see above)*

PREPARATION
Soak the dried mushrooms in warm water for 30 minutes. Then discard the hard stalks and cook the caps in the mushroom stock until the stock has almost gone (about 15 minutes). Cool and slice the caps finely. Wash and rub the melon strips with the salt, then soak in cold water for 5 minutes. Place in a pan of boiling water and boil for 15 minutes. Drain and put into a clean pan with the *dashi* and sugar. Simmer until the melon strips are soft, then add the soy sauce and *mirin*. Simmer for another 5 minutes, then leave to cool in the stock. When cold, cut into 15-cm (6-inch) lengths. Wash and trim the chrysanthemum or spinach leaves, discarding any tough stalks or ribs. Blanch in lightly salted water for about 3 minutes, then refresh in cold water and drain well. Toast the shiny side of the *nori* sheets over a high flame for about 10 seconds until they turn purple. Cut the cold omelettes into thin shreds.

Assemble all the vegetables and a bowl of vinegar and water with which to dampen your hands. Lay one sheet of *nori* on the rolling mat. Cover with a layer of rice about 1 cm (⅓ inch) thick, leaving a bare 3 cm (1 inch) at the bottom and top of the *nori* free of rice. Arrange a line of mushroom strips, egg shreds, melon strips and spinach across the centre of the rice, using about one-quarter of the prepared vegetables. Holding the line of vegetables firmly in place with your finger-tips, use your thumbs to push up the bamboo mat so that the edge of the *nori* folds over to close with the edge furthest from you, making a cylinder of rice and *nori* around the vegetables. Press gently on the mat to firm up the roll, which should be about 5 cm (2 inches) in diameter. Unroll the mat and place the roll on a dry plate. Cut into 1-cm (½-inch)-thick slices with a wet knife. Repeat with the other three sheets of *nori*.

Chirashi sushi

JAPANESE

INGREDIENTS
15 g (½ oz) dried melon strips
6 dried mushrooms
2 squares fried beancurd (page 83)
SIMMERING STOCK
600 ml (2½ cups, 1 pint) dashi
45 ml (3 tablespoons) caster sugar
15 ml (1 tablespoon) mirin
30 ml (2 tablespoons) Japanese soy sauce
50 g (2 oz) french beans
pinch salt
2 eggs, made into egg shreds (page 37)
sushi *rice (see above)*
pickled ginger for garnish

PREPARATION
Wash and rub the dried melon strips with the salt, then soak in cold water for 5 minutes. Rinse well, then put into a pan of boiling water and boil for 15 minutes. Lift out and cut into very thin strips. Soak the dried mushrooms in warm water for 30 minutes, then discard the hard stalks and cut the caps into thin slices. Cut the fried beancurd cubes into similar-sized shreds. Put the melon strips, mushrooms and beancurd into the simmering stock and bring to the boil. Simmer for 4 minutes. Leave to cool in the simmering stock. Wash and trim the french beans and boil in lightly salted water for 5 minutes. Cut into 2-cm (½-inch) lengths. Prepare the egg shreds as directed.

When the *sushi* rice is ready add the mushrooms, beancurd and melon shreds and mix well with about 15 ml (1 tablespoon) of the simmering stock. Arrange in four separate bowls or picnic boxes and garnish each helping with the french beans, egg shreds and pickled ginger.

Fukusa sushi

JAPANESE

If you have any *chirashi sushi* left over, you can make these egg-covered bundles to serve for a cold lunch. The egg represents a silk cloth covering the filling (traditionally, the manner in which gifts were wrapped in Japan).

INGREDIENTS

4 size 2 eggs, made into 6 thin omelettes (page 37)
chirashi sushi *(see above)*
pickled ginger shreds or thin strips nori

PREPARATION

Make the thin omelettes and leave to cool. Have ready the *chirashi sushi* as directed in the previous recipe. Shape about 45 ml (3 tablespoons) of the *sushi* into a rectangle about 3 × 6 cm (1 × 2½ inches), using your hands dampened with a vinegar-and-water mixture. Put one rice rectangle on to the centre of an omelette and fold over each side in turn to make a soft parcel about 7 cm (3 inches) square. Garnish the top with shreds of ginger and, if you like, fold over strips of *nori* to bind the parcel. Serve either on individual plates or for a picnic.

Inari sushi

JAPANESE

INGREDIENTS

10 cakes aburage
SIMMERING STOCK FOR ABURAGE
300 ml (1¼ cups, ½ pint) dashi
75 ml (5 tablespoons) caster sugar
45 ml (3 tablespoons) Japanese soy sauce
5 g (¼ oz) dried melon strips
salt
50 g (2 oz) carrot
STOCK FOR MELON STRIPS
200 ml (7 fl oz) dashi
30 ml (2 tablespoons) caster sugar
30 ml (2 tablespoons) soy sauce
10 ml (2 teaspoons) poppy seeds or sesame seeds
sushi *rice (see above)*
pickled ginger

PREPARATION

Cut the *aburage* cakes into half across and open each square pouch. Remove any extra-soft beancurd. Soak the *aburage* in a pan of boiling water for a minute, then drain well. Put into a pan with the *dashi* and sugar and boil gently for 5 minutes. Then add the soy sauce and simmer until the sauce has almost gone (use a drop lid to cover while cooking) and leave to cool in the pan. Meanwhile wash and rub the melon strips with a little salt. Rinse well and soak in cold water for 5 minutes, then place in a pan of boiling water and simmer for 15 minutes. Lift out and cut into minute pieces. Scrape and cut the carrot into tiny fragments. Put both the melon and carrot into the *dashi* and bring to the boil. Add the caster sugar and simmer for another 2 minutes, then add the soy sauce. Continue simmering until the sauce has reduced to about 45 ml (3 tablespoons).

Toast the poppy seeds in a dry pan until they dance. Finally, mix the *sushi* rice with the carrot, melon and remaining sauce. Add the poppy seeds.

Roll a small portion of this mixture into a ball between the hands and slide it into an *aburage* pocket. Close the pocket by folding in the sides and turning down the top flat like an envelope. Arrange the packets on individual plates or in picnic boxes and serve garnished with ginger.

EGG ROLLS

Korean egg roll

INGREDIENTS
5 eggs
100 g (4 oz) spinach
30 ml (2 tablespoons) sesame oil
5 dried mushrooms
100 g (4 oz) carrot
30 ml (2 tablespoons) vegetable oil
salt and pepper
2 sheets nori, *toasted (pages 36–7)*

PREPARATION
Beat the eggs very well, then leave to stand. Wash the spinach and tear into 5-cm (2-inch) pieces, discarding the tough central veins. Boil in lightly salted water for 4 minutes, then refresh in cold water and drain very well. Mix with 5 ml (1 teaspoon) sesame oil and a little salt and pepper. Soak the dried mushrooms in warm water for 45 minutes. Then discard the hard stalks and cut the caps into thin shreds. Scrape and cut the carrot into matchsticks. Heat the vegetable oil in a large frying-pan and stir-fry the mushroom and carrot strips separately. Lift out and season each with 5 ml (1 teaspoon) sesame oil and a little salt and pepper. Wipe clean the heated frying-pan and coat with 7.5 ml (1½ teaspoons) sesame oil. Pour in half the beaten egg, reduce the heat and cook until nearly set. Lay one sheet of *nori* on top of the egg. Lift the pan away from the heat, and quickly arrange half the mushroom, carrot and spinach on the *nori.* Roll up the egg around the filling into a sausage. Seal the loose flap with a little beaten egg. Return to the heat for a few moments to cook the seal, then lift out and leave to cool. Coat the pan with 7.5 ml (1½ teaspoons) more sesame oil and repeat with the remaining half of the egg and filling. When the rolls are cool, cut into 2-cm (¾-inch)-thick slices. Arrange flat on a plate so that the brightly coloured filling shows. Serve with Japanese soy sauce.

Japanese egg roll

INGREDIENTS
10 g (½ oz) carrot
10 g (½ oz) french beans
salt
10 ml (2 teaspoons) caster sugar
5 ml (1 teaspoon) Japanese soy sauce
5 eggs
45 ml (3 tablespoons) dashi
oil for frying

PREPARATION
Scrape the carrot and cut into 5-cm (2-inch)-long batons about 1 cm (⅓ inch) wide. Trim the french beans and cut into 5-cm (2-inch) lengths. Cook the carrots in a little boiling water for 5 minutes. Then add a pinch of salt and 5 ml (1 teaspoon) sugar. Simmer for a minute, then add the soy sauce and the french beans. Simmer until both the beans and carrots are cooked (about 4 minutes). Drain and leave to cool. Meanwhile, beat the eggs with the *dashi*, remaining 5 ml (1 teaspoon) sugar and a little salt to taste.

Heat a large frying-pan and lightly wipe with oil. Pour in one-third of the beaten egg and cook as an omelette over a moderate heat. When the bottom is set, arrange two rows of carrot and beans across the centre of the pan and fold the omelette over into a half-moon. Move the folded omelette down the pan and wipe more oil over the bottom of the pan before returning the omelette to its original position. Add another 75 ml (5 tablespoons) egg to the empty half of the pan and cook until the bottom is set. Then arrange more carrots and beans across the omelette and fold it over on top of the first omelette. Wipe the pan with oil again and repeat making the half-omelettes and folding them over on top of the previous ones until the egg is finished. All this should be done as quickly as possible over a moderate heat, since the eggs must not be overcooked. Immediately you have finished the last omelette, turn the whole bundle of omelettes on to a rolling mat and roll up into a sausage about 5 cm (2 inches) thick. Leave to cool in the mat. (When you roll up the omelettes they should ooze a little juice.) Serve cold, cut into slices and garnish with a small mound of grated white radish and chilli ('autumn leaves': see bottom of page 82).

Making egg rolls

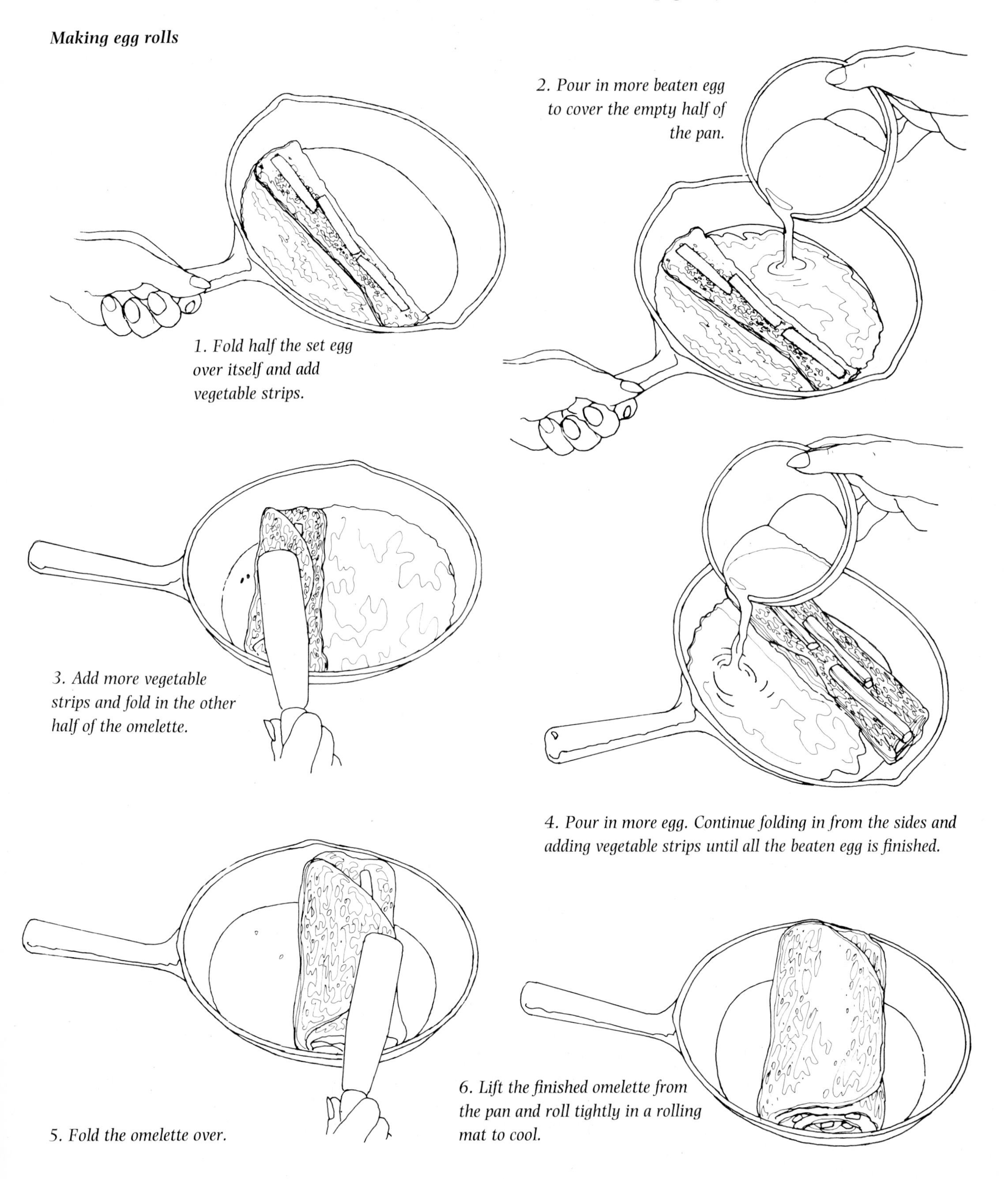

1. Fold half the set egg over itself and add vegetable strips.

2. Pour in more beaten egg to cover the empty half of the pan.

3. Add more vegetable strips and fold in the other half of the omelette.

4. Pour in more egg. Continue folding in from the sides and adding vegetable strips until all the beaten egg is finished.

5. Fold the omelette over.

6. Lift the finished omelette from the pan and roll tightly in a rolling mat to cool.

SIDE SALADS

These salads have a range of unfamiliar and sometimes exotic dressings, ranging from an egg and vinegar cream to a sweet *miso* and sesame sauce and a spicy curry dressing. Any of them can be served with main dishes, and we have found that Japanese salads blend particularly well into Western meals. However, while they can usually be combined with Chinese dishes, their delicate flavouring does not mix well with South East Asian cooking.

Broccoli and black fungus salad

JAPANESE

INGREDIENTS

200 g (7 oz) purple sprouting broccoli
15 ml (1 tablespoon) black fungus
100 g (4 oz) white radish
pinch salt

DRESSING

1 egg yolk
45 ml (3 tablespoons) rice vinegar
30 ml (2 tablespoons) dashi
15 ml (1 tablespoon) mirin
1.5 ml (¼ teaspoon) salt
5 ml (1 teaspoon) caster sugar

PREPARATION

Trim the broccoli and blanch in boiling water for 30 seconds. Refresh in cold water and drain well. Cut into 5-cm (2-inch) lengths. Soak the black fungus in warm water for 20 minutes, then discard the hard parts and blanch in boiling water for 1 minute. Rinse in cold water and drain. Cut into thin strips. Peel and cut the white radish into matchsticks. Sprinkle with salt and leave to drain for about 30 minutes. Rinse in cold water and drain well. Beat all the ingredients of the dressing together and cook in a double boiler, stirring all the time until the mixture thickens. Do not use too high a heat or the egg may curdle. When the mixture is thick and creamy, lift from the heat and leave to cool.

Just before the meal, mix the vegetables together and divide between four small serving bowls. Spoon over the dressing and serve.

Urap (warm vegetable salad)

INDONESIAN

Urap is a salad of lightly cooked vegetables served while still warm. There are no strict rules governing which vegetables can be used, but usually there are at least three different varieties, mostly green-leaved. Choose three or more from spinach, water-spinach, watercress, beansprouts, cucumber, chayote, snow peas, french beans, Chinese leaves, purslane or even *choisam*.

INGREDIENTS

2 cloves garlic, crushed
2 fresh chillis, de-seeded and finely chopped
flesh of half a coconut, freshly grated
salt and sugar to taste

PREPARATION

Prepare the garlic, chillis and coconut. When ready, trim and if necessary slice the vegetables. Blanch in boiling water, then drain well. Mix while still warm in a bowl with the grated coconut, crushed garlic and finely chopped chillis. Add brown sugar and salt to taste and serve immediately.

Gado-gado

INDONESIAN

This salad can be served as a side salad in a main meal, coming either before or after the other dishes, in which case this recipe is sufficient for four. However, more usually it is served as a one-dish snack lunch, in which case the quantities are sufficient for two people, or one very hungry person.

INGREDIENTS

250 g (8 oz) water-spinach or 100 g (4 oz) Chinese leaves
100 g (4 oz) beansprouts
100 g (4 oz) soapy potatoes
100 g (4 oz) french beans
4 squares fried beancurd, bought-in or deep-fried at home (see page 83)
100 g (4 oz) cucumber
1 small bunch watercress
2 hard-boiled eggs

DRESSING

100 g (4 oz) peanuts
oil for deep frying
4 macadamia nuts or brazil nuts
2 cloves garlic
1.5–2.5 ml ($\frac{1}{4}$–$\frac{1}{2}$ teaspoon) chilli powder
1.5 ml ($\frac{1}{4}$ teaspoon) salt
1.5 ml ($\frac{1}{4}$ teaspoon) brown sugar
100 ml ($3\frac{1}{2}$ fl oz) santan *or 35 g ($1\frac{1}{2}$ oz) creamed coconut*
15 ml (1 tablespoon) lemon or lime juice
15 ml (1 tablespoon) fried onion shreds (page 42)

PREPARATION

Wash the water-spinach and cut into short lengths before blanching in boiling water for 2 minutes. Refresh in cold water and drain well. If using Chinese leaves, wash and cut into bite-sized pieces, then blanch in boiling water for about 1 minute. Refresh in cold water and drain well. Wash and pick over the beansprouts and blanch in boiling water. Refresh under the cold tap and leave to drain. Cook the potato, unpeeled, in boiling water, then skin and cut into bite-sized pieces. Top and tail the beans and cut into 4-cm ($1\frac{1}{2}$-inch) lengths. Cook in lightly salted water for 5 minutes, then drain and allow to cool. Cut the fried beancurd squares into halves. Cut the cucumber, unpeeled, into batons. Pick over and wash the watercress. Drain well. Shell the hard-boiled eggs and cut into halves.

When the salad ingredients are all prepared make the dressing. Skin and deep-fry the peanuts until golden (about 3 minutes), then leave to cool. Deep-fry the macadamia or brazil nuts for about 4 minutes. Lift out and drain. Put the garlic, chilli powder, fried nuts, salt and sugar into a food processor (or use a pestle and mortar) and blend to a smooth paste. Mix with 300 ml (1 cup, $\frac{1}{2}$ pint) water, or 400 ml ($1\frac{3}{4}$ cups, $\frac{2}{3}$ pint) if using creamed coconut, and tip into a pan. Bring to the boil, stirring all the time, then leave to simmer for 5 minutes. Stir in the *santan* or creamed coconut and lift from the heat. Arrange concentric rings of the different vegetables on a large plate. Return the pan to a low heat and bring almost to the boil, stirring all the time. Lift from the heat and stir in the lemon juice. Pour over the salad. Garnish with the fried onion and serve at once. If preferred, serve the dressing separately.

Alternative dressing for gado-gado

INGREDIENTS

150 g (5 oz) peanuts, skinned and deep-fried, or 45 ml (3 tablespoons) peanut butter
5 ml (1 teaspoon) brown sugar
1–2 chillis, to taste, or 1.5 ml ($\frac{1}{4}$ teaspoon) chilli powder
2 pete *or French pickled gherkins*
juice of 1 lemon
1 lime or bay leaf

PREPARATION

Put the peanuts, sugar, chillis and gherkins into a food processor (or use a pestle and mortar) and blend into a cream with 200 ml ($\frac{3}{4}$ cup, 7 fl oz) water and the lemon juice. Put the mixture into a pan and bring to the boil with the lime leaf. Simmer for 5 minutes, then adjust the seasoning if necessary with salt and sugar. When the salad has been arranged on the serving plate, pour over the hot sauce and serve.

Vinegared turnips

JAPANESE

This dish will keep for up to three weeks.

INGREDIENTS

450g (1 lb) young turnips
20ml (4 teaspoons) salt

DRESSING

75ml (5 tablespoons) caster sugar
150ml (⅔ cup, 5fl oz) rice vinegar
2.5ml (½ teaspoon) Japanese soy sauce

2 dried chillis, or 3-cm (1-inch) square yuzu *or lemon peel and 3cm (1 inch)* konbu

PREPARATION

Peel and cut the tops off the turnips. Turn upside down and stand between two chopsticks on a chopping board. Using a thin, sharp knife, slice the turnip at 2-mm (1/12-inch) intervals down to the chopsticks, which act as guards to prevent your cutting right through the turnip. Then turn the turnip between the chopsticks and slice again at right angles to the previous cuts (see page 39). Repeat with the other turnips. Soak in 300ml (1¼ cups, ½ pint) water and the salt for 30 minutes. Then squeeze dry and cut into quarters or eighths, depending on the size of the turnip. Put into a clean bowl and pour over the dressing. De-seed and finely chop the chillis, or finely slice the *yuzu* peel and *konbu*, and add to the turnips. Mix carefully and cover the bowl with clingwrap. Leave in the refrigerator for at least 5 days before eating. Every 2–3 days mix with a clean spoon to make sure the turnips remain in contact with the dressing.

Persimmon and white radish salad

JAPANESE

INGREDIENTS

150g (5oz) white radish
1 small, firm persimmon
2.5ml (½ teaspoon) salt
7.5ml (½ tablespoon) lemon juice

DRESSING

30ml (2 tablespoons) rice vinegar
15ml (1 tablespoon) mirin
pinch caster sugar

PREPARATION

Peel the white radish and persimmon and cut into matchsticks about 5cm (2 inches) long. Mix the salt with the white radish and marinate for 10 minutes. Rinse in cold water and squeeze dry. Meanwhile, pour the lemon juice over the persimmon and chill in the refrigerator. Mix the dressing and add to the squeezed-out white radish. Leave for an hour in the refrigerator. Drain and mix with the persimmon. Serve in small individual bowls.

This salad will keep for several days in the refrigerator.

Beancurd salad

JAPANESE

INGREDIENTS
350 g (12 oz) cotton beancurd
25 g (1 oz) small green pepper
2 spring onions
25 g (1 oz) wakame *seaweed*
DRESSING
45 ml (3 tablespoons) rice vinegar
5 ml (1 teaspoon) Japanese soy sauce
2.5 ml (½ teaspoon) mirin
15 g (½ oz) red pickled ginger shreds to garnish

PREPARATION
Dip the beancurd in boiling water for 30 seconds, then cool immediately in cold water. Drain well. Wash and de-seed the small green pepper, then cut into very thin rings. Chop the spring onions finely. Dip the *wakame* in boiling water for 1 minute and refresh at once under the cold tap. Drain well and cut into 5-cm (2-inch) lengths. Mix the dressing.

Divide the *wakame* between four individual serving plates. Put the beancurd squares on the *wakame* and pour over the dressing. Arrange some pepper rings, chopped onion and red pickled ginger shreds on each square of beancurd.

Cucumber and wakame salad

JAPANESE

INGREDIENTS
180 g (6 oz) cucumber
15 ml (1 tablespoon) salt
15 g (½ oz) dried wakame *seaweed*
DRESSING
30 ml (2 tablespoons) Japanese soy sauce
30 ml (2 tablespoons) rice vinegar
10 ml (2 teaspoons) caster sugar
15 ml (1 tablespoon) white sesame seeds, toasted and ground
ginger shreds to garnish

PREPARATION
Roll the cucumber in salt and leave for 10 minutes. Rinse well and cut into 3-cm (1-inch)-long batons about 1 cm (½ inch) wide. Rinse the *wakame* in cold water and blanch in boiling water for 1 minute. Dip immediately in cold water. Drain and cut into 4-cm (1½-inch) lengths. Mix the dressing.

Just before the meal, arrange the *wakame* and cucumber on four separate small plates and spoon over the dressing. Garnish each helping with a few shreds of finely cut ginger.

Persimmons with beancurd dressing (kakino shiroae)

JAPANESE

INGREDIENTS
2 persimmons
180 g (6 oz) cotton beancurd
30 ml (2 tablespoons) sesame seeds
15 ml (1 tablespoon) caster sugar
15 ml (1 tablespoon) white miso
2.5 ml (½ teaspoon) salt

PREPARATION
Peel the persimmons and cut into very thin slices. Dip the beancurd into boiling water for 1 minute, then drain and put into a food processor. Toast the sesame seeds in a dry frying-pan over a moderate heat until they turn gold and start to dance. Then turn out on to a board and crush with a rolling-pin. Add to the beancurd together with the sugar, *miso* and salt. Work into a smooth paste. Mix the persimmon slices in the paste, divide between four small serving bowls and serve.

Cucumber and dried mushroom salad with miso

JAPANESE

INGREDIENTS
250g (8oz) cucumber
10ml (2 teaspoons) salt
3 dried mushrooms
100ml (3½ fl oz) dashi
15ml (1 tablespoon) Japanese soy sauce
15ml (1 tablespoon) caster sugar
10ml (2 teaspoons) sake
DRESSING
30ml (2 tablespoons) white sesame seeds
15ml (1 tablespoon) white miso
15ml (1 tablespoon) caster sugar
15ml (1 tablespoon) Japanese soy sauce
toasted nori *shreds to garnish (page 36)*

PREPARATION
Slice the cucumber very thinly and soak in 600ml (1 pint) cold water and the salt for 10 minutes. Then drain well. Soak the dried mushrooms in warm water for 30 minutes, then discard the hard stalks and cut the caps into thin slices. Place in a pan with the *dashi*, soy sauce, caster sugar and *sake* to simmer until almost all the stock has gone. Leave in the pan to cool. Toast the sesame seeds in a dry frying-pan until they turn golden and start to dance. Turn out on to a flat board and crush with a rolling-pin, or use a pestle and mortar. Blend the crushed sesame seeds with the *miso*, sugar and soy sauce into a smooth paste. Just before serving, mix the cucumber and mushrooms with the sauce and divide between four small serving dishes. Garnish with a few shreds of toasted *nori*.

Watercress and fried beancurd salad

JAPANESE

INGREDIENTS
150g (5oz) watercress
2 cubes fried beancurd, either bought or fried at home (page 83)
DRESSING
45ml (3 tablespoons) dashi
30ml (2 tablespoons) Japanese soy sauce
5ml (1 teaspoon) mirin

PREPARATION
Wash and pick over the watercress and blanch in boiling water for 20 seconds. Refresh in cold water and drain well. Break the watercress stalks into 6-cm (2½-inch) sections. Put the beancurd squares in a dry frying-pan and cook over a low heat on all sides until darkened in colour (do not allow to burn); alternatively, brown lightly under a grill. Then cut them into batons 1 × 5cm (⅓ × 2 inches). Mix the dressing and pour over the beancurd and watercress. Serve at room temperature divided between four small bowls.

OPPOSITE *Making sweet and sour vegetarian 'spareribs' (Chinese, page 95), using wheat-flour protein (gluten) and bamboo shoots. Also shown: cellophane greens (Chinese, page 57): shredded spinach deep-fried until crisp and served with a vinegar and soy sauce dressing.*

OVERLEAF, LEFT *'A thousand grasses' (Japanese, page 104): steamed individual savoury egg custards garnished with shreds of orange peel and served in the cups in which they are cooked; stuffed cucumber with a corn sauce (Chinese, page 106): lengths of cucumber stuffed with chestnut purée and served in a bright yellow creamed corn sauce; and avocado and* wakame *salad (Japanese, page 113);* wakame *seaweed and fresh grapefruit segments mixed with a dressing of lime juice, oil and soy sauce and piled into halved avocados.*

OVERLEAF, RIGHT *Mixed vegetable soup (page 148), a hearty Chinese soup with baby corn cobs, tomato, Sichuan preserved vegetable, fresh mushrooms, carrots and vegetarian 'ham' in a vegetable stock.*

Beansprout salad

KOREAN

INGREDIENTS

300 g (10 oz) beansprouts (preferably soya)
1 litre (4 cups, 1¾ pints) water
pinch salt
15 ml (1 tablespoon) sesame seeds, toasted
15 ml (1 tablespoon) sesame oil
5 ml (1 teaspoon) salt

PREPARATION

Wash and trim the beansprouts. Bring the water to the boil with a pinch of salt and add the beansprouts. Boil gently for 15 minutes, then drain well. Mix with the toasted sesame seeds and sesame oil. Season with the salt to taste.

Reserve the cooking liquor to use as a vegetarian stock.

Spiced cucumber salad

MALAYSIAN

INGREDIENTS

300 g (10 oz) cucumber
40 ml (2½ tablespoons) rice vinegar
pinch salt
25 g (1 oz) red onion
3 cloves garlic
45 ml (3 tablespoons) oil
10 ml (2 teaspoons) sugar
pinch pepper
2.5 ml (½ teaspoon) turmeric
2.5 ml (½ teaspoon) ground coriander
40 ml (2½ tablespoons) lemon or lime juice

PREPARATION

Cut the cucumber into quarters lengthways and discard the seeds, then cut into ½-cm (¼-inch)-thick slides. Put into a pan with just enough water to cover and add the rice vinegar. Bring to the boil and simmer until the cucumber is slightly transparent (about 10 minutes). Drain and mix with the salt. Slice the onion and garlic very thinly. Heat the oil in a wok or large frying-pan and stir-fry the onion and garlic over a low heat until lightly browned (about 8 minutes). Lift out with a slotted spoon and leave on one side. Put the sugar, pepper and turmeric into the remaining oil and stir-fry for another minute over a moderate heat. Pour in the lemon juice and mix in the cucumber. Remove from the heat and leave to cool. Before serving, garnish with the reserved onion and ginger.

NAMURA (SMALL SALADS)

Japan has had many contacts over the centuries with Korea, her nearest neighbour on the Asian mainland. As a result of the relationship between them they share many traditional customs, including foods and eating habits. These *namuru* dishes would not seem out of place in a Japanese meal, but in that context only one would be served at a time, while in a Korean meal it is more normal to serve a whole selection of tiny salads with a main dish, such as a Korean mixed grill (page 56) or with rice.

OPPOSITE *A tray of Japanese salads and appetizers. Spinach and* nori *rolls (page 116): lightly cooked spinach rolled in* nori *and served with a tart, lemony dressing. Red and white salad (page 116): finely shredded carrot and white radish served chilled in a sweet and sour dressing. Egg roll (pages 122–3): lightly cooked omelettes filled with carrots and beans and allowed to cool in a roll before being sliced and served. Pickled ginger (page 136): shredded young ginger shoots pickled with sugar and vinegar.*

Cucumber namuru

KOREAN

INGREDIENTS
250 g (8 oz) cucumber
30 ml (2 tablespoons) sesame oil
60 ml (4 tablespoons) water
10 ml (2 teaspoons) soy sauce
pinch salt
5 ml (1 teaspoon) very finely chopped garlic
15 ml (1 tablespoon) sesame seeds, toasted (page 36)

PREPARATION
Cut the cucumber into quarters lengthways, then into 3-cm (1-inch) pieces. Heat the sesame oil in a frying-pan over a low heat and stir-fry the cucumber batons for about 2 minutes. Add the water, soy sauce, garlic and salt. Simmer gently until the pan is almost dry without letting the cucumber burn. Remove from the heat and stir in the sesame seeds. Serve cold.

Spinach namuru

KOREAN

INGREDIENTS
200 g (7 oz) fresh spinach
pinch salt
DRESSING
10 ml (2 teaspoons) white sesame seeds, toasted
15 ml (1 tablespoon) sesame oil
2 cloves garlic, crushed
5 ml (1 teaspoon) salt

PREPARATION
Wash and trim the spinach. Cook in salted boiling water for about 4 minutes, then refresh under cold water. Drain well and cut into 3-cm (1-inch) lengths. Mix the dressing and pour over the spinach. Serve cold.
NOTE In an alternative Japanese family recipe for spinach salad, the spinach is cooked in the same way but is then sprinkled with 5 ml (1 teaspoon) soy sauce. It is served with a dressing of toasted sesame seeds, soy sauce, sugar and *dashi*.

White radish namuru

KOREAN

INGREDIENTS
300 g (10 oz) white radish
10 ml (2 teaspoons) sesame oil
5 ml (1 teaspoon) caster sugar
2.5 ml (½ teaspoon) salt
5 ml (1 teaspoon) white sesame seeds, toasted

PREPARATION
Peel and cut the white radish into batons ½ cm (¼ inch) across and 4 cm (1½ inches) long. Mix with the sesame oil in a bowl, coating well. Tip into a dry frying-pan with the sugar and salt. Cook over a low heat until soft but still firm (about 20 minutes). (If necessary add a little water to the pan.) Mix in the toasted sesame seeds and put into small serving bowls. Leave until cold before serving.

Aubergine namuru

KOREAN

INGREDIENTS
300 g (10 oz) aubergine
10 ml (2 teaspoons) salt
DRESSING
15 ml (1 tablespoon) sesame oil
15 ml (1 tablespoon) sesame seeds, toasted
30 ml (2 tablespoons) soy sauce
5 ml (1 teaspoon) crushed garlic
pinch chilli powder (optional)

PREPARATION
Cut the aubergine into slices and soak in salted water for 20 minutes, putting a plate on top to hold them under the water. Then drain and transfer to a pan of lightly salted boiling water. Cook for 10 minutes, or until soft. Drain and squeeze dry. Tear into shreds and mix with the dressing. Serve cold.

COLD MAIN DISHES

Many of the dishes in this section contain beancurd or other protein foods, which means that although served cold they can be considered as main dishes when planning a meal. It is of considerable advantage to the cook to include such a dish in a Far-Eastern meal if the other dishes in the meal are complicated or need a lot of last-minute attention.

Family aubergines

CHINESE

This dish may be served hot if preferred.

INGREDIENTS
300 g (10 oz) aubergines
salt
90 ml (6 tablespoons) oil
2 spring onions, cut into 1-cm (½-inch) lengths
45 ml (3 tablespoons) light soy sauce
15 ml (1 tablespoon) sugar
pinch salt and pepper

PREPARATION
Cut the aubergine into rounds about 1 cm (⅓ inch) thick and cut a diagonal criss-cross on the top of each slice, without cutting right through. Soak the slices in a bowl of lightly salted water for 30 minutes with a plate on top to keep the slices under the water's surface. Drain. Heat the oil in a wok or large frying-pan and gently fry the aubergines over a moderate heat until soft (about 15 minutes). Press out the oil and lift from the pan. Stir-fry the onion pieces in the remaining oil, then add the soy sauce and sugar. Return the aubergines to the pan over a moderate heat and season with pepper and salt. Cook for a further 2 minutes until the aubergines are well coated in the sauce. Leave to cool before serving.

Beancurd and basil salad

CHINESE

INGREDIENTS

350g (12oz) beancurd
20g (3–4oz) basil or mint leaves
5ml (1 teaspoon) grated ginger
salt to taste
15ml (1 tablespoon) sesame oil

PREPARATION

Dip the beancurd in boiling water for 30 seconds, then in cold water to cool quickly. Drain well and cut into 1-cm (½-inch) cubes. Blanch the basil in boiling water for about 15 seconds, then refresh in cold water. Chop finely. Arrange the beancurd on a plate, garnish with the basil and grated ginger. Season with salt and dribble over the sesame oil.

Beancurd salad with sesame sauce

CHINESE

INGREDIENTS

350g (12oz) beancurd
25g (1oz) preserved Sichuan vegetable
30ml (2 tablespoons) sesame paste
15ml (1 tablespoon) sesame oil
2.5ml (½ teaspoon) sugar
pinch salt

PREPARATION

Dip the beancurd into boiling water for 30 seconds, then immediately cool in cold water and drain well. Cut into 1-cm (½-inch) dice. Wash the preserved Sichuan vegetable and chop very finely. Mix the sesame paste and sesame oil, then season with sugar and salt. Stir in the preserved vegetable and spoon over the beancurd dice.

Cold beancurd salad

KOREAN

INGREDIENTS

8 squares fried beancurd
100g (4oz) cucumber
100g (4oz) carrot
3 eggs
4 spring onions

DIPPING SAUCE

45ml (3 tablespoons) Japanese soy sauce
5ml (1 teaspoon) chilli oil
2.5ml (½ teaspoon) sugar

or

45ml (3 tablespoons) Japanese soy sauce
15ml (1 tablespoon) sesame oil
2.5ml (½ teaspoon) sugar

PREPARATION

Cut the beancurd squares into thin slices. Cut the cucumber and carrot into separate piles of matchsticks. Make two-colour omelettes (see page 37) and cut into matchsticks, keeping the colours separate. Wash and trim the spring onions and tie each into a little bundle. Arrange the beancurd in the centre of a large plate. Arrange around it the various coloured strips, laying them all straight in small blocks of colour. Put the spring onion bundles on the beancurd and serve with one of the dipping sauces.

Celery and beancurd salad

CHINESE

This is a summer salad.

INGREDIENTS
180 g (6 oz) beancurd
4 sticks celery
3 slices ginger, finely chopped
2 spring onions, finely chopped
DRESSING
5 ml (1 teaspoon) soy sauce
15 ml (1 tablespoon) sesame oil
pinch salt, pepper and sugar to taste

PREPARATION
Dip the beancurd in boiling water for 30 seconds, then immediately refresh in cold water and drain well. Cut into 1-cm (½-inch) cubes. Wash and trim the celery and cut into 3-cm (1-inch) lengths. Boil in lightly salted water until just transparent (about 4 minutes). Refresh in cold water and drain. Take care not to overcook the celery: it should remain crisp. Mix the celery with the beancurd and garnish with the ginger and onion. Pour over the dressing and chill well before serving.

'Ham' and peanut salad

CHINESE

INGREDIENTS
100 g (4 oz) cucumber
150 g (5 oz) vegetarian 'ham' (page 100)
50 g (2 oz) salted peanuts
DRESSING
5 ml (1 teaspoon) chilli oil
10 ml (2 teaspoons) soy sauce
5 ml (1 teaspoon) rice vinegar
pinch sugar to taste
5 ml (1 teaspoon) sesame oil

PREPARATION
Wash the cucumber and dice it and the 'ham' into 1½-cm (½-inch) cubes. Mix with the salted peanuts in a serving bowl and pour over the dressing.

'Ham' salad

CHINESE

INGREDIENTS
100 g (4 oz) vegetarian 'ham' (page 100)
50 g (2 oz) celery
DRESSING
5 ml (1 teaspoon) soy sauce
10 ml (2 teaspoons) sesame oil
5 ml (1 teaspoon) chilli oil (optional)
2.5 ml (½ teaspoon) salt
pinch sugar and Sichuan pepper

PREPARATION
Cut the 'ham' into matchsticks. Wash and cut the celery into similar-sized pieces. Mix the dressing, adjusting the seasoning to taste. Arrange the 'ham' and celery on a serving plate and pour over the dressing. Serve.

Water-spinach with garlic sauce

CHINESE

INGREDIENTS

350g (12oz) water-spinach
5ml (1 teaspoon) salt

DRESSING

45ml (3 tablespoons) soy sauce
15ml (1 tablespoon) rice vinegar
15ml (1 tablespoon) sesame oil
5ml (1 teaspoon) grated garlic

PREPARATION

Wash and trim the water-spinach. Blanch in boiling water for 1 minute, then refresh under the cold tap. Drain and cut into 3-cm (1-inch) sections. Mix the dressing and pour over the water-spinach.

Ginger spinach salad

CHINESE

INGREDIENTS

450g (1 lb) fresh spinach
50g (2oz) ginger
25ml (1½ tablespoons) red vinegar
10ml (2 teaspoons) sesame oil
salt

PREPARATION

Wash the spinach and discard any old leaves. Blanch in lightly salted boiling water for 3–4 minutes, then refresh immediately in cold water and drain well. Cut into 4-cm (1½-inch) lengths. Grate the ginger and strain off the juice. Mix the ginger juice with the vinegar and sesame oil. Season to taste with salt and pour this dressing over the cold chopped spinach. Serve.

PICKLES

Among the best features of a Japanese meal are the pickles that are served with the rice. These vegetable pickles are usually sour (with vinegar) or salted, although the Japanese also have a number of strong-smelling fermented pickles. They go very well with Japanese tea, drunk without milk, and we have found that many people in the West will eat them not just at the end of a meal but throughout, given the chance. Many pickles are made at home in Japan, and this section includes a range of recipes for them. Excellent pickles can also be bought in small packets from Japanese grocers in the West. Once opened they keep for a long time in the refrigerator.

No Korean meal could possibly be served without at least one dish of pickled vegetables, called *kimchi*. More usually two or three different *kimchi* are served with every meal. Fresh vegetables are very difficult to grow during the long, hard Korean winters and these vegetable pickles, many of which are made during the summer and autumn from fresh vegetables and allowed to mature during the winter, provide many of the vitamins, including vitamin C, and minerals which would otherwise be lacking from the Korean diet.

Kimchi originally came from China, but even before Buddhism was established in Korea, the Koreans were pickling vegetables. They used fish and meat as well as salt for the ferment. When mixed with garlic the pickles were said to have a 'stinking' flavour. By the beginning of the seventeenth century, with the arrival of chillis from America via Japan, *kimchi* developed into the hot pickles that are so popular today.

Indonesian *sambals*, more closely related to a dipping sauce or a condiment than a pickle, are eaten in very small quantities to add extra bite or seasoning to the main dishes in the meal. It is possible to buy some ready-made *sambals* in jars, and unless you are very keen to try making your own you will find that bought *sambals* can save you a lot of time. They too will keep well.

Pickled aubergine with ginger

JAPANESE

INGREDIENTS

250g (8oz) aubergine
10g (½ oz) ginger
10ml (2 teaspoons) salt
15ml (1 tablespoon) Japanese soy sauce

PREPARATION

Wash and cut the aubergine into quarters lengthways, then slice finely. Shred the ginger. Mix the aubergine slices and the ginger with the salt by hand in a bowl. Place a plate immediately on top of the aubergine and place a weight on top. Leave for 5 hours.

Afterwards, squeeze out and discard the liquid and mix the aubergine with the soy sauce. Serve on individual small plates.

Pickled cabbage

JAPANESE

INGREDIENTS

200g (7oz) cabbage (a hearted, not a Dutch, cabbage)
3 stalks fresh sweet basil
7.5ml (1½ teaspoons) salt
15ml (1 tablespoon) black sesame seeds

DIPPING SAUCE

30ml (2 tablespoons) Japanese soy sauce
15ml (1 tablespoon) lemon juice

PREPARATION

Wash the cabbage and discard the stalks. Slice the green leaves finely. Chop the basil. Mix the cabbage with the basil and the salt, then cover with a weighted plate and leave for 3 hours. Squeeze out the liquid from the cabbage and serve divided between four small plates garnished with the sesame seeds. Serve the dipping sauce in separate side dishes.

NOTE 5ml (1 teaspoon) dried basil may be substituted for the fresh basil in this recipe.

Pickled cucumber

JAPANESE

INGREDIENTS

180g (6oz) cucumber
15ml (1 tablespoon) salt
20ml (4 teaspoons) Japanese soy sauce
2.5ml (½ teaspoon) caster sugar

PREPARATION

Cut the cucumber into quarters lengthways and rub each section with the salt. Press between two weighted-down plates for 2 hours. Then rinse, pat dry and cut into 3-cm (1-inch) lengths. Serve in four small bowls with the soy sauce and sugar dressing.

Sichuan pickled red chillis

CHINESE

This pickle is better when made with red chillis rather than the sharper-flavoured green chillis usually sold in the UK. However, green chillis may be used if red are not available.

INGREDIENTS

100 g (4 oz) large mild chillis
10 ml (2 teaspoons) rice wine
10 ml (2 teaspoons) sea salt
2.5 ml (½ teaspoon) Sichuan peppercorns
2 slices ginger
300 ml (1¼ cups, ½ pint) boiled water

PREPARATION

Wash and dry the chillis carefully, leaving whole. Prick all over with the point of a needle. Sterilize a small bowl in the oven for about 20 minutes, then mix the remaining ingredients in it and put in the chillis. Place a small, clean saucer on top to keep them below the water's surface. Cover the bowl with clingwrap and leave at room temperature for 2 days. Taste the marinade: if it tastes sour, remove the clingwrap and put in the refrigerator for 4 days before eating (if not sour enough, leave for another day at room temperature before putting into the refrigerator).

These chillis will keep for several weeks in the refrigerator, so long as they are left uncovered.

NOTE A very similar dish is made in Korea, using mixed vegetables and following the same principle of souring: see spring *kimchi*, page 138.

Pickled ginger

JAPANESE

INGREDIENTS

125 g (4 oz) fresh young ginger
20 ml (4 teaspoons) salt
100 ml (3½ fl oz) rice vinegar
30 ml (2 tablespoons) caster sugar
a few drops edible red colouring or beetroot juice

PREPARATION

Peel the ginger very finely and cut with the grain of the ginger into paper-thin vertical slices. Blanch in boiling water for 2 minutes, then drain and put into 300 ml (1¼ cups, ½ pint) cold water with the salt. Soak for 1 hour. Meanwhile, mix the vinegar and sugar in a pan and boil to dissolve the sugar. Allow to cool. Drain the ginger and mix with the vinegar, sugar and colouring. Cover and leave in the refrigerator for at least 24 hours before using. This pickled ginger will keep for months in the refrigerator.

White radish pickle

JAPANESE

INGREDIENTS

250 g (8 oz) white radish
5 white radish leaves (optional)
10 ml (2 teaspoons) salt
zest ½ lemon, finely shredded

PREPARATION

Peel the white radish and cut into batons about ½ cm (¼ inch) across and 3 cm (1 inch) long. Chop the leaves into 1-cm (½-inch) pieces. Blanch the leaves and white radish in boiling water for 1 minute, then drain well.

Mix the white radish and the leaves very thoroughly with the salt in a bowl, then place a weighted plate on top and leave for 3 hours. Drain well. Serve garnished with the finely shredded zest of lemon in four separate small bowls.

Vinegared white radish

JAPANESE

INGREDIENTS

450g (1 lb) white radish
25ml (1½ tablespoons) salt
200g (7oz) caster sugar
150ml (⅔ cup, 5fl oz) rice vinegar

PREPARATION

Wash and trim the white radish and cut into slices about ½cm (¼ inch) thick. Mix very thoroughly with the salt in a glass or china bowl and leave for 24 hours to soften. Then drain well and squeeze dry in a clean cloth. Put the sugar and vinegar in a pan and bring to the boil to dissolve the sugar. Place the radish slices in a clean screw-topped storage jar and pour over the vinegar and sugar syrup. Fasten the lid and leave in the refrigerator for at least 10 days before eating.

This pickle will keep for several months in the refrigerator.

NOTE For a crisper pickle reduce the sugar to 150g (5oz).

Sambal jenggot (chilli-coconut sauce)

INDONESIAN

This *sambal* goes particularly well with *sayur bening* or any rather bland vegetable stew or soup.

INGREDIENTS

180g (6oz) fresh coconut flesh
1 clove garlic
2 chillis (ideally one hot and one mild), de-seeded
15ml (1 tablespoon) dark soy sauce
brown sugar and salt to taste

PREPARATION

Remove the coconut from the shell and take off as much of the thin inner brown skin as possible. Put the pieces of coconut flesh in a food processor and chop finely, then add the garlic, de-seeded chillis and soy sauce and work into a grainy paste. Season with brown sugar and salt to taste.

Sambal pecal (chilli-peanut relish)

INDONESIAN

This *sambal* goes very well with both raw and cooked vegetables and can be used either as a dressing for a salad or as a dip.

INGREDIENTS

75g (3oz) peanuts
oil for deep frying
45ml (3 tablespoons) tamarind juice
3 chillis, de-seeded
1 very small clove garlic
5ml (1 teaspoon) brown sugar
10ml (2 teaspoons) light soy sauce
1.5ml (¼ teaspoon) salt

PREPARATION

Skin the peanuts, then deep-fry in hot oil over a moderate heat until golden brown (about 3 minutes). Lift out immediately and drain well. Grind in a food processor or with a pestle and mortar into a fine sand. Add the remaining ingredients together with 15ml (1 tablespoon) water and continue working into a stiff, slightly grainy paste. Add a little more water if necessary.

Sambal tomat (tomato chilli)

INDONESIAN

This *sambal* goes particularly well with vegetable stews, but it does not keep for more than about 3 days, even in the refrigerator.

INGREDIENTS
180g (6oz) tomatoes
3 chillis
pinch salt
5ml (1 teaspoon) soy sauce
5ml (1 teaspoon) granulated sugar

PREPARATION
Put the tomatoes and chillis into a steamer and steam for about 7 minutes. Leave to cool for a few minutes, then skin and de-seed the tomatoes and de-seed the chillis. Put the tomato flesh and chillis with the remaining ingredients into a food processor and grind to a fine, smooth paste.

Spring kimchi

KOREAN

INGREDIENTS
350g (12oz) Chinese leaves
125g (4oz) carrots
50g (2oz) white radish
3 fresh chillis
6 slices ginger
2 cloves garlic
3 spring onions
30ml (2 tablespoons) sea salt
600ml (2½ cups, 1 pint) boiled water

PREPARATION
Wash, dry and cut the Chinese leaves into bite-sized pieces. Scrape and dice the carrot and white radish. Wash, de-seed and slice the chillis finely. Chop the ginger and garlic. Cut the spring onions into thin shreds. Mix the salt with the boiled water in a clean china or glass bowl and add the chillis, garlic, ginger and onions. Stir well, then add the prepared vegetables. Place a clean saucer on top of the vegetables to keep them under the marinade. Cover the bowl with clingwrap and keep at room temperature. After 2 days taste the marinade. If it tastes sour put the pickle, uncovered, in the refrigerator; if not sour, leave for another 24 hours. This pickle can be eaten after 4 days. It will keep for a week or more in the refrigerator, uncovered.

White turnip kimchi

KOREAN

INGREDIENTS
250g (8oz) white turnips
2 chillis, chopped
2 cloves garlic, chopped
25ml (1½ tablespoons) salt

PREPARATION
Wash, peel and cut the turnips into halves. Mix with 15ml (1 tablespoon) salt and leave to marinate for 24 hours. Then, reserving the salty water which has collected at the bottom of the bowl, rinse the turnips and slice into ½-cm (¼-inch)-thick slices. Put with the chillis and garlic into a clean jar and add 10ml (2 teaspoons) salt. Pour in the reserved salty water and add sufficient cold boiled water to cover the turnip slices. Cover the jar loosely and leave in a cool place for 3–4 days before eating.

This *kimchi* will keep for at least 2 weeks.

Aubergine kimchi

KOREAN

INGREDIENTS
450 g (1 lb) aubergines
4 spring onions
1 chilli
25 ml (1½ tablespoons) Japanese soy sauce
7.5 ml (1½ teaspoons) chilli powder
10 ml (2 teaspoons) grated garlic
pinch salt

SEASONING SAUCE
200 ml (1 scant cup, ⅓ pint) Japanese soy sauce
7.5 ml (1½ teaspoons) caster sugar
7.5 ml (1½ teaspoons) rice vinegar
7.5 ml (1½ teaspoons) chilli powder (or double quantity for a really hot pickle)

PREPARATION
Wash and deeply score the aubergines all over. Boil in lightly salted water until soft (about 15 minutes). Drain very well. Meanwhile, chop the spring onions and chilli very finely. Mix together with the soy sauce, chilli powder, garlic and salt. When the aubergines are cool enough to handle, stuff the onion and chilli mixture into the scores on the aubergines. Put into a pot or glass casserole and pour over the seasoning sauce. Put a weighted plate on the aubergines to press down. Leave in a cool place overnight. Eat after 24 hours.

This pickle will keep for several weeks.

Mixed vegetable kimchi

KOREAN

INGREDIENTS
500 g (1 lb) Chinese leaves
500 g (1 lb) white radish
75 g (3 oz) carrot
40 g (1½ oz) red onion
2 cloves garlic
200 g (7 oz) cooked rice
salt
4 litres (16 cups, 7 pints) water

PREPARATION
Wash the Chinese leaves and cut into 2-cm (½-inch) pieces. Scrape and slice the white radish and carrot into thin slices about 2 cm (¾ inch) square. Slice the onion and garlic very finely. Sprinkle 30 ml (2 tablespoons) salt over the white radish and Chinese leaves, mix well and leave to marinate for 1 hour. Meanwhile, cook the rice in the measured water over a very low heat until the rice falls into a paste (about 1 hour). Add a pinch of salt and drain through a fine sieve or cheesecloth. Leave the rice water to cool. Rinse the white radish and Chinese leaves, then drain well and mix all the vegetables in a clean bowl. Pour over the rice water. Cover the bowl and leave at room temperature for 3 days before eating. (In warm weather, place the bowl in the refrigerator.)

10 Soups

Soups form the principal drink in many Far-Eastern meals. At a family meal the Chinese would drink only soup – not tea, nor anything stronger. Such a soup is served together with the other dishes and people help themselves to small quantities of it throughout the meal; alternatively, the soup can be served at the end of the meal. It is unthickened and usually contains only scraps of whatever the housewife has to hand whilst she is preparing the meal. This soup would not count as a dish on its own. However, soups for more formal meals, called 'big soups', are served as a separate course and considered dishes in their own right. In very large-scale dinners several soups may be served during the course of the meal, ranging in style from a thickened stock containing many, often expensive, ingredients to a sugar-sweet soup which may on occasion mark the beginning of the end of a big banquet.

In Japanese meals there is also a distinction between a family soup and a soup for a grander occasion, although here the roles are reversed, with thick soups for family meals and thin ones at formal meals. The Japanese, unlike the Chinese, often drink tea with their rice at family meals. A soup enriched with fermented soya-bean paste, *miso*, is usually served at family meals, whilst a delicately garnished clear soup, rather like a consommé, is drunk as a separate course in a formal meal. Clear soups can, however, also be served at family meals.

The Indonesians on the other hand do not make a clear distinction between a soup and a wet stew, and they have no tradition of the consommé style of soup. Even at a feast a stew with a lot of gravy is always among the dishes provided. All the recipes for Indonesian soups-cum-stews appear in Chapter 6.

STOCKS

One of the most important elements in a successful Chinese or Japanese vegetarian meal is the soup. A good soup depends on a good stock; no matter what garnishes are added, if the stock is poor, the soup will taste feeble. The basic Chinese vegetarian stock, called white bean stock, is made from soya beansprouts, while in Japan seaweed is used to make stock. Both give excellent results. Although the Chinese traditionally add MSG to enrich the flavour of their vegetarian stocks, this ingredient is not included in the recipes that follow, in deference to the general trend against such additives in the West. However, a small quantity of MSG will certainly improve the flavour of all Chinese vegetarian soups.

Beansprouts

Soya beansprouts can be bought fresh from most Chinese grocers, particularly at the weekend, and are also quite easy to grow at home, as follows.

Soak 150g (5oz) soya beans in water overnight, then spread out on a dampened towel in a box. Store in a dark place and water at least once a day (depending on the temperature). Wait until the sprouts are 12–15 cm (6 inches) high, then cut and use as required.

Mung beansprouts can be grown in the same way. They are ready for cutting when they are about 6 cm (2½ inches) high.

Soya beans are tougher than mung beansprouts. They can stand cooking for a long time and still be good to eat. Drain and serve with a dressing of sesame oil, soy sauce and vinegar.

White bean stock

CHINESE

INGREDIENTS

300 g (10 oz) soya beansprouts
4 dried mushrooms, soaked in 200 ml (1 cup, 7 fl oz) warm water for 30 minutes
15 g (½ oz) Western onion
1 slice ginger
2 cloves garlic
1.5 ml (¼ teaspoon) Sichuan peppercorns
30 ml (2 tablespoons) rice wine
5 ml (1 teaspoon) salt
15 ml (1 tablespoon) light soy sauce

PREPARATION

Rinse the soya beans and place, with the dried mushrooms and the mushrooms soaking water, in 2 litres (7½ cups, 3 pints) water. Add the remaining ingredients and bring to the boil. Skim off the foam and cover the pan with a lid. Simmer for 1 hour. Season to taste and use as required.

If desired, add the peel of white radish, 25 g (1 oz) carrots and 25 g (1 oz) bamboo shoots to this stock. It does not keep very well and should be used as soon as possible after it is made for its delicate flavour to be at its best.

Soya-bean stock

CHINESE

INGREDIENTS

180 g (1 cup, 6 oz) soya beans
10 g (⅓ oz) ginger, cut into slices
10 Sichuan peppercorns or black peppercorns
2 spring onions or 20 g (¾ oz) Western onion
1 clove garlic

PREPARATION

Wash the beans and soak overnight in 2 litres (8 cups, 3 pints) cold water. The next day add the remaining ingredients. Bring to the boil, then turn down the heat and skim the stock carefully. Cover the pan and simmer until the beans are soft (this may take up to 2 hours, depending on the freshness of the beans). Then strain the stock through a sieve and use as required.

Mushroom stock

CHINESE

The water in which dried mushrooms have been soaked makes a very good stock on its own. Rinse the mushrooms well, soak for about 45 minutes then use the mushrooms as required and strain off the soaking water to use as directed.

Mushroom, soya bean and red date stock

CHINESE

This is an expensive stock, suitable for a special meal or dinner party. It has an attractive, slightly smoky undertone

INGREDIENTS

60 g ($\frac{1}{3}$ cup, 2 oz) soya beans
20 g ($\frac{3}{4}$ oz) dried mushrooms (broken bits and odd stalks)
4 red dates
10 g ($\frac{1}{3}$ oz) ginger, cut into slices
1 clove garlic
2 spring onions

PREPARATION

Soak the soya beans overnight in cold water, rinse and drain. Put into 1 litre (4 cups, $1\frac{3}{4}$ pints) water. Soak the mushrooms in 200 ml (1 cup, 7 fl oz) warm water for 30 minutes. Strain the water and add the mushrooms and the strained water to the soya beans. Soak the red dates for 4 hours, then drain and add to the pan with the remaining ingredients. Bring to the boil, skim off the scum and cover the pan. Simmer for 1 hour, strain and use as required.

White radish vegetarian stock

CHINESE

The peppery bite of the radish is noticeable in this stock, and for this reason it is better used for a strong-flavoured soup than a delicate one. It must be made freshly when required, for it develops a strong overtone of cabbage when it is stale.

INGREDIENTS

200 g (7 oz) white radish
1 slice ginger
2 spring onions
1 clove garlic
5 black peppercorns
2 litres ($7\frac{1}{2}$ cups, 3 pints) water
salt to taste
5 ml (1 teaspoon) sesame oil

PREPARATION

Cut the white radish into thin slices. Put the ginger, spring onions, garlic and peppercorns with the water into a pan. Add the white radish. Cover the pan and bring to the boil, then lower the heat and simmer gently for 1 hour. Strain through a sieve and season the stock to taste with salt and sesame oil. Use as required.

Konbu dashi

JAPANESE

Konbu dashi is the basic stock for all Japanese cooking and soups. Another, quicker, version appears on page 37.

INGREDIENTS

40 g ($1\frac{1}{2}$ oz) dried konbu
1 litre (4 cups, $1\frac{3}{4}$ pints) water

PREPARATION

Wipe the *konbu* with a damp cloth and place in the water. Leave at room temperature overnight (or for at least 8 hours). Then remove the *konbu* and use the stock as required. This stock should be made fresh as required.

JAPANESE MISO SOUPS

***Adding* miso**

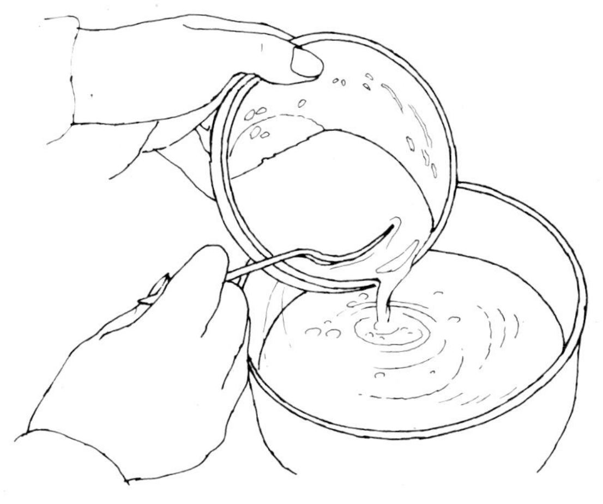

Mix the miso *with a little* dashi *before adding it to the hot soup.*

Miso soup has been the standard Japanese family soup for centuries. It is drunk both at breakfast and at the main meal of the day. *Miso* gives soup a rich, savoury flavour as well as thickening it.

There are four varieties: white *miso*; red *miso*, which is darker and saltier; a stronger-flavoured variety, almost black in colour, called *hatcho*; and a very sweet pale cream variety called *kyomiso*. Not all *miso* is to Western taste, but several different brands of the different kinds of *miso* are on sale in Western health-food stores and Japanese shops, so you have the opportunity to choose which you prefer. Unless the recipe specifies which variety, use your own favourite. The flavour of *miso* changes if it is boiled, so it should only be added to the soup at the last minute, just before serving. It must be very thoroughly blended with a small quantity of the *dashi* before it is added to the body of the soup otherwise the soup will become lumpy.

Miso soups are always garnished with seasonal vegetables or other foods such as beancurd, eggs or seaweed. Vegetables which need cooking can be cooked in the *dashi* before the *miso* is added, while soft ingredients such as beancurd or *wakame* can be arranged directly in the warmed soup bowls and the hot soup labelled over them. Japanese soups are served in small individual soup bowls and drunk straight from the bowl. No spoon is used. Any larger pieces of garnish are eaten with chopsticks from the soup.

Miso and beancurd soup

JAPANESE

INGREDIENTS

900 ml (3¾ cups, 1½ pints) dashi
½ packet silk beancurd
45 ml (3 tablespoons) miso
2 spring onions, finely sliced
pinch one-spice pepper (optional)

PREPARATION

Bring all but 100 ml (½ cup, 3½ fl oz) of the *dashi* to the boil. Mix the reserved *dashi* with the *miso* in a small bowl. Cut the silk beancurd into 1-cm (½-inch) cubes, holding it on the flat of your hand. Slide into the boiling stock. After the soup has returned to the boil, lift from the heat and add the *miso* mixture. Return to the heat and bring almost to boiling point. Ladle into four separate heated serving bowls, add the spring onions and one-spice pepper and serve.

Miso soup with eggs

JAPANESE

INGREDIENTS

8–10 chives, or green parts of spring onions
4 egg yolks
900 ml (3¾ cups, 1½ pints) dashi
75 ml (5 tablespoons) miso

PREPARATION

Rinse and cut the chives into 4-cm (1½-inch) lengths. Put one egg yolk with a portion of the chives in the bottom of each soup bowl, taking care not to break them. Mix 100 ml (½ cup, 3½ fl oz) *dashi* with the *miso* into a smooth paste. Bring the rest of the *dashi* to the boil. Stir in the *miso* and immediately lift from the heat. Pour over the egg yolks and serve at once.

Mixed vegetable soup with miso and beancurd

JAPANESE

INGREDIENTS

150 g (5 oz) cotton beancurd
3 dried mushrooms
150 g (5 oz) potato
100 g (4 oz) white radish
75 g (3 oz) carrot
40 g (1½ oz) scorzonera or salsify (optional)
30 ml (2 tablespoons) oil
900 ml (3¾ cups, 1½ pints) dashi
60 ml (4 tablespoons) hatcho *or red* miso

PREPARATION

Wrap the beancurd tightly in a towel and press beneath a board for 1 hour. Cut into thin oblongs 3 × 4 cm (1 × 1½ inches). Soak the dried mushrooms in warm water for 30 minutes, then discard the hard stalks and cut the caps into thin slices. Peel the potato, white radish and carrot and cut into thin oblongs like the beancurd. Peel and slice the scorzonera into thin flakes, under water to prevent discolouring. Heat the oil in a saucepan and stir-fry the scorzonera, mushroom and carrots over a moderate heat for about 2 minutes. Tip in the *dashi*, potato and white radish. Simmer, covered, for about 15 minutes. When all the vegetables are cooked, remove a cupful of the stock to mix with the *miso*. Slide in the beancurd. Blend the *miso* with the stock into a smooth paste and pour into the pan. Bring almost to boiling point and serve in four separate bowls.

Miso and dried melon soup

JAPANESE

INGREDIENTS

40 cm (16 inches) dried winter melon strips
5 ml (1 teaspoon) salt
SIMMERING STOCK FOR WINTER MELON
300 ml (1⅓ cups, ½ pint) water
15 ml (1 tablespoon) caster sugar
15 ml (1 tablespoon) Japanese soy sauce
15 ml (1 tablespoon) mirin
900 ml (3¾ cups, 1½ pints) dashi
120 ml (8 tablespoons) kyomiso *(sweet white* miso*)*
15 ml (1 tablespoon) mirin
5 ml (1 teaspoon) Japanese soy sauce

PREPARATION

Rub the winter melon strips with the salt, then rinse well. Soak in cold water for 5 minutes, then boil in fresh water for 15 minutes. Drain and put into a clean pan with the simmering stock. Bring to the boil, cover the pan and reduce the heat. Simmer until the melon strips are soft (about 40 minutes), adding more water if necessary. When soft, drain and cut into 12-cm (4-inch) lengths. Tie each length into a knot and put into four warmed soup bowls. Bring the *dashi* to the boil, reserving about 100 ml (½ cup, 3½ fl oz) to mix with the *miso*. Season with *mirin* and soy sauce. Blend the reserved *dashi* with the *miso* into a smooth paste and stir into the soup. Lift from the heat and ladle over the knots of winter melon. Serve at once.

JAPANESE CLEAR SOUPS

Clear soups are usually reserved for formal dinners in Japan, although they may be served at family meals. The choice of garnish is most important, since the appeal of a clear soup lies in its looks. Almost any seasonal vegetable, as well as beancurd or eggs, can be used. There should be at least two different ingredients in the garnish chosen to complement each other in colour, shape and texture.

Clear soup with silk beancurd and chrysanthemum leaves

JAPANESE

INGREDIENTS

1 packet silk beancurd
75 g (3 oz) fresh chrysanthemum leaves or spinach
900 ml (3¾ cups, 1½ pints) dashi
2.5 ml (½ teaspoon) salt
15 ml (1 tablespoon) Japanese soy sauce
wasabi *mustard*

PREPARATION

Cut the silk beancurd into four equal squares and carefully slide one into each soup bowl. Wash the chrysanthemum leaves and par-boil in lightly salted water for 1 minute; refresh in cold water and drain well. Bring the *dashi* to the boil and season with salt and soy sauce. Arrange one chrysanthemum leaf beside each square of beancurd and put a tiny mound of *wasabi* mustard on to each beancurd square. Carefully pour over the boiling *dashi* so as not to disturb the arrangement in the bowl. Serve immediately.

Wakame and silk beancurd soup

JAPANESE

INGREDIENTS

1 strand dried or salted wakame
900 ml (3¾ cups, 1½ pints) dashi
5 ml (1 teaspoon) Japanese soy sauce or a light soy sauce
salt to taste
½ packet silk beancurd
5 ml (1 teaspoon) hair-like shreds of lemon or lime peel

PREPARATION

Rinse the *wakame* and soak in cold water for 5 minutes. Discard the hard rim and cut the *wakame* into 4-cm (1½-inch) lengths. Bring the *dashi* to the boil and season with salt and soy sauce to taste. Hold the silk beancurd on the flat of your hand and cut into 1-cm (⅓-inch) cubes. Slide carefully into the stock. Divide the *wakame* between the heated soup bowls and ladle the soup over it, taking care not to break the beancurd cubes. Garnish with a few shreds of lemon peel and serve.

Clear soup with egg slices

JAPANESE

INGREDIENTS

3 eggs
5 ml (1 teaspoon) caster sugar
750 ml (3 cups, 1¼ pints) water
8-cm (2½-inch) square konbu
5 ml (1 teaspoon) salt
900 ml (3¾ cups, 1½ pints) dashi
5 ml (1 teaspoon) Japanese soy sauce
5 ml (1 teaspoon) salt
4 sprigs watercress, each about 5 cm (2 inches) long

PREPARATION

Beat the eggs with the sugar. Bring the water to the boil with the *konbu* and salt. Check the seasoning, then drop in the beaten egg. Lift from the heat and drain the egg in a sieve lined with a cloth. Quickly put the egg on to a bamboo rolling mat and roll up into a cylinder. Allow to cool in the mat. When cold cut into 1-cm (½-inch) slices.

Just before the meal bring the *dashi* to the boil. Season to taste with the soy sauce and salt. Arrange two slices of egg and a sprig of watercress in the bottom of each soup bowl. Ladle over the hot *dashi* and serve at once.

Dried gluten and snow peas clear soup

JAPANESE

INGREDIENTS

4 dried gluten, in either small balls or flower-shapes
8 snow peas
900 ml (3¾ cups, 1½ pints) dashi
shreds yuzu *or lemon peel to garnish*
caster sugar, salt and Japanese soy sauce to taste

PREPARATION

Soak the gluten for up to 1 hour until soft. Wash and trim the snow peas and blanch in lightly salted boiling water for 2 minutes. Refresh in cold water and drain well. Bring the *dashi* to the boil, add the gluten and return to the boil. Arrange two snow peas in each soup bowl with the shreds of *yuzu* or lemon peel. Lift out the gluten and add to the arrangement in the bowls. Season the *dashi* to taste with sugar, salt and soy sauce, then very carefully pour over the gluten and snow peas in the soup bowls.

Egg soup

JAPANESE

INGREDIENTS

4 eggs
2 sprigs watercress
900 ml (3¾ cups, 1½ pints) dashi
5 ml (1 teaspoon) Japanese or light soy sauce
salt to taste
25 ml (1½ tablespoons) kudzu *flour or potato flour mixed with 15 ml (1 tablespoon) water*

PREPARATION

Beat the eggs. Rinse and cut the watercress into 3-cm (1-inch) lengths. Bring the *dashi* to the boil and season to taste with the soy sauce and salt. Thicken the soup with the *kudzu* flour paste, then add the beaten egg and watercress. Bring just to the boil and lift from the heat. Take care not to overcook the eggs.

Beancurd and leek soup

KOREAN

INGREDIENTS

1 small leek (white parts only)
900 ml (3¾ cups, 1½ pints) well-seasoned white bean stock
15 ml (1 tablespoon) Japanese soy sauce
1 fresh chilli
1 packet silk beancurd

PREPARATION

Wash and trim away any dark leaves from the leek and cut into elongated slices about ½ cm (¼ inch) thick. Bring the stock to the boil and season with the soy sauce and very finely shredded chilli to taste. Hold the beancurd on the flat of your palm and cut into four equal cubes. Slide into the stock. Add the leek slices and return to a very gentle boil for about 3 minutes. Divide between four separate serving bowls and serve.

CHINESE FAMILY SOUPS

The simplest family soups in China may be nothing but boiling water seasoned with soy sauce, garlic and sesame oil, or even just cabbage and water. However, they are more usually made with scraps of meat or fish mixed with some vegetables to give a colourful and decorative appearance. Some are made with beancurd rather than meat or fish. Soups such as these are never served in restaurants because they are considered too simple; they belong entirely to the field of domestic cookery. This section's recipes, while following in the spirit of Chinese family soups, are generally more elaborate and extravagant than these would normally be.

Soup in a Chinese family meal is served in a big bowl either at the same time as the other dishes or after they are finished at the end of the meal.

Three-colour egg soup

CHINESE

INGREDIENTS

2 tomatoes
1 piece wood ears
50 g (2 oz) spinach
1 spring onion
900 ml (3¾ cups, 1½ pints) well-seasoned stock
salt and pepper to taste
10 ml (2 teaspoons) cornflour mixed with 15 ml (1 tablespoon) water
1 large egg, beaten
5 ml (1 teaspoon) sesame oil

PREPARATION

Skin and de-seed the tomatoes. Cut the flesh into 1-cm (⅓-inch) squares. Soak the wood ears in warm water for 30 minutes. Rinse well and cut into thin strips. Wash the spinach, remove any tough veins and tear into small pieces. Chop the onion into 1.5-cm (½-inch) lengths. Bring the stock to the boil, add the tomatoes, spring onion, wood ears and spinach. Return to the boil, adjust the seasoning and thicken with the cornflour paste. Stream in the beaten egg and lift the pan from the heat. Pour on the sesame oil and serve. This soup cannot be re-heated.

Spiced vegetable and silk noodle soup

CHINESE

INGREDIENTS

15 g (½ oz) Sichuan preserved vegetable
50 g (2 oz) vegetarian 'ham'
25 g (1 oz) cucumber
10 g (⅓ oz) silk noodles
900 ml (3¾ cups, 1½ pints) stock
5 ml (1 teaspoon) soy sauce
salt and pepper to taste
15 ml (1 tablespoon) finely chopped spring onion
5 ml (1 teaspoon) sesame oil

PREPARATION

Rinse the Sichuan preserved vegetable and cut into very thin slices, 1½ cm (½ inch) wide and 3 cm (1 inch) long. Cut the vegetarian 'ham' and cucumber into similar-sized slices. Cut the silk noodles into 3-cm (1-inch) lengths and soak in warm water for 10 minutes. Bring the stock to the boil and add the Sichuan preserved vegetable, 'ham', silk noodles and cucumber. Return to the boil and adjust the seasoning to taste. Serve sprinkled with finely chopped onion and sesame oil.

NOTE Failing vegetarian 'ham', add 40 g (1½ oz) bamboo shoots, thinly sliced.

Mixed vegetable soup

CHINESE

INGREDIENTS

10 baby corn cobs
1 tomato
25 g (1 oz) Sichuan preserved vegetable
25 g (1 oz) fresh mushrooms
25 g (1 oz) carrot
salt
25 g (1 oz) vegetarian 'ham', sliced, or bamboo shoots
900 ml (3¾ cups, 1½ pints) stock
salt, sugar and freshly ground black pepper to taste

PREPARATION

Cut each baby corn cob lengthways in half. Skin the tomato and cut into 1-cm (⅓-inch)-thick slices. Cut each slice in half. Rinse and thinly slice the Sichuan preserved vegetable. Wipe the mushrooms, trim and slice. Scrape the carrot and cut into thin slices. Par-boil in lightly salted water, then drain well. Bring the stock to the boil, add the vegetables and return to the boil before adjusting the seasoning. Serve.

Tiger lily and wood ears soup

CHINESE

INGREDIENTS

15 g (½ oz) dried lily buds
15 g (½ oz) wood ears
180 g (6 oz) beancurd
900 ml (3¾ cups, 1½ pints) vegetarian stock
5 ml (1 teaspoon) light soy sauce
5 ml (1 teaspoon) sesame oil
pinch salt
freshly ground black pepper

PREPARATION

Soak the lily buds for 30 minutes in hot water. Then rinse, drain and cut off the hard stalk ends. Soak the wood ears separately in warm water for 30 minutes, then rinse and discard any hard bits. Cut into thin slices. Cut the beancurd into slices 5 mm (¼ inch) thick and about 2.5 cm (1 inch) square. Bring the stock to the boil and add the lily buds and wood ears. Simmer for 5 minutes until the buds are beginning to open, then slide in the beancurd and season to taste with the soy sauce, salt and pepper. Serve hot.

Three-colour beancurd soup

CHINESE

INGREDIENTS

100 g (4 oz) beancurd
100 g (4 oz) tomatoes
900 ml (3¾ cups, 1½ pints) stock
25 g (1 oz) frozen peas
pinch freshly ground black pepper
15 ml (1 tablespoon) cornflour mixed with 30 ml (2 tablespoons) water
5 ml (1 teaspoon) finely chopped spring onion
5 ml (1 teaspoon) finely chopped ginger
5 ml (1 teaspoon) sesame oil

PREPARATION

Cut the beancurd into 1-cm (½-inch) cubes. Skin and de-seed the tomatoes and cut the flesh into 1-cm (½ inch) pieces. Bring the stock to the boil and add the beancurd, tomatoes and frozen peas. Check the seasoning and stir in the pepper. Thicken with the cornflour paste and just before serving scatter over the spring onions, ginger and sesame oil.

Fried beancurd with mustard greens

CHINESE

INGREDIENTS

4 squares fried beancurd
75g (3oz) canned mustard greens
50g (2oz) bamboo shoots
5 canned straw mushrooms or fresh button mushrooms
900ml (3¾ cups, 1½ pints) unsalted *stock*
15ml (1 tablespoon) light soy sauce
10ml (2 teaspoons) rice wine
pinch sugar
salt and freshly ground pepper

PREPARATION

Soak the fried beancurd in hot water to remove the oil. Then pat dry and cut into thin slices. Rinse the mustard greens and cut into thin strips. Cut the bamboo into thin slices. Cut the mushrooms into halves. Bring the stock to the boil and add the mustard greens, fried beancurd, bamboo shoots and mushrooms. Adjust the seasoning, taking care not to add too much salt as the mustard greens are already salty, and serve.

NOTE Another version of this recipe uses 40g (1½oz) fresh spinach and 25g (1oz) fresh mushrooms instead of mustard greens and canned straw mushrooms. The stock for this version of the recipe may be fully seasoned. Prepare as above.

Another recipe for mustard-green soup excludes the beancurd. Use 75g (3oz) mustard greens, 2 dried mushrooms, 50g (2oz) cucumber and 900ml (3¾ cups, 1½ pints) unsalted stock seasoned only with sugar and freshly ground pepper. Discard any leafy parts of the mustard greens and soak the stalks in cold water for 1 minute to remove the salt; then slice thinly. Soak the dried mushrooms and discard the hard stalks before slicing the caps. Cut the cucumber into thin batons. Cook as above.

Frozen beancurd soup

CHINESE

INGREDIENTS

180g (6oz) frozen beancurd (page 89)
25g (1oz) Sichuan preserved vegetable
25g (1oz) bamboo shoots
900ml (3¾ cups, 1½ pints) vegetarian stock
salt to taste
5ml (1 teaspoon) sesame oil

PREPARATION

Pour boiling water over the frozen beancurd to thaw, then cut into thin strips. Cut the Sichuan vegetable and bamboo shoots into matchsticks. Put the beancurd and vegetables into a dry wok or frying-pan over a moderate heat and stir-fry for about 30 seconds with a pinch of salt. Pour in the stock and bring to the boil. Simmer for about 5 minutes, then serve sprinkled with sesame oil.

BIG CHINESE SOUPS

'Big' soups in Chinese terms are those with a wide range of, or expensive, ingredients, or both; sometimes, but not always, the stock is thickened with potato flour or cornflour. These soups are regarded as important dishes and are usually served alone. Most restaurant soups are of this kind, but in family cooking they are kept for special occasions. Several other recipes for 'big' soups appear at the end of the chapter on steaming (Chapter 8).

Straw mushrooms and crispy rice soup

CHINESE

INGREDIENTS

1 can straw mushrooms
750 ml (3¼ cups, 1¼ pints) good stock
5 ml (1 teaspoon) ginger juice
5 ml (1 teaspoon) rice wine
50 g (2 oz) rice crust (see pages 153–4)
oil for deep frying
5 ml (1 teaspoon) sesame oil
15 ml (1 tablespoon) finely chopped green tops of spring onions

PREPARATION

Drain the mushrooms and tip the water from the can into the stock. Bring to the boil, if possible, in a casserole. Season with the ginger juice and rice wine and add the mushrooms. Check the seasoning and simmer for about 4 minutes. Meanwhile, heat the oil and deep-fry the rice crust until it is golden brown. Have ready a big heated soup bowl. Drain the rice for a few seconds only, then place in the soup bowl. Take it immediately to the table with the casserole of boiling stock. In front of the diners pour the soup over the fried rice. As the soup hits the rice it crackles and splutters. Garnish with the sesame oil and chopped green onion.

NOTE If using fresh mushrooms in place of the canned straw mushrooms, wipe the caps, trim the stalk ends and stir-fry with 15 ml (1 tablespoon) oil until soft; then tip into 900 ml (30 fl oz, 1½ pints) stock. Check the seasoning and simmer as above.

Silver wood ears and straw mushroom soup

CHINESE

INGREDIENTS

15 g (½ oz) silver wood ears
900 ml (3¾ cups, 1½ pints) white bean stock
12 canned straw mushrooms
salt and pepper to taste

PREPARATION

Soak the wood ears in warm water for 30 minutes. Discard the hard or discoloured bits and tear the rest into separate leaves. Bring the stock to the boil and add the silver wood ears. Cover and simmer for 1 hour. Then check the seasoning and add the straw mushrooms. Cook for a further 2 minutes before serving.

Take care when cooking this soup not to let the stock boil once the vegetables have been added, or it will develop a foam which spoils the look of the soup. The finished soup should be quite clear and very light in colour.

Sea tangle soup

CHINESE

INGREDIENTS

beancurd 'fish' balls (page 104)
25 g (1 oz) carrot
25 g (1 oz) bamboo shoots
4 baby corn cobs
900 ml (3¾ cups, 1½ pints) stock
salt, sugar and freshly ground black pepper to taste
10 ml (2 teaspoons) sesame oil

PREPARATION

Make the 'fish' balls as directed. Peel the carrot and cut it and the bamboo shoots into thinly sliced flower-shapes (page 39). Cut the corn cobs into halves lengthways. Bring the stock to the boil and add all the vegetables. Adjust the seasoning to taste, drop in the 'fish' balls, sprinkle with sesame oil and serve.

Winter melon and soya bean soup

CHINESE

INGREDIENTS

75g (3oz) soya beans
200g (7oz) fresh winter melon
4 dried mushrooms
10cm (4 inches) kelp
30ml (2 tablespoons) oil
2 slices ginger
salt to taste

PREPARATION

Wash the soya beans and soak in 600ml (2½ cups, 1 pint) water overnight. The next day soak the dried mushrooms for 1 hour in 600ml (2½ cups, 1 pint) warm water, then drain and reserve the soaking water. Discard the hard stalks and cut the mushroom caps into halves. Peel and cut the winter melon into 2-cm (1-inch) cubes. Put the soya beans and their soaking water into a pan with the reserved mushroom water and the kelp. Bring slowly to the boil. (At this point you can remove the kelp if you do not like a rather strong iodine flavour.) Skim the stock and continue to boil gently until the beans are nearly cooked. Meanwhile, heat the oil in a wok or frying-pan and stir-fry the ginger and mushrooms. Add the winter melon and stir-fry for another 2 minutes. When the soya beans are soft, tip the stir-fried vegetables into the pan and continue simmering until the winter melon is soft and the beans are falling apart. Add more water if necessary while cooking and season with salt to taste before serving.

NOTE If you wish to use canned winter melon, drain it first, then very carefully remove the peel from each slice and cut the flesh into cubes. Do not stir-fry, but add to the soup at the very last minute.

Hot and sour soup

CHINESE

INGREDIENTS

250g (8oz) beancurd
25g (1oz) pickled bamboo
3 pieces wood ears
3 dried mushrooms
50g (2oz) spinach leaves
2 spring onions
15g (½ oz) ginger
30ml (2 tablespoons) coriander
900ml (3¾ cups, 1½ pints) vegetarian stock

SEASONING SAUCE

10ml (2 teaspoons) soy sauce
25ml (5 teaspoons) rice vinegar
2ml (⅓ teaspoon) freshly ground white pepper

15ml (1 tablespoon) cornflour mixed with 20ml (4 teaspoons) water
1 egg, beaten
2.5ml (½ teaspoon) sesame oil

PREPARATION

Press the beancurd between two plates for 1 hour. Prepare the pickled bamboo as directed on page 14 and cut in thin shreds. Soak the wood ears and dried mushrooms separately in warm water for 30 minutes. Rinse the wood ears and discard any hard bits, then cut into thin strips. Discard the hard stalks of the mushrooms and cut the caps into thin slices. Wash and remove the tough veins from the spinach leaves, then cut the leaves into bite-sized pieces. Chop the spring onions, ginger and coriander very finely. Cut the beancurd into matchsticks. Bring the soup stock to the boil and slide in the beancurd, wood ears, mushrooms and bamboo shreds. Return to the boil and add the seasoning sauce. Adjust the flavour with salt and pepper. Thicken the soup with the cornflour paste. Just before serving stream in the beaten egg and stir in the onion, ginger and coriander together with the sesame oil.

Creamed corn soup

CHINESE

INGREDIENTS

75g (3oz) potato
25g (1oz) vegetarian 'ham'
25g (1oz) bamboo shoots
75g (3oz) Western onion
30ml (2 tablespoons) oil
200g (1 cup, 7oz) creamed corn
900ml (3¾ cups, 1½ pints) stock
20ml (4 teaspoons) frozen peas (preferably petits pois*)*
salt and freshly ground pepper

PREPARATION

Peel the potato and cut it into 7-mm (¼-inch) cubes. Cut the vegetarian 'ham', bamboo shoots and onion into similar-sized pieces. Heat the oil in a saucepan and stir-fry the onion, then add the rest of the vegetables including the corn but not the peas. Pour in the stock and bring to the boil. Cover and simmer until the potatoes are cooked (about 12 minutes). Add the frozen peas and season with salt and pepper to taste. Serve.

Snow soup with fresh mushrooms

CHINESE

INGREDIENTS

25g (1oz) fresh mushrooms
2 egg whites
15g (½ oz) vegetarian 'ham' (optional) or an additional 15g (½ oz) bamboo shoots
15g (½ oz) bamboo shoots
900ml (3¾ cups, 1½ pints) well-seasoned stock
salt and papper to taste
15ml (1 tablespoon) finely chopped coriander

PREPARATION

Wipe, trim and cut the mushrooms into thin slices. Beat the egg whites with 15ml (1 tablespoon) cold water until stiff. Slice the vegetarian 'ham' and bamboo shoots thinly. Bring the stock to the boil and add the mushrooms, bamboo shoots and vegetarian 'ham'. Return to the boil and adjust the seasoning. Slide in the stiffly beaten egg whites and lift the pan from the heat. Spoon some of the hot stock over the egg to cook it. Tip into a heated soup bowl, making sure that the vegetables sink to the bottom and are not caught on top of the egg white. Sprinkle with coriander and serve at once. This soup cannot be re-heated.

11

Rice, Noodles and Bread Buns

It is a remarkable feature of East Asian life that in spite of the vast geographical and climatic ranges, the preferred food staples of all the regions remain the same: rice and noodles. Rice is grown in a broad band stretching from South East Asia to the north of Honshu in Japan, including the southern two-thirds of China and southern Korea. Wheat is grown in the remaining northern areas, and its flour used for bread and noodles.

Two distinct types of rice are used as a staple in the Far East: long-grained rice, known as Indica, and short-grained rice, called Japonica. Japan, Korea and some parts of eastern China prefer short-grained rice, while South East Asia and southern China in particular prefer the long-grained variety. Brown (unrefined) rice is not eaten in the Far East, except by a few very Western-conscious Japanese families. It carries with it too many overtones of poverty and hardship to be acceptable to the mass of the people. Glutinous rice is a different variety. It has a rounder, whiter grain than either of the other two varieties, and is much stickier when cooked. It is grown throughout the Far East, primarily for wine; it is also used in many sweet rice dishes and for festival foods, but never at an ordinary meal.

COOKING RICE

Rice is not difficult to cook successfully provided a few basic rules are followed. Always wash it very thoroughly to remove any loose starch before cooking; do not cook it in too much water – about 3 cm (1 inch) above the level of the rice in the pan is a good rough guide; and always ensure that the rice has time to finish cooking in its own heat, in a pan covered with a tight-fitting lid, after the heat has been turned off. Nowadays many people in the Far East, particularly in Japan and Hong Kong, use an electric rice-cooker which cooks the rice automatically and keeps it warm until required. These can be bought in the West.

Cooked rice can be stored for several days in a covered container in the refrigerator. (Rice kept too long at room temperature can cause food poisoning.) Cold rice for frying should be broken up into separate grains before it is put into the pan. Cooked rice re-heats very well. Add about 15 ml (1 tablespoon) water to every 150 g (5 oz) cooked rice and put it, in a covered casserole, in a pre-heated oven (180°C, 350°F, Gas 4) for 20 minutes. In the Far East it is customary to allow 150 g (¾ cup, 5 oz) dry rice per person at a main meal. This of course may be varied according to individual requirements.

Most Far-Eastern people eat simple boiled rice to accompany cooked dishes; fried rice and other kinds of special rice dishes are either for festivals or meals in themselves. However the silver and gold rice, the rice with broad beans and even the rice with bamboo shoots, recipes for which are given below, may be served with other dishes at a meal.

Rice crust

Originally rice crust – called *gwoba* in Chinese – was the rice which stuck to the bottom of the pan when it was boiled, and these recipes were ways of using up what otherwise might be wasted. However, it has become a special delicacy, partly because it takes time and trouble to get the rice dried to the right texture: dry, but not hard or shrunken. A little practice can produce excellent results and soups made with rice crust are quite out of the ordinary.

INGREDIENTS
150 g (⅔ cup, 5 oz) long-grain rice
225 ml (1 cup, 8 fl oz) water

PREPARATION
Wash the rice very thoroughly in several lots of water. Put into a thick-bottomed pan with the measured water and bring to the boil. Cover with a lid and simmer for 35 minutes over a very low heat. Take off the lid and leave overnight in a cool, dry place. The next day, lift out of the pan and store.

If you have a microwave oven, you can make rice crust by spreading out plain boiled rice in a layer about 1 cm (⅓ inch) deep and letting it dry in the oven (on a low setting).

Plain boiled rice

INGREDIENTS
600 g (3 cups, 21 oz) rice
950 ml (3¾ cups, 1¼ pints) water

SERVES 4–6

PREPARATION
Wash the rice in several lots of water, swirling it round vigorously to remove the loose starch. Drain well after the last washing and if possible leave to stand for 30 minutes before putting it into a thick-bottomed pan with the measured water. Bring quickly to the boil, then cover the pan and simmer over a reduced heat until all the water has gone (about 15 minutes). Then turn the heat to the lowest possible setting and continue cooking the rice with the lid on for another 10 minutes. Turn off the heat and without lifting the lid leave the rice for another 10 minutes to dry in its own heat.

Silver and gold

CHINESE AND INDONESIAN

INGREDIENTS
300 g (1¼ cups, 10 oz) rice
475 ml (2¼ cups, 15 fl oz) water
250 g (8 oz) loose grains of fresh corn

PREPARATION
Wash the rice in several lots of water, then drain well. Cook in the measured water in a thick-bottomed pan until the water has all gone. Meanwhile, cook the corn in boiling water for 3 minutes, then drain well. When the water has gone from the rice add the corn and cover the pan with a tight-fitting lid. Lower the heat as far as possible and cook for another 10 minutes. Turn off the heat, and without lifting the lid leave to rest for 10 minutes. Mix the rice and corn together before serving.

NOTE An alternative version of this recipe can be made with leftover rice and frozen corn. Use equal volumes of rice and corn. Put into a bowl with 15 ml (1 tablespoon) water for each 125 g (4 oz) of the grains. Put into a steamer and steam over a high heat for 20 minutes, or cover with tinfoil and put into a pre-heated oven (190°C, 375°F, Gas 5) for 30 minutes.

Nasi gurih (coconut rice)

INDONESIAN

INGREDIENTS

300 g ($1\frac{1}{4}$ cups, 10 oz) long-grained rice
400 ml ($1\frac{3}{4}$ cups, 14 fl oz) santan
1 bay leaf
pinch salt

PREPARATION

Wash the rice thoroughly in several lots of water and leave to drain for 30 minutes. Place in a thick-bottomed pan with the *santan*, bay leaf and salt. Bring to the boil and boil gently until the *santan* has disappeared (about 10 minutes). Stir the rice round and cover with a tight-fitting lid. Reduce the heat as far as possible and continue cooking for another 10 minutes.

Rice with broad beans

CHINESE

INGREDIENTS

45 ml (3 tablespoons) oil
150 g (5 oz) fresh shelled broad beans
100 ml (4 fl oz) well-seasoned stock
500 g (3 cups, 1 lb) cooked long-grain rice
freshly ground white pepper

PREPARATION

Heat a wok or large frying-pan with the oil and stir-fry the broad beans for 2 minutes. Then add the stock and boil gently until the beans are just cooked (about 5 minutes). Mix in the rice, cover the pan closely and turn down the heat. Simmer for another 5 minutes, then serve sprinkled with freshly ground white pepper.

Rice with bamboo shoots

JAPANESE

INGREDIENTS

450 g (2 cups, 1 lb) short-grained rice
600 ml ($2\frac{1}{2}$ cups, 1 pint) water
150 g (5 oz) bamboo shoots
1 sheet aburage *or 3 squares deep-fried beancurd*
200 ml (1 scant cup, 7 fl oz) dashi
15 ml (1 tablespoon) Japanese soy sauce
15 ml (1 tablespoon) mirin
30 ml (2 tablespoons) sake
2.5 ml ($\frac{1}{2}$ teaspoon) salt

PREPARATION

Wash the rice very thoroughly in several lots of water. Drain well and leave to soak in the measured water for 1 hour in a large, heavy saucepan. Meanwhile, slice the bamboo shoots and cut the *aburage* into thin strips. Put the *dashi*, soy sauce and *mirin* into a pan with the bamboo shoots and *aburage*. Bring to the boil, then simmer for 5 minutes. Pour this mixture, including the liquid, on the rice and add the *sake* and salt. Bring the pan to the boil, cover and simmer over a low heat for 10 minutes. Then turn off the heat and leave for 15 minutes, still covered with the lid. Just before serving mix the bamboo and *aburage* into the rice.

CELEBRATION RICE

Until this century there was a tradition, dating from 2000 BC, of serving red beans and rice at the time of the winter solstice in China, and today in Japan and Korea red rice is still cooked and eaten on special occasions such as the first birthday of a son or a child's first day at school. In Indonesia yellow, not red, is the festival colour and yellow rice is served at major festival dinners.

Nasi kuning (yellow rice)

INDONESIAN

INGREDIENTS

300g ($1\frac{1}{4}$ cups, 10oz) long-grained rice
400ml ($1\frac{3}{4}$ cups, 14fl oz) santan
5ml (1 teaspoon) turmeric
2 slices laos *or ginger*
1 bay leaf, or use a citrus leaf
pinch salt
pinch lemon grass powder (optional)

PREPARATION

Wash the rice very thoroughly in several lots of water, then soak in clean cold water for 30 minutes. Drain very well and put it into a thick-bottomed pan with the remaining ingredients. Bring to the boil, then lower the heat and boil gently until the *santan* has disappeared (about 10 minutes). Stir the rice, cover with a tight-fitting lid and continue to cook over the lowest possible heat for a further 8–10 minutes.

Red rice

KOREAN

INGREDIENTS

350g ($1\frac{1}{2}$ cups, 12oz) glutinous rice
50g (2oz) red adzuki beans
10ml (2 teaspoons) black sesame seeds, toasted
sea salt

PREPARATION

Boil the beans in a large pan of water for 3 minutes, then drain and add 1.25 litres (5 cups, $1\frac{3}{4}$ pints) fresh cold water. Bring to the boil again and boil for about 45 minutes, until the beans are soft but still grainy. Strain off the beans and reserve the water. Put the beans in a bowl covered in clingwrap to prevent drying out. Make the reserved water up to 450ml (2 cups, $\frac{3}{4}$ pint). Wash the glutinous rice very thoroughly in several lots of water, drain and put into the reserved bean water to soak overnight. The next day spread a cloth over the base of a steamer. Drain the rice, mix with the red beans and spread them over the cloth in the steamer. Reserve the soaking water. Steam the rice and beans for 1 hour over a high heat. If the rice and beans look dry during the steaming, sprinkle with the reserved water. When completely soft, lift out from the steamer very carefully and divide between four bowls. Garnish with the sesame seeds and sea salt and serve hot.

RICE DISHES FOR SNACK MEALS

This section includes two recipes for fried rice, one from Indonesia and the other from China. Neither dish is served as a staple at a main meal but as a light snack or luncheon dish. The Indonesian *nasi goreng* is not a complete one-dish meal on its own, but a tasty way of serving rice with a fried egg or similar side dish, while Chinese fried rice is a complete meal on its own. The two dishes start from very different positions although they seem so similar in their modern manifestations. The Indonesian recipe's purpose is primarily to flavour the rice, but the Chinese version, which should never have soy sauce in it, developed from a very old recipe in which each grain of rice was coated in egg.

Also included in this section are Japanese rice cakes and a breakfast dish made with rice, egg and *nori* seaweed.

Fried rice

CHINESE

INGREDIENTS

3 dried mushrooms
3 spring onions
3 large eggs
salt
60 ml (4 tablespoons) oil
500 g (3 cups, 1 lb) cold cooked long-grain rice
30 ml (2 tablespoons) frozen green peas
pepper to taste

PREPARATION

Soak the dried mushrooms in warm water for 30 minutes, then discard the hard stalks and chop the caps coarsely. Chop the spring onions finely and beat the eggs with a pinch of salt. Heat the oil in a wok or large frying-pan and stir-fry half the chopped spring onions for 15 seconds. Then add the mushrooms, beaten eggs and peas and stir-fry over a moderate heat until the egg just begins to set. Mix in the rice and continue to stir-fry for another 3 minutes. Adjust the seasoning and serve garnished with the remaining chopped onions.

Nasi goreng (fried rice)

INDONESIAN

INGREDIENTS

75 g (3 oz) red onion
1 clove garlic
2 fresh chillis
45 ml (3 tablespoons) oil
500 g (3 cups, 1 lb) cooked long-grained rice
15 ml (1 tablespoon) dark soy sauce
5 ml (1 teaspoon) brown sugar
salt
onion flakes (page 42), omelette shreds (page 37) and sliced tomatoes and cucumber to garnish

PREPARATION

Slice the onion very finely and chop the garlic and chillis. Heat the oil in a large frying-pan or wok and stir-fry the onion, garlic and chillis over a moderate heat until soft (about 7 minutes). Mix in the rice and continue to stir-fry for another 4–5 minutes. Season with the soy sauce, sugar and salt and serve on a hot dish garnished with shreds of omelette and onion flakes and surrounded by slices of tomato and cucumber.

Rice cakes

Cakes of cooked rice are a feature of Japanese luncheon boxes and Japanese cold quick meals. They are easily made and can be served cold with a light lunch or even provide a snack by themselves. They would not however be served in place of rice in a main meal.

INGREDIENTS
300g (1¼ cups, 10oz) short-grained rice
440ml (2 cups, 14 fl oz) water
8 pickled sour plums
nori
salt

MAKES 8

PREPARATION
Wash the rice very thoroughly in several lots of water, then leave it to soak in the measured water for 30 minutes. Bring to the boil, cover with a lid and cook on a reduced heat for 5 minutes, or until all the water has gone. Then, keeping the pan tightly covered, reduce the heat as far as possible and cook for another 15 minutes. Turn off the heat and leave for 10 minutes without lifting the lid.

While still hot, spoon 45ml (3 tablespoons) rice into a bowl. Put one pickled plum in the middle and cover with another 30ml (2 tablespoons) rice. Dampen your hands and put a pinch of salt in the palm of your left hand. Pick up the rice with the pickled plum and shape into a ball, pressing firmly but taking care not to squash the grains of rice. Continue rolling and squeezing until the rice forms a solid ball. Then mould into a triangular shape with a flat top and bottom, using the flattened palm of one hand and the forefinger and thumb of the other hand to shape the three sides (see illustration). Cut 2 squares of *nori* and decorate the top and bottom of the rice cake with these. Make another 7 rice cakes in the same way. Serve cold.

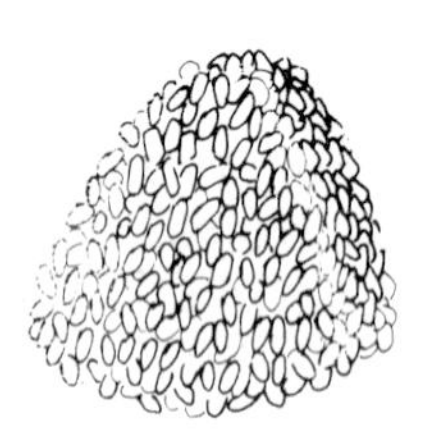

Shaping a rice ball
Using salted, dampened hands, shape the ball of rice into a flattened triangle with the palm of one hand and the forefinger and thumb of the other.

Grilled rice cakes

JAPANESE

INGREDIENTS
short-grained rice
45ml (3 tablespoons) white miso
45ml (3 tablespoons) caster sugar

PREPARATION
Cook the rice as directed in the previous recipe. Dampen your hands, put a pinch of salt in the palm of your left hand, then shape 75ml (5 tablespoons) rice into a flattened round cake, rather like a rissole in shape. When the rice is all shaped, cook the cakes in a dry frying-pan over a low heat until golden brown on both sides. Paint one side of each with a mixture of the *miso* and sugar and put under a heated grill for a few moments until the *miso* mixture starts to bubble. Serve immediately or allow to cool and serve cold.

Rice with egg and nori

JAPANESE

This is a breakfast dish in Japan, but it could equally well be served as a quick luncheon snack. In Korea rice, without the egg, is often served with small sheets of *nori* at a main meal.

INGREDIENTS

plain boiled short-grained rice (see page 154), freshly cooked
4 eggs
12 small sheets nori
Japanese soy sauce

PREPARATION

Give each diner a bowl of hot freshly cooked rice together with an egg and three sheets of *nori*. The diner breaks the egg into the rice and mixes it in with his chopsticks: the heat of the rice cooks the egg. The rice and egg is seasoned to taste with soy sauce, and the occasional mouthful of rice wrapped up in a sheet of the *nori*.

NOODLES

Noodles are particularly popular in northern China and Japan; in Korea people prefer to eat rice but usually serve noodles at least once a week as the staple for a main meal. (In Indonesia, noodles are never served as a staple – only as a special snack meal.) There are three different kinds of noodle in the regions: plain noodles made from wheat flour, egg noodles made with wheat flour, and buckwheat noodles, called *soba* in Japan. Plain noodles are called *udon* in Japan and come in varying widths, each of which has its own name such as *somen* (thinner) and *kishimen* (broader). Each of these varieties of noodle may be served plain as the main staple of a meal, although the Japanese would seldom eat *soba* in such a way; they can otherwise be served with a sauce or in a soup as a light snack or lunch on their own. People's appetites for noodles vary considerably, but in this section we have allowed 500 g (1 lb) noodles for 4 people; this may be cut to 350 g (12 oz) without changing the recipe in any other respect.

Cooking Chinese buckwheat noodles or Japanese soba

Boil a large pan of water, then lift from the heat and add the noodles. Return to a high heat. When the water boils again pour in 100 ml (½ cup) cold water and bring back to the boil. Repeat the adding of cold water and returning to the boil 2–3 times. The noodles should cook for 7 minutes in all. When ready they are firm but not hard in the centre. Take care not to overcook. Drain in a sieve and rinse quickly in cold running water. Drain well and serve as directed.

Cooking Chinese plain noodles or Japanese udon

Heat a large pan of water to just below boiling point. Add the noodles and bring quickly to the boil. Boil for 5–6 minutes (or less, depending on the thickness and variety of the noodles) until still firm but not hard in the centre. Do not allow to overcook. Drain well and rinse in cold water to remove any loose starch. Dip momentarily in boiling water to re-heat. Serve as directed.

Cooking egg noodles

Cook in boiling water until tender, drain and toss in a little oil. (There is no need to rinse egg noodles.)

Sauce for noodles

CHINESE

Serve plain or egg noodles mixed with this sauce instead of rice as a staple.

INGREDIENTS

75 ml (5 tablespoons) groundnut oil
30 ml (2 tablespoons) finely chopped onion
15 ml (1 tablespoon) grated ginger
30 ml (2 tablespoons) soy sauce
pinch salt

PREPARATION

Heat the oil in a wok or large frying-pan and mix in the onion and ginger. Lift from the heat and stir in the soy sauce. Toss the hot drained noodles in the sauce before serving.

NOODLE DISHES AS SNACKS

All the dishes in this section are suitable for light snack meals or luncheons.

Moon noodles

JAPANESE

INGREDIENTS

450 g (1 lb) udon
SOUP STOCK
1600 ml (7 cups, $2\frac{2}{3}$ pints) dashi
150 ml (10 tablespoons) Japanese soy sauce
45 ml (3 tablespoons) mirin
4 eggs
spring onions, finely chopped, and seven-spice pepper to garnish

PREPARATION

Cook the noodles as directed on page 160, then re-heat in boiling water. Meanwhile, bring the soup stock to the boil. Divide the drained noodles between four soup bowls and quickly break an egg into the centre of each. Immediately pour over the boiling soup stock. Garnish with the chopped spring onion and seven-spice pepper and serve.

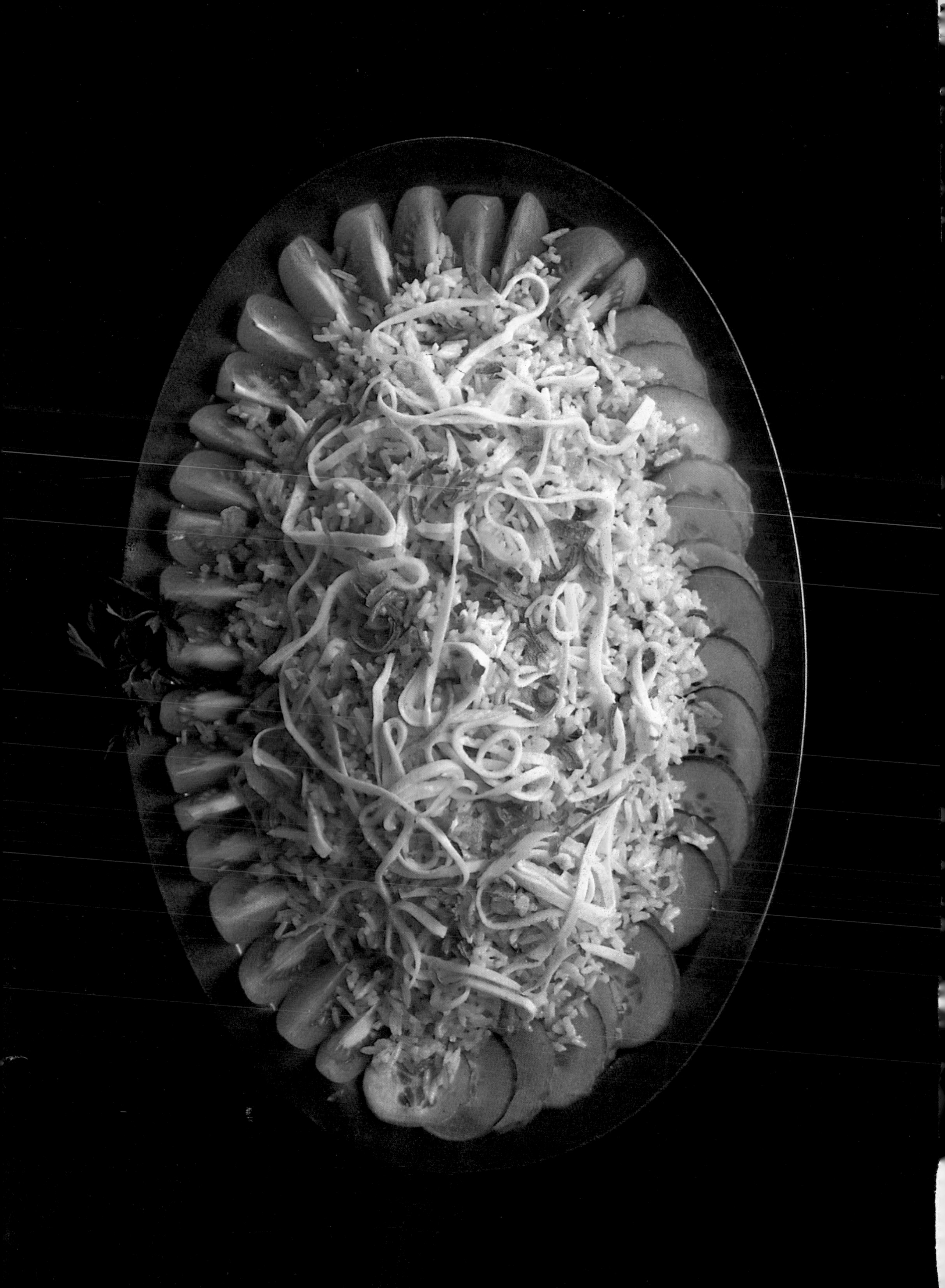

Noodles with a chilli sauce

CHINESE

INGREDIENTS

50g (2oz) Sichuan preserved vegetable
150g (5oz) vegetarian 'ham'
100g (4oz) cucumber
75g (3oz) bamboo shoots
75g (3oz) carrot
45ml (3 tablespoons) oil

SEASONING SAUCE

15ml (1 tablespoon) chilli-bean sauce (halve quantity for a milder dish)
30ml (2 tablespoons) barbecue sauce
10ml (2 teaspoons) soy sauce
6 spring onions, finely chopped
5ml (1 teaspoon) sugar
150ml (⅔ cup, 5fl oz) water

500g (1lb) noodles
15ml (1 tablespoon) sesame oil

PREPARATION

Rinse the Sichuan preserved vegetable and cut into 1-cm (½-inch) dice. Cut the vegetarian 'ham', cucumber, bamboo shoots and carrot into similar-sized dice. Par-boil the carrot for 3 minutes, then drain well. Heat the oil in a wok or saucepan and add the seasoning sauce over a low heat. Then add the vegetables and boil gently for 2 minutes. Meanwhile, bring a large pan of water to the boil and cook the noodles until just soft. Drain well, toss in the sesame oil and divide between four heated plates. Spoon a quarter of the vegetables and sauce on top of each helping and serve at once.

Kitsune noodles

JAPANESE

INGREDIENTS

2 sheets aburage *or 6 squares fried beancurd*

SIMMERING STOCK

100ml (½ cup, 4fl oz) dashi
15ml (1 tablespoon) caster sugar
15ml (1 tablespoon) Japanese soy sauce

SOUP STOCK

1½ litres (6 cups, 1¾ pints) dashi
60ml (4 tablespoons) Japanese soy sauce
20ml (4 teaspoons) caster sugar
10ml (2 teaspoons) sake

salt to taste
450g (1lb) soba *noodles*
50g (2oz) spring onions, finely chopped

PREPARATION

Pour boiling water over the *aburage* or fried beancurd to remove any oiliness. Cut into halves and cook gently in the simmering stock for about 10 minutes. Meanwhile, bring the soup stock to the boil and cook the *soba* as directed on page 159. Divide the noodles between four large heated bowls and put the *aburage* strips on top. Pour over the boiling soup stock and garnish with the finely chopped spring onions. Serve at once.

OPPOSITE PAGE 160 *Cucumber and dried mushroom salad (page 174), a simple Japanese salad of sliced cucumber and dried mushrooms in a fresh sesame sauce served in a red lacquer bowl according to the traditional style of the Daitokuji temple near Kyoto.*

OPPOSITE THIS PAGE Nasi goreng *(page 157), the famous Indonesian fried rice dish, seasoned with onion and chillis and garnished with egg shreds, onion flakes, slices of tomato and cucumber.*

Vegetarian temple noodles

CHINESE

This recipe comes from the Buddhist temple at Quanzhou in southern Fujian and rejoices in the name 'purple clouds with three fairies'.

INGREDIENTS

250g (8oz) soya beansprouts
8 dried mushrooms
50g (2oz) choisam *or spinach or watercress*
3 slices ginger
25g (1oz) celery
500g (1lb) plain noodles
45ml (3 tablespoons) peanut oil
25ml (1½ tablespoons) light soy sauce
200ml (1 cup, ⅓ pint) stock

PREPARATION

Wash the beansprouts and take off the roots. Soak the dried mushrooms in warm water for 30 minutes, then discard the hard stalks and cut the caps into thin slices. Wash and cut the *choisam*, or green vegetable, into 3-cm (1-inch) lengths. Shred the ginger and celery finely. Put the noodles into boiling water for 3 minutes, then lift them out, drain and toss in 15ml (1 tablespoon) peanut oil. Heat the remaining 30ml (2 tablespoons) oil in a wok or saucepan. Put in the ginger shreds and sliced mushrooms and stir-fry for 15 seconds. Add the *choisam*, cook for 30 seconds, then add the soy sauce and stock. Bring to the boil. Add the beansprouts and cook for 1 minute. Then add the noodles, mix well and serve on four warmed plates sprinkled with the chopped celery.

STEAMED BREADS

In China and Korea freshly cooked warm bread buns are eaten with main meals in place of either rice or noodles. These buns are particularly good with dishes which have plenty of gravy. The buns must be eaten hot, straight from the steamer, or they become heavy and sad. The recipe given below for open-flower buns is a Cantonese version of a rather sweet bread bun which is common in western China, and is particularly useful because the buns can be made very quickly.

Open-flower buns

CHINESE

INGREDIENTS

35g (1½ oz) white fat
360g (13oz) plain flour
120g (4½ oz) caster sugar
20ml (4 teaspoons) baking powder
225ml (8 fl oz) warm milk
flour for dusting

PREPARATION

Have 16 small squares of non-stick parchment and a pan of boiling water ready for steaming the buns before mixing the dough. Rub the fat into the flour and mix in the sugar and baking powder. Pour in the warm milk and mix well into a sticky dough. Dust your hands with the dry flour and shape the dough into a sausage. Cut into 16 equal portions. Roll each portion into a ball and stand them on the parchment squares in a steamer without allowing them to touch. Slash a cross on the top of each bun and steam for 25 minutes over a high heat. Serve hot.

These buns can be deep-frozen after cooking, then re-steamed straight from the freezer for 10 minutes.

Steamed vegetarian jiaozi

CHINESE

Jiaozi are a robust 'people's food' in northern China, eaten not only for snacks but also for whole main meals. Some Chinese have formidable appetites when it comes to *jiaozi*, eating up to 80 or 100 at one sitting. The *jiaozi* houses of northern China correspond to the fish and chip shops of Britain, and *jaozi* have much the same status there as fish and chips in the food of the UK.

Most *jiaozi* are boiled and are bought by weight. However, the recipe that follows is for steamed *jiaozi*, which are a little more delicate. Their advantage is that they can be frozen after the skins are filled (before they are cooked), unlike boiled *jiaozi* skins, and then steamed straight from the freezer when required. Leftover steamed *jiaozi* can be re-heated by being deep-fried.

INGREDIENTS

JIAOZI SKINS

12 g (½ oz) white fat
100 g (3½ oz) plain flour
100 g (3½ oz) strong flour
100–120 ml (3½–4 fl oz) boiling water

FILLING

300 g (10 oz) Chinese broccoli
4 dried mushrooms
15 g (½ oz) silk noodles
2 eggs
30 ml (2 tablespoons) sesame oil
30 ml (2 tablespoons) vegetable oil
30 ml (2 tablespoons) soy sauce
2.5 ml (½ teaspoon) salt

DIPPING SAUCE

60 ml (4 tablespoons) light soy sauce
20 ml (4 teaspoons) rice vinegar
20 ml (4 teaspoons) sesame oil
10 ml (2 teaspoons) chilli-bean paste (double the quantity for a hotter dip)

PREPARATION

Rub the fat into the flours, then mix in the boiling water. Knead to a smooth dough. Cover with clingwrap and leave for 2 hours.

Meanwhile make the filling. Wash and blanch the broccoli in boiling water for 3 minutes. Then rinse under cold water, drain and chop finely. Squeeze the chopped greens dry in a cloth. Soak the mushrooms in warm water for 30 minutes, discard the hard stalks and chop the caps finely. Soak the silk noodles in warm water for 10 minutes, drain well and chop into ½-cm (¼-inch) lengths. Beat the eggs with 5 ml (1 teaspoon) sesame oil. Heat the vegetable oil in a pan and scramble the eggs. Turn out when just set and leave to cool. Mix the vegetables, silk noodles and egg together and season with soy sauce, salt and the remaining sesame oil.

After the dough has rested, roll out on a floured board into a cylinder and cut into 40 slices. Roll each slice into a slightly domed round about 7 cm (2¾ inches) in diameter with the centre thicker than the edges. Put about 25 ml (1½ tablespoons) of the filling on the centre of one skin. Fold up the skin into a half-moon shape so that the edges meet. Pinch in the centre of the half-moon to seal, then pleat the side of the skin nearest you about three times towards the right and seal this pleated edge against the lower edge. Then pleat the left-hand edge about 3 times and seal that against the left-hand edge furthest from you, to form the shape of a tiny Cornish pasty. Repeat with the remaining skins. Stand the *jiaozi* on a damp cloth in a steamer, without allowing them to touch. Steam over a high heat for 20 minutes and serve immediately with the dipping sauce.

Korean filling for steamed jiaozi

This *jiaozi* filling dates from the sixteenth century before there were any chillis in Korea. At that time vinegar was one of the most important seasonings for Korean foods. Use this recipe with the *jiaozi* skins described above.

INGREDIENTS

2 dried mushrooms
15 ml (1 tablespoon) black fungus
100 g (4 oz) cucumber
25 g (1 oz) straw mushrooms
25 g (1 oz) pine kernels
2.5 ml (½ teaspoon) salt
15 ml (1 tablespoon) rice wine
pinch sugar
45 ml (3 tablespoons) sesame oil

DIPPING SAUCE

45 ml (3 tablespoons) red vinegar
45 ml (3 tablespoons) Japanese soy sauce

PREPARATION

Soak the dried mushrooms and black fungus separately in warm water for 30 minutes. Discard the hard mushroom stalks and cut the caps into very fine slices. Rinse the black fungus and discard any hard bits, cut into fine shreds. Cut the cucumber and straw mushrooms into fine shreds. Mix with the remaining ingredients, except the sesame oil. Fill the *jiaozi* skins as directed above and steam for 20 minutes. Then paint each *jiaozi* with the sesame oil and serve hot with the dipping sauce.

Mantou (steamed bread buns)

CHINESE

INGREDIENTS

7.5 ml (1½ teaspoons) dried yeast
450 ml (1⅞ cups, 14 fl oz) warm water
5 ml (1 teaspoon) sugar
750 g (5 cups, 1½ lb) strong flour
2.5 ml (½ teaspoon) salt

PREPARATION

Put the yeast, water and sugar in a bowl in a warm place and leave until foaming. Put the flour and salt in a large bowl and make a well in the middle. Pour in the yeast mixture and work into a smooth dough. Lift out of the bowl and knead well. Return the dough to the bowl, cover with a plastic sheet and leave to rise in a warm place. When doubled in size, roll into a cylinder about 4 cm (1½ inches) in diameter and cut into 16 equal slices, each about 5 cm (2 inches) wide. Put the slices on to squares of non-stick parchment and leave to prove in a warm place for 30 minutes. Have ready a pan of boiling water, arrange the bread buns in the trays of a steamer without touching and steam for 20 minutes over fast-boiling water. Remove the paper bases as soon as the buns are cooked and serve hot.

These buns can be deep-frozen after cooking, then re-heated in a steamer for about 7 minutes straight from the freezer.

12

Temple Cooking

The highest form of vegetarian cooking in the Far East is temple cooking, developed by the Buddhists centuries ago and still highly influential. The reasons for this lie deep in the past of China and Japan, the countries with which temple cooking is most closely associated.

VEGETARIANISM IN CHINA

Vegetarianism was not a new concept in China when the teachings of Buddha arrived there from India at about the time of Christ: at least 500 years earlier filial duty had decreed that people should abstain from eating meat after the death of a close relative, and special vegetarian dishes were prepared for mourning periods in the family (vegetarian mourning dishes are still served in Japan today).

According to one story about the arrival of Buddhism in China, the then Emperor of China dreamt for several nights running of a man dressed in gold holding a bow and arrows and pointing to the West. Eventually the Emperor sent an embassy to India. On the way the ambassadors met two men bringing Buddhist scriptures and images on a white horse. The ambassadors escorted these men back to the court at Loyang, where they were given a temple to live in which was called the White Horse monastery.

Buddhism spread widely in China among both rich and poor during the first centuries after Christ, although meat-eating was never completely abandoned by the rich. The poor in China, on the other hand, had little choice but to follow a diet of grain and vegetables, so Buddhism demanded little sacrifice from them.

By the eighth century Buddhist monasteries were commonly founded by groups of tradesmen – even butchers. The Emperor decreed that such monasteries must keep open house for travellers, and the monasteries, on their own initiative but partly to attract fresh benefactors, developed a style of vegetarian cooking which equalled – even surpassed – ordinary restaurant food in quality. This was 'temple' cooking.

The two cornerstones of temple cooking were beancurd and gluten. Beancurd, derived from soya beans, had been discovered in about AD 300. This extraordinarily versatile high-protein food was the basis for many new sophisticated vegetarian dishes, while gluten – the protein from wheat flour – was discovered in about 1200, adding yet another ingredient to the range of vegetarian foods. By the twelfth century a wide range of vegetarian snacks and other dishes was on sale in the vegetarian restaurants specializing in temple cooking.

At this time Buddhism and the dietary restraints associated with it were very fashionable among the upper classes in China. Temple cooking became so skilled that mock meats, closely resembling what they imitated in texture, appearance and taste, were made, usually with beancurd – particularly beancurd skin. Flavouring was generally very light, with no onions, garlic, leeks or coriander, but a strong dependence upon pickled vegetables, especially Sichuan pickled vegetable, mushrooms, fungi and soya-bean products such as soy sauce. Monosodium glutamate was another produce of soya beans which became a traditional Chinese flavouring and was widely used by temple cooks. It is interesting to note that in an old-fashioned Buddhist cookbook written in the 1950s no onions are included in any dish but coriander is mentioned as a possible garnish on several occasions.

In fact most Chinese cooks at all levels used relatively little seasoning until after the Second World War – partly, no doubt, from motives of economy. But since the 1950s there has been a noticeable upturn in seasoning levels in Chinese food, which has sharpened the distinction between traditional vegetarian food, now considered very old-fashioned in style, and modern cookery.

Since the Liberation in 1949 cookery books in China have tended to feature meatless rather than specifically Buddhist recipes. Generally the policy has been to encourage non-meat-eating in this vast land where meat is perpetually scarce. During the earlier decades of the twentieth century meat-eating, even by well-to-do Chinese families, was considered an unnecessary extravagance, and it was not customary to serve meat at home unless there were visitors or it was a special occasion. Nowadays, with the new prosperity in China, many families may buy a chicken once a week in the free market in addition to their ration of pork, while in Hong Kong people eat meat at every meal, often in greater quantities than would be usual in the West.

However, nowadays in Hong Kong and Taiwan it has become very fashionable to visit temples and eat the traditional vegetarian foods served there. Obviously the scale of such meals varies with the size of the diner's purse. In every culture a meal served for a special dinner, the underlying purpose of which may be to impress or placate, is worlds away from an ordinary family meal. The difference is not just a matter of scale. Usually at a formal dinner the dishes are made from expensive ingredients or require elaborate preparation and skilled cooking. The Chinese have a vast range of dishes that are generally reserved for formal meals. Below we provide instructions for a modified version of a Buddhist temple meal which it is possible to prepare and cook at home, if you so wish. Of course, any of the recipes can be used as part of a less ambitious meal.

Chinese temple meal

Serves 8

☐ Cold-meat plate, served as a starter

Four quickly cooked dishes, brought to the table together:
☐ Dry-fried bamboo and red-in-snow
☐ Braised quail eggs and straw mushrooms
☐ Fried vegetarian abalone
☐ Braised mushrooms and vegetables

Three big dishes, each served separately:
☐ Vegetarian 'shark's-fin' soup
☐ 'Big pot' or casserole, e.g. Buddha leaps over the wall
☐ Whole-fish dish, e.g. sweet and sour vegetarian 'fish'

Another soup, to clear the palate, e.g. sea tangle soup (page 150, using double quantities for 8) or snow soup with fresh mushrooms (page 152)

During the meal you may if you wish serve plain boiled rice or steamed Chinese bread (*mantou*), or finish with a bowl of fried rice (page 157) for anyone who is still hungry.

Cold-meat plate

Serves 8

INGREDIENTS

100g (4oz) vegetarian 'ham' (page 100)
100g (4oz) vegetarian 'chicken' (page 101)
100g (4oz) smoked vegetarian 'goose' (page 102)
8 squares fried beancurd
steamed black mushrooms (page 108)
5g (¼oz) black hair fungus

SEASONING SAUCE

5ml (1 teaspoon) light soy sauce
5ml (1 teaspoon) rice vinegar
2.5ml (½ teaspoon) sesame oil

cold stuffed egg roll (pages 122–3)
100g (4oz) cucumber

PREPARATION

Slice the prepared vegetarian meats and beancurd. Soak the black hair fungus in simmering but not boiling water for 3 minutes. Drain well and reserve the water. Tease out the threads of the black fungus so that they separate easily when served. Mix the seasoning sauce with 45ml (3 tablespoons) of the reserved water and return the black fungus to the sauce to marinate until required.

Before serving, lift out and drain. Cut the egg rolls into slices. Shape the cucumber into fans. Arrange the meat, beancurd and egg slices decoratively on a plate together with the black hair fungus and mushrooms. Garnish with the cucumber fans.

Dry-fried bamboo and red-in-snow

Serves 8

INGREDIENTS

75g (3oz) canned red-in-snow
350g (12oz) bamboo shoots
200ml (1 cup, 7fl oz) sesame oil
200ml (1 cup, 7fl oz) vegetable oil
salt and pepper

PREPARATION

Soak the red-in-snow in cold water for 5 minutes to remove some of its saltiness. Then drain well and pat very dry in a cloth. Cut the bamboo shoots into small slices. Heat the sesame and vegetable oils together in a deep-frying pan and when moderately hot deep-fry the red-in-snow until golden brown (this could take up to 10 minutes). Lift out the red-in-snow and drain. Allow the oil to cool, then return the pan to the heat and deep-fry the bamboo shoots for 5 minutes until golden brown. Lift out and drain. Using a clean wok or frying-pan without any oil, stir-fry the bamboo shoots and red-in-snow with a pinch of salt and pepper until heated through. Serve at once. Take care not to over-salt this dish: red-in-snow is itself salty.

Braised quail eggs and straw mushrooms

Serves 8

INGREDIENTS

24 fresh quail eggs
oil for deep frying

SEASONING SAUCE

- *7.5 ml (1 $\frac{1}{2}$ teaspoons) cornflour*
- *30 ml (2 tablespoons) soy sauce*
- *2.5 ml ($\frac{1}{2}$ teaspoon) sugar*
- *15 ml (1 tablespoon) rice wine*
- *100 ml ($\frac{1}{2}$ cup, 4 fl oz) stock*
- *salt and pepper to taste*

250 g (8 oz) choisam
2.5 ml ($\frac{1}{2}$ teaspoon) salt
1 can straw mushrooms

PREPARATION

Boil the eggs for 2 minutes, then cool quickly by dipping in cold water before shelling. Heat the oil until moderately hot in a deep-fat pan and deep-fry the eggs until golden brown. Lift out and drain well. Mix the seasoning sauce. Wash the *choisam* and cut into 6-cm (2$\frac{1}{2}$-inch) lengths. Add the salt and 5 ml (1 teaspoon) oil to a pan of boiling water and blanch the *choisam* in this for 2 minutes. Then drain well, arrange round the edge of a heated serving plate and keep warm. Heat a wok or large frying-pan with 30 ml (2 tablespoons) oil and stir-fry the straw mushrooms for a few seconds. Add the eggs and the seasoning sauce. Bring to the boil and check the seasoning. Spoon the eggs and mushrooms into the centre of the serving dish and pour over the sauce. Serve hot.

NOTE You can use 12 size 1 hen's eggs, which are about double the size of quail's eggs, instead of 24 quail eggs.

Fried vegetarian abalone

Serves 8

INGREDIENTS

8 large dried mushrooms
150 g (5 oz) large yam
2.5 ml ($\frac{1}{2}$ teaspoon) salt
25 g (1 oz) water chestnuts
50 g (2 oz) celery
2.5 ml ($\frac{1}{2}$ teaspoon) salt
pinch sugar
pinch five-spice powder
5 ml (1 teaspoon) rice wine
45 ml (3 tablespoons) plain flour plus some for dusting mushrooms
25 g (1 oz) slivered almonds
oil for deep frying

PREPARATION

Soak the dried mushrooms in hot water for about 1 hour, then discard the hard stalks and drain the caps. Peel the yam and soak in salted water for 30 minutes. Transfer to a saucepan with just sufficient fresh water to cover and bring to the boil. Cover the pan and simmer until the yam is soft (about 20 minutes). Drain and cool. Meanwhile chop the water chestnuts and celery into minute pieces. Mash the yam in a food processor, or with a potato masher, and beat in the water chestnuts, celery and seasonings of salt, sugar, five-spice powder and rice wine. Dust the insides of the drained mushroom caps with a little flour and put 15 ml (1 tablespoon) of the yam stuffing into each. Coat each mushroom and its filling in the flour, then stick the almond flakes all over the yam filling. Heat the oil until very hot and deep-fry the mushrooms over a high heat until golden brown. Serve at once.

Braised mushrooms and vegetables

Serves 8

INGREDIENTS

4 dried mushrooms

SIMMERING STOCK FOR DRIED MUSHROOMS

5 ml (1 teaspoon) light soy sauce
5 ml (1 teaspoon) sugar
1.5 ml (¼ teaspoon) sesame oil

15 g (½ oz) silver wood ears

SIMMERING STOCK FOR WOOD EARS

200 ml (1 cup, 7 fl oz) stock
5 ml (1 teaspoon) sugar
5 ml (1 teaspoon) rice wine
pinch salt

25 ml (1½ tablespoons) black fungus

SIMMERING STOCK FOR BLACK FUNGUS

200 ml (1 cup, 7 fl oz) well-seasoned stock

25 g (1 oz) carrot

SIMMERING STOCK FOR CARROT

150 ml (¾ cup, 5 fl oz) stock
5 ml (1 teaspoon) sugar
5 ml (1 teaspoon) rice wine
pinch salt

25 g (1 oz) bamboo shoots
15 g (½ oz) preserved needle mushrooms
2 preserved oyster mushrooms
8 straw mushrooms
5 water chestnuts
2 squares fried beancurd

SIMMERING STOCK FOR BEANCURD

100 ml (½ cup, 4 fl oz) stock
5 ml (1 teaspoon) light soy sauce
5 ml (1 teaspoon) rice wine

75 g (3 oz) broccoli
150 g (¾ cup, 5 fl oz) well-seasoned stock
4 baby corn cobs
60 ml (4 tablespoons) oil
pinch salt and sugar
10 ml (2 teaspoons) sesame oil

PREPARATION

Soak the dried mushrooms in warm water for 30 minutes, then discard the hard stalks and cut the caps into quarters. Simmer the caps gently in the prepared stock for 5 minutes. Drain before using.

Soak the silver wood ears in warm water for 20 minutes, then rinse thoroughly and discard any hard or discoloured bits. Tear into separate leaves. Simmer in the prepared stock for 15 minutes, then leave in the stock until required.

Soak the black fungus in warm water for 20 minutes, then rinse carefully and discard any hard bits. If any piece is very big, cut it in half. Simmer in the prepared stock for 10 minutes, then leave until required.

Peel the carrot and cut into flower-shaped slices (see illustration on page 39). Simmer in the prepared stock for 7 minutes, or until just soft. Drain.

Cut the bamboo shoots into flat slices. Pour boiling water over the needle mushrooms and leave to drain. Rinse the oyster mushrooms and cut into quarters. Cut each water chestnut into 3 round slices. Simmer the fried beancurd for about 3 minutes in the prepared stock, then drain and cut into slices. Wash and tear the broccoli into small florets, discarding any long stalks. Poach in 150 ml (¾ cup, 5 fl oz) stock for 3 minutes, then drain. Cut each baby corn cob into half. (All this preparation can be done well in advance of the meal.)

Just before serving, heat the oil in a wok or large frying-pan and add all the prepared vegetables and mushrooms except the needle mushrooms. Stir-fry for 20 seconds over a high heat, season with a pinch of salt, sugar and the sesame oil and serve at once garnished with the needle mushrooms.

Vegetarian 'shark's-fin' soup

Serves 8

INGREDIENTS

20 g ($\frac{3}{4}$ oz) silk noodles
5 dried mushrooms
40 g ($1\frac{1}{2}$ oz) bamboo shoots
15 g ($\frac{1}{2}$ oz) Sichuan preserved vegetable
50 g (2 oz) Chinese leaves
1 sheet dried beancurd skin
oil for deep frying
1200 ml (5 cups, 2 pints) vegetarian stock
15 ml (1 tablespoon) cornflour mixed with 30 ml (2 tablespoons) water
7.5 ml ($1\frac{1}{2}$ teaspoons) soy sauce
salt and sugar to taste
red vinegar

PREPARATION

Cut the silk noodles into 3-cm (1-inch) lengths with a sharp pair of scissors and soak in warm water for 10 minutes. Soak the dried mushrooms in hot water for 30 minutes, then discard the hard stalks and cut the caps into thin slices. Cut the bamboo shoots and Sichuan preserved vegetable into matchsticks. Slice the Chinese leaves finely. Deep-fry the dried beancurd skin over a moderate heat until crisp (about 30 seconds), then drain and crumble. Stir-fry the mushrooms, bamboo shoots, Sichuan vegetable and Chinese leaves together in 15 ml (1 tablespoon) oil for about 15 seconds. Tip in the stock and drained silk noodles. Bring to the boil and add the crumbled beancurd skin. Thicken the soup with the cornflour paste and adjust the seasoning. Serve with small bowls of red vinegar at the side for the diners to add as they choose.

Buddha leaps over the wall

Serves 8

INGREDIENTS

4 dried mushrooms

MARINADE

10 ml (2 teaspoons) soy sauce
5 ml (1 teaspoon) sugar
2.5 ml ($\frac{1}{2}$ teaspoon) sesame oil
pinch five-spice powder

30 ml (2 tablespoons) cornflour
oil for deep frying
50 g (2 oz) raw gluten made with strong flour
75 g (3 oz) yam
10 g ($\frac{1}{2}$ oz) dried melon strips (Chinese variety)
100 g (4 oz) vegetarian 'chicken'
100 g (4 oz) beancurd
50 g (2 oz) pickled mustard greens
25 g (1 oz) bamboo shoots
12 straw mushrooms
600 ml ($2\frac{1}{2}$ cups, 1 pint) stock
10 ml (2 teaspoons) light soy sauce
5 ml (1 teaspoon) sugar
2.5 ml ($\frac{1}{2}$ teaspoon) salt
10 ml (2 teaspoons) sesame oil
freshly ground black pepper

PREPARATION

Soak the dried mushrooms in warm water for 30 minutes, then discard the hard stalks and pat the caps dry. Marinate for 10 minutes, then drain and coat the mushroom caps in cornflour. Deep-fry in hot oil until golden brown. Drain well. Shape the gluten into round balls about 2 cm ($\frac{1}{2}$ inch) in diameter. Drop into the hot oil and deep-fry until puffed up. Lift out and drain. Peel the yam and cut into wedge-shaped pieces. Deep-fry for 5 minutes, then drain and steam over a high heat for 10 minutes. Soak the dried melon strips in boiling water for 5 minutes, then cut into 3-cm (1-inch) lengths. Cut the vegetarian 'chicken' into $1\frac{1}{2}$-cm ($\frac{1}{2}$-inch)-thick slices. Cut the beancurd into $1\frac{1}{2}$-cm ($\frac{1}{2}$-inch) cubes. Rinse and drain the pickled mustard greens. Slice it and the bamboo shoots finely.

When all the vegetables are prepared arrange the pieces of yam in the bottom of an earthenware casserole or Chinese sand-pot. Then add the remaining vegetables and pour over the stock. Cover with the lid, put into a steamer and steam for 1 hour over a moderate heat. Season the stock with the sugar, soy sauce, salt, sesame oil and pepper to taste. Serve very hot.

Sweet and sour vegetarian 'fish'

This dish is difficult to make look convincing, mainly on account of the quality of dried beancurd available in the West. Dried beancurd is very brittle: it breaks and cracks easily. Unfortunately many of the sheets on sale in the West are badly cracked at the time of purchase and the tears cannot be repaired. However, the dish tastes very good. (If you wish to practise handling beancurd skin, a simpler version of this dish appears on page 102.

The 'fish' is easier to eat cut into slices. If your finished shape is not recognizably fish-like, slice it before serving. If the shape is good, take a sharp knife to the table and cut it after your guests have seen the complete 'fish'.

Serves 8

INGREDIENTS

15 ml (1 tablespoon) wood ears
50 g (2 oz) konnyaku *or 25 g (1 oz) pine kernels*
25 g (1 oz) carrot
pinch salt and sugar
450 g (1 lb) potatoes
2 sheets dried beancurd skin without holes
75 ml (5 tablespoons) cornflour mixed with 75 ml (5 tablespoons) water

VEGETABLES FOR THE SAUCE

2 dried mushrooms
25 g (1 oz) bamboo shoots
25 g (1 oz) green pepper, de-seeded
25 g (1 oz) carrot

SAUCE

75 ml (5 tablespoons) sugar
75 ml (5 tablespoons) rice vinegar
15 ml (1 tablespoon) tomato paste
5 ml (1 teaspoon) salt
15 ml (1 tablespoon) potato flour
75 ml (5 tablespoons) water

SEASONING FOR MASHED POTATOES

15 ml (1 tablespoon) soy sauce
15 ml (1 tablespoon) sesame oil
pinch salt and pepper
2 green peas (optional)
oil for deep frying

PREPARATION

Soak the wood ears in warm water for 20 minutes, then rinse and discard any hard bits. Chop finely. If using *konnyaku*, blanch in boiling water for 3 minutes, then dry in a dry pan over a low heat. Chop finely. If using pine kernels, deep-fry until golden brown, then drain and chop. Scrape and boil the carrot with a pinch of salt and sugar until soft (about 10 minutes). Drain and chop finely. Wash and boil the potatoes in their skins until cooked. Soak the beancurd sheets in warm water in a flat dish for about 6 minutes, until soft. Pat dry very gently and trim away any hard edges. Mix the cornflour paste.

To make the sauce, soak the dried mushrooms in warm water for 30 minutes, then discard the hard stalks and slice the caps finely. Reserve the soaking water. Cut the bamboo shoots, green pepper and carrot into thin matchsticks. Mix the sauce ingredients in a small bowl.

When the potatoes are cooked, peel and mash well – in a food processor if available. If they are very dry add a little of the mushroom soaking water. Beat in the *konnyaku*, or pine kernels, wood ears and carrot and season with the soy sauce, sesame oil, salt and pepper. Lay out one sheet of the softened beancurd and paint all over with the cornflour paste. Place the potato mixture lengthwise down the centre of the beancurd skin and mould into the shape of a fish. Fold over the edges of the beancurd skin to cover all the potato, and press into the fish-shape against the filling. Lay out the other beancurd skin and paint with the cornflour paste. Place on top of the 'fish', covering the join of the first sheet of beancurd. Press again into the shape of a fish, and seal carefully underneath. Press in the two green peas for eyes.

Heat 15 ml (1 tablespoon) oil in a wok or large frying-pan and stir-fry the sauce vegetables for a few minutes. Pour in the seasoning sauce and bring to the boil. Lift from the heat and put on one side. Heat a pan of oil for deep-frying until moderately hot (160°C, 325°F) and deep-fry the 'fish' until golden brown (about 5 minutes). Lift out and drain for a few minutes before placing on a heated serving plate. Return the sauce to the boil and spoon over the 'fish'. Serve at once.

JAPANESE VEGETARIAN COOKING

Buddhism came to Japan from China and Korea during the seventh century. An Imperial edict of that time forbade the eating of any meat except by the sick. However, less than a hundred years later chicken and fish were both exempted from this rule, together with deer – called 'mountain whales' to excuse their slaughter by an aristocracy unwilling to give up hunting. A stricter interpretation of Buddhist law came in the twelfth century with the spread of Zen Buddhism in Japan. The Zen Buddhists re-introduced a rigid vegetarian diet, not wholly successfully. None the less, Japan's vegetarian tradition has remained remarkably strong at all levels until the present century. The aversion to killing four-legged animals for food – particularly cattle – remained prevalent among the Japanese until the mid-nineteenth century, when a visitor was told: 'The Japanese do not eat cows. The cows do their duty; they bear calves, they give milk. It is sinful to take it. The cows require it to raise their calves, and because of this they are not allowed to work. The bulls do their work; they labour at the plough, they get thin, you cannot eat them. It is not just to kill a beast that does its duty.'

Until the middle of the last century the leatherworkers, who handled dead animals and were also the executioners, were a serf caste in Japan. Their occupation and status were hereditary: they were not allowed to conceal their origins and they were forbidden to live with others not of their caste. When the strict vegetarian laws were abolished in Japan in about 1850, these people became the butchers, handling and selling meat as a closed-caste profession. It was not until almost a century later that all caste distinctions were removed from Japanese society. Even today in Japan there is resistance, particularly by older people, to eating red meat other than occasionally; they consider it unhealthy and prefer to eat fish or chicken.

The Zen Buddhists also laid down rules governing the preparation and cooking of foods, their colour and flavouring, and the seasons at which they might be eaten. They decreed that every meal should include the five flavours – bitter (soy sauce), salty (salt), sweet (sugar), hot (ginger or chilli) and sour (vinegar) – together with the five colours – red, green, yellow, black and white – and the five methods of preparing foods – raw, simmered, grilled, fried and steamed. The tea-ceremony cuisine based on these rules, which developed in the temples at that time, is still profoundly influential in both *haute cuisine* and domestic cookery in Japan today.

The tea ceremony combines ritual with calm surroundings to promote inner peace and tranquillity among the participants. The two main styles of tea-ceremony cooking are Daitokuji, developed in the fourteenth century at the Daitokuji temple near Kyoto, and Fucharyori, developed in the sixteenth century at the Obakusan temple near Tokyo. Both of these were intended specifically to accompany, and to extend the existing ritual of, the tea ceremony, and they are believed by many to be the foundation of Japanese national cuisine. However, they do differ in certain respects. While the Daitokuji style is distinguished by its individual servings in an elaborate place-setting, the Fucharyori style was based almost entirely on contemporary Chinese vegetarian cookery, and retained the Chinese practice of serving all the foods in big dishes in the centre of the table from which the diners would help themselves. This style of meal is still served at the

Obakusan shrine after an important ceremony or thanksgiving. The dishes are brought to the table in courses, one after the other. They are still known by their Chinese names and many of them are typical of the style of cooking still prevalent in eastern China today.

The tea ceremony is governed by very detailed regulations not only for the preparation of the food but for its presentation, serving and even its eating. For example, beautiful lacquer bowls are very important to the atmosphere of a Daitokuji meal (see photograph opposite page 160).

The Japanese today still hold the mastery of these regulations in high regard; indeed, some people spend years perfecting the art. Although, therefore, it would be impossible to explain in the context of this book exactly how the rituals are carried out we have reproduced below typical Daitokuji and Fucharyori menus with recipes for the dishes listed. Each dish will serve four, and any of them can be served separately, of course, at a less formal meal.

A Daitokuji meal

Serves 4
(All but the soup are served together, in the positions around the diner indicated in the diagram.)

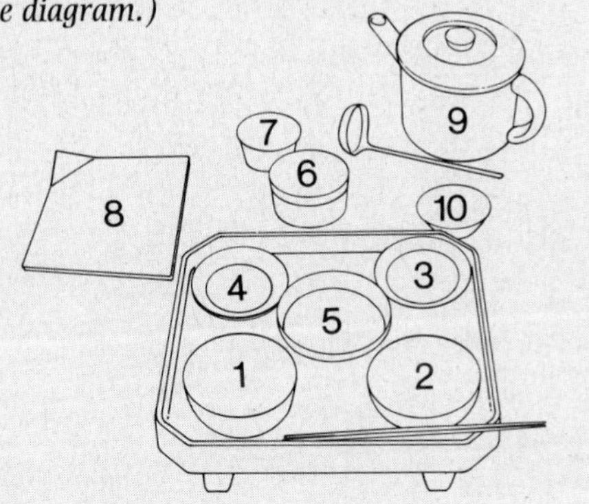

☐ Rice (bowl no. 1) (page 154)
☐ White radish and *wakame* soup with *miso* (bowl no. 2)
☐ Cucumber and dried mushroom salad (bowl no. 3)

☐ *Seven foods, mainly grilled and simmered* (served together in one bowl: no. 4), including stir-fried gluten balls, beancurd cake, grilled beancurd skin, simmered mushrooms, simmered yams, simmered fried aubergines, and pickled ginger

☐ *Aburage* rolls (bowl no. 5)
☐ Sesame *tofu* (bowl no. 6)
☐ Clear soup with green grapes (bowl no. 7)
☐ Fried 'nibbles' (bowl no. 8) including sweet walnuts, pieces of *konbu* and green chillis
☐ Pickles (bowl no. 10), e.g. pickled perilla seeds or other bought pickle
☐ Rice soup (no. 9)

A Fucharyori meal

Serves 4
(Serve each dish as a separate course.)

☐ Green tea and a sweet cake, served in the tea-ceremony manner
☐ Cold *hors d'oeuvre* plate
☐ Clear soup, with beancurd and ginko nuts
☐ *Seven simmered foods*, including *hirouzu* (beancurd balls), simmered aubergines, *aburage* rolls, simmered mushrooms, simmered bamboo shoots, simmered lotus root, marinated chillis, garnish of ginko nuts and pine-needles, and pickles
☐ Steamed dish or sesame *tofu* (page 177)
☐ Braised mixed vegetables
☐ *Tempura* (deep-fried fish)
☐ Chrysanthemum leaves with a walnut dressing (salad)
☐ Lohan's delight (vegetable stew)
☐ Fruit
☐ Tea rice

White radish and wakame soup with miso

INGREDIENTS

10g (⅓oz) dried wakame
75g (3oz) white radish
40g (1½oz) carrot
900ml (3¾ cups, 1½ pints) dashi
60ml (4 tablespoons) miso

PREPARATION

Rinse the *wakame* and soak in cold water for 5 minutes before removing the hard rim and cutting the fronds into 4-cm (1½-inch) diamonds. Peel and cut the white radish into matchsticks. Peel the carrot and cut into similar-sized pieces. Bring the *dashi* to the boil, reserving 100ml (½ cup, 3½ fl oz) to mix with the *miso*. Cook the white radish and carrot in the *dashi* for about 5 minutes. Blend the *miso* into the reserved *dashi* and mix into the soup. Add the *wakame* and immediately lift from the heat. Serve in four heated soup bowls.

Cucumber and dried mushroom salad

INGREDIENTS

4 dried mushrooms

SIMMERING STOCK

100ml (½ cup, 3½ fl oz) dashi
7.5ml (1½ teaspoons) caster sugar
5ml (1 teaspoon) sake
2.5ml (½ teaspoon) Japanese soy sauce

1 small cucumber
15ml (1 tablespoon) salt
75ml (5 tablespoons) toasted sesame seeds (page 36)
7.5ml (1½ teaspoons) Japanese soy sauce
7.5ml (1½ teaspoons) caster sugar

PREPARATION

Soak the dried mushrooms in warm water for 30 minutes, then discard the hard stalks and cook the caps in the simmering stock until the liquid has almost gone. Pat the caps dry and slice finely. Cut the cucumber in half lengthwise and discard all the seeds. Slice very finely and sprinkle with the salt. Leave to marinate for 20 minutes, then rinse well and squeeze dry. Crush the freshly toasted sesame seeds with a rolling-pin on a flat surface into a smooth paste. Mix with the soy sauce and sugar. Mix the cucumber and mushrooms in the sesame sauce and serve.

Grilled and simmered foods

Traditionally the beancurd cake, gluten balls, beancurd skin, aubergines, yams and mushrooms are all arranged with a little pickled ginger, either home-made (see recipe on page 136) or bought, in a lacquer bowl (no. 4 in the diagram). The recipes below are for the foods in season during the summer; during the autumn burdock and chillis would take the place of the aubergines and ginger.

Stir-fried gluten balls

INGREDIENTS

120g (4oz) raw gluten made with strong flour
60ml (4 tablespoons) dashi
45ml (3 tablespoons) Japanese soy sauce
30ml (2 tablespoons) mirin
15ml (1 tablespoon) oil

PREPARATION

Divide the raw gluten into four and shape each portion into a ball. Bring the *dashi* to the boil with the soy sauce and *mirin* and drop in the gluten balls. Lower the heat and simmer until the stock has almost gone. Lift out the gluten balls. Heat the oil in a frying-pan and stir-fry the gluten until golden brown. Serve cold or hot.

Beancurd cake

INGREDIENTS

180g (6oz) beancurd
65g ($2\frac{1}{2}$ oz) sugar
15ml (1 tablespoon) Japanese soy sauce

PREPARATION

Wrap the beancurd in a clean cloth and gently squeeze to remove excess moisture. Put the beancurd in a food processor and blend with the sugar and soy sauce into a smooth paste. Oil the bottom of a small omelette pan and spoon in the paste. Smooth over to make a flat cake, and using a piece of tinfoil press down to make sure no bubbles remain in the beancurd. Cook over a very low heat for about 20 minutes, then turn over and cook the other side until lightly browned. Lift out and leave to cool. Cut into four triangles.

Grilled beancurd skin

INGREDIENTS

1 sheet beancurd skin

SIMMERING STOCK

45ml (3 tablespoons) dashi
30ml (2 tablespoons) Japanese soy sauce
15ml (1 tablespoon) mirin

PREPARATION

Damp the beancurd skin until it becomes soft, then roll tightly into a cylinder. Cut into four lengths and cook in the simmering stock for about 10 minutes over a low heat. Leave the rolls to cool in the remaining stock. Then thread on to a skewer and grill under a moderate heat. Serve hot.

Simmered mushrooms

INGREDIENTS

4 dried mushrooms
15ml (1 tablespoon) caster sugar
15ml (1 tablespoon) sake
25ml ($1\frac{1}{2}$ tablespoons) Japanese soy sauce

PREPARATION

Soak the mushrooms in 200ml (1 cup, $\frac{1}{3}$ pint) warm water for 6 hours. Remove the hard stalks and put into a small pan with enough of the water in which they were soaked to cover. Bring to the boil and cook for 2 minutes. Add the sugar, *sake* and soy sauce, turn down the heat and simmer for a further 2 minutes. Remove from the heat and allow the mushrooms to cool in the cooking liquor.

Simmered yams

INGREDIENTS

4 small yams (edoes)
15 ml (1 tablespoon) mirin
15 ml (1 tablespoon) caster sugar
15 ml (1 tablespoon) sake
SIMMERING STOCK
  200 ml (1 cup, ⅓ pint) dashi
  25 ml (1½ tablespoons) caster sugar
  7.5 ml (1½ teaspoons) Japanese soy sauce
  15 ml (1 tablespoon) sake
pinch salt

PREPARATION

Peel the yams and cut into 4 equal-sized, flat-sided oblongs. Soak in water for 20 minutes, then rinse well to eliminate some of the stickiness. Put into a bowl with the *mirin*, sugar and *sake*. Add just sufficient water to cover and steam over a high heat until the yams are soft (about 15 minutes). Meanwhile, put the simmering stock into a saucepan and bring to the boil. When the yams are cooked add to the pan, without their cooking liquor, and simmer for 10 minutes.

Simmered fried aubergines

INGREDIENTS

180 g (6 oz) aubergine
5 ml (1 teaspoon) salt
SIMMERING STOCK
  300 ml (1¼ cups, ½ pint) dashi
  15 ml (1 tablespoon) caster sugar
  15 ml (1 tablespoon) mirin
  45 ml (3 tablespoons) Japanese soy sauce
  1 chilli, de-seeded and chopped
oil for deep frying

PREPARATION

Without peeling the aubergine cut into batons about 3 cm (1 inch) wide and 7 cm (3 inches) long. Lightly score the skin and soak in lightly salted water for 30 minutes, covering with a plate to keep the batons under the surface. Mix the simmering stock in a saucepan and bring to the boil; leave to simmer gently. Heat the oil in a deep-frying pan. Pat the aubergine batons dry and deep-fry until soft, then gently press out the surplus oil; simmer in the prepared stock for 2 minutes. Serve hot, without the stock.

Aburage rolls

INGREDIENTS

10 g (½ oz) carrot
4 large thick dried mushrooms
150 g (5 oz) fresh spinach
1 sheet dried beancurd skin
STOCK FOR MUSHROOMS AND CARROT
  100 ml (½ cup, 4 fl oz) dashi
  10 ml (2 teaspoons) Japanese soy sauce
  5 ml (1 teaspoon) caster sugar
  pinch salt
1 sheet aburage
STOCK FOR ABURAGE ROLL
  100 ml (½ cup, 4 fl oz) dashi
  5 ml (1 teaspoon) caster sugar
  5 ml (1 teaspoon) Japanese soy sauce
  5 ml (1 teaspoon) sake
  pinch salt

PREPARATION

Peel the carrot and cut into a pencil-sized strip about 14 cm (5 inches) long. Soak the dried mushrooms for 30 minutes in warm water, then discard the hard stalks. Wash the spinach and tear out the tough central veins. Blanch in lightly salted boiling water for 2 minutes. Refresh in cold water. Squeeze dry. Rinse the beancurd skin in warm water, then leave on one side. Cook the carrot and mushrooms in the simmering stock over a low heat for 10 minutes. Lift out the carrot and mushroom and cut the mushroom into thin slices. Meanwhile, soak the beancurd skin in the remaining stock for 10 minutes. Lift out and roll into a pencil-sized cylinder. Soak the spinach in the remaining stock for 10 minutes, then squeeze into a bundle 14 cm (5 inches) long.

Cut the top, bottom and one side from the *aburage* and open out into a flat sheet about 14 cm (5 inches) square. Place on a rolling mat with the white (inner) side up. Arrange the carrot stick, mushrooms, beancurd roll and spinach bundle across the *aburage* and roll up around the filling, using the bamboo mat to help make an even, tight roll. Tie at 5-cm (2-inch) intervals.

Put the roll into the prepared stock in a saucepan and simmer for 20 minutes. Remove the string and cut into four equal portions. Serve hot with the cut sides up.

Sesame tofu

INGREDIENTS

100g (4oz) white sesame seeds
100g (4oz) kudzu *flour*
15ml (1 tablespoon) mirin
wasabi *mustard*

PREPARATION

Toast the sesame seeds over a moderate heat in a dry pan until they start to dance and turn golden brown. Tip out on to a flat surface and crush with a rolling-pin to an oily paste. Mix this paste with the *kudzu* flour and slowly add the water, stirring all the time, to make sure the batter is smooth. Cook this batter over a moderate heat, stirring constantly, until it starts to boil. Then lift from the heat and add the *mirin* and another 200ml (1 cup, ⅓ pint) water, a little at a time. Mix well between each addition. Wet a 15-cm (5-inch)-square cake-tin, or failing that a 400-g (1-lb) loaf-tin, and quickly pour in the mixture, discarding any batter that is sticking to the bottom of the pan. Put into the refrigerator to cool and leave for at least 1 hour to set. Cut into four squares and serve one to each plate with a little soy sauce and a cone of *wasabi* mustard.

Clear soup with green grapes

INGREDIENTS

4 green grapes
800ml (3½ cups, 1⅓ pints) dashi
5ml (1 teaspoon) salt

PREPARATION

Peel the grapes and remove their stones. Put one grape in each soup bowl. Bring the *dashi* to the boil, season to taste with the salt and pour into each soup bowl over the grapes. Serve hot.

Fried nibbles

These three fried items are arranged on a plate 24cm (8 inches) square (no. 8 in the diagram).

INGREDIENTS

8 pieces konbu, *2 × 3cm (¾ × 1 inch)*
4 green chillis
oil for deep frying
12 sweet walnuts (see below)

PREPARATION

Wipe the *konbu* and cut into the individual pieces. Drop into moderately hot oil and deep-fry until the pieces rise to the surface. Drain well. Serve cold. Slit the chillis, from their pointed ends, into four quarters, leaving them joined at the stalks. De-seed. Drop into hot oil and deep-fry for about 30 seconds. Lift out and drain. Assemble with the previously prepared walnuts.

Sweet walnuts

INGREDIENTS

75g (3oz) walnuts
60ml (4 tablespoons) water
60ml (4 tablespoons) sugar
oil for deep frying

PREPARATION

Put the nuts with the water and sugar into a small pan and bring to the boil. Simmer for 5 minutes over a low heat, then lift from the heat and leave to marinate for 4 hours in the syrup. Turn the nuts in the syrup from time to time to make sure they are well coated. Heat the oil until very hot, then, over a *low* heat, deep-fry the walnuts for about 4 minutes until golden brown. Lift out and leave to drain. Serve cold.

Rice soup

INGREDIENTS

15ml (1 tablespoon) Japanese round-grained rice
400ml (2 cups, $\frac{2}{3}$ pint) hot water
pinch salt

PREPARATION

Wash the rice and drain well. Put into a clean, dry frying-pan and toast over a moderate heat until lightly browned all over. Then pour in the hot water and add the salt. Simmer until the rice is soft (about 10 minutes). Serve this 'soup' at the end of the meal. (Take care if using a tea-pot for this soup that it is quite clean before you pour in the soup.)

Cold hors d'oeuvre plate

INGREDIENTS

30 soya beans
oil for deep frying
SEASONING SAUCE
20ml (4 teaspoons) miso
30ml (2 tablespoons) caster sugar
15ml (1 tablespoon) sake
30ml (2 tablespoons) green peas
1 small piece wood ears
15ml (1 tablespoon) Japanese soy sauce
15ml (1 tablespoon) sake
pinch sugar

PREPARATION

Soak the beans overnight, then boil in fresh water until soft. Drain and leave on a towel to dry. Deep-fry in hot oil for a few seconds, then drain well. Mix with the seasoning sauce.

Boil the peas in lightly salted water until cooked, then drain well. Soak the wood ears in warm water for 20 minutes, then rinse and cut into very fine strips. Put with the soy sauce and *sake* in a small saucepan and bring to the boil. Add the sugar and simmer for another minute. Drain the wood ears and mix with the green peas. Serve, arranged carefully, in one dish with the soya beans.

Clear soup with beancurd and ginko nuts

INGREDIENTS
100 g (4 oz) beancurd
pinch salt and sugar
pinch black sesame seeds, toasted
5 ml (1 teaspoon) grated yam
5 g (¼ oz) ginger
4 stalks mitsuba *or blanched parsley or coriander*
800 ml (3½ cups, 1⅓ pints) dashi
5 ml (1 teaspoon) Japanese soy sauce
salt
oil for deep frying
4 ginko nuts

PREPARATION
Wrap the beancurd lightly in a cloth and leave to drain for 30 minutes. Then squeeze in the cloth to remove as much water as possible. Put in a food processor with a pinch of salt and sugar, the black sesame seeds and the grated yam. (This last ingredient will help bind the beancurd together.) Work into a smooth paste. Cut the ginger into hair-like shreds. Chop the *mitsuba*, parsley or coriander. Heat the *dashi* and adjust the seasoning with soy sauce and salt. Shape the beancurd into a triangular roll and cut into four equal lengths. Heat the oil until moderately hot and deep-fry the beancurd until golden brown. Lift out and drain. Arrange one triangle in each soup bowl with a ginko nut, a few shreds of ginger and the green *mitsuba*. Re-heat the *dashi* and divide between the soup bowls. Serve hot.

Simmered foods

The seven different items in this dish, each cooked according to a separate recipe, are arranged on one big plate and served cold. Try to use the different colours and shapes of the food to the best advantage when you arrange them and serve the foods without their simmering stocks. At this time also bring to the table one or two small bowls of pickles (bought).
Hirouzu (beancurd balls) (page 86)
Simmered fried aubergines (page 176)
Aburage rolls (page 176)
Simmered mushrooms (page 175)
Simmered bamboo shoots (see below)
Simmered lotus root (see below)
Marinated chillis (see below)
Ginko nuts with pine-needles, to garnish (see below).

Simmered bamboo shoots

INGREDIENTS
75 g (3 oz) bamboo shoot
5 ml (1 teaspoon) caster sugar
15 ml (1 tablespoon) Japanese soy sauce
pinch salt
15 ml (1 tablespoon) sake
dashi

PREPARATION
Cut the pointed end of the bamboo shoot in half lengthwise and the remaining part into slices 1 cm (¼ inch) thick. Put into a pan with the seasonings and add enough *dashi* to cover. Bring to the boil, then simmer for 15 minutes. Leave to cool in the stock.

Simmered lotus root

INGREDIENTS

50 g (2 oz) canned or fresh lotus root
45 ml (3 tablespoons) caster sugar
pinch salt
100 ml (1 cup, 3½ fl oz) rice vinegar
100 ml (1 cup, 3½ fl oz) dashi

PREPARATION

If using fresh lotus root, peel off the skin. Cut the lotus into wedges, place with the remaining ingredients in a pan and cook for 10 minutes. Leave to cool in the stock.

Marinated chillis

INGREDIENTS

4 fresh green chillis
oil for deep frying
15 ml (1 tablespoon) Japanese soy sauce

PREPARATION

Slash the pointed end of the chillis and deep-fry in hot oil for about 30 seconds. Then drain well and leave to marinate in the soy sauce for at least 30 minutes.

Garnish of ginko nuts and pine-needles

Fresh ginko nuts are much better than canned ones for this garnish, but not essential. The pine-needles must be collected fresh from a wood or garden. If necessary this garnish may be omitted.

INGREDIENTS

4 ginko nuts
5 ml (1 teaspoon) oil
pine-needles, washed and dried

PREPARATION

Fry the ginko nuts in a frying-pan with a little oil until lightly browned. Make a small hole through each with a skewer or toothpick and thread each one on to a pine-needle.

Braised mixed vegetables

INGREDIENTS

2 dried mushrooms
3 pieces wood ears
20 g (¾ oz) lily buds
100 g (4 oz) lotus root
15 g (½ oz) carrot
50 g (2 oz) bamboo shoots
15 g (½ oz) broad beans
45 ml (3 tablespoons) oil

SEASONING SAUCE

300 ml (1¼ cups, ½ pint) dashi
15 ml (1 tablespoon) caster sugar
5 ml (1 teaspoon) Japanese soy sauce
15 ml (1 tablespoon) sake

10 ml (2 teaspoons) cornflour mixed with 10 ml (2 teaspoons) water

PREPARATION

Soak the dried mushrooms and wood ears separately in warm water for 20 minutes. Discard the hard stalks of the mushrooms and cut the caps into thin slices. Rinse the wood ears, discard any hard bits and cut into thin strips. Soak the lily buds in warm water for 20 minutes, then tie each one in a knot. Cut the lotus root, carrot and bamboo shoots into matchsticks. Heat the oil in a large frying-pan and stir-fry all the vegetables together for about 2 minutes. Pour in the seasoning sauce and bring to the boil. Thicken with the cornflour paste and serve hot.

Tempura

INGREDIENTS

4 sour plums
75 ml (5 tablespoons) caster sugar
200 g (7 oz) pumpkin

STOCK FOR COOKING PUMPKIN

300 ml (1¼ cups, 10 fl oz) dashi
30 ml (2 tablespoons) caster sugar
30 ml (2 tablespoons) Japanese or light soy sauce
30 ml (2 tablespoons) sake

200 g (7 oz) white-fleshed sweet potato

STOCK FOR SWEET POTATO

300 ml (1¼ cups, 10 fl oz) dashi
30 ml (2 tablespoons) caster sugar
30 ml (2 tablespoons) Japanese soy sauce
30 ml (2 tablespoons) sake

200 g (7 oz) bamboo shoots

STOCK FOR BAMBOO SHOOTS

300 ml (1¼ cups, 10 fl oz) dashi
30 ml (2 tablespoons) caster sugar
30 ml (2 tablespoons) Japanese soy sauce
pinch salt

4 large dried mushrooms

STOCK FOR DRIED MUSHROOMS

100 ml (3½ fl oz) mushroom soaking water
15 ml (1 tablespoon) mirin
15 ml (1 tablespoon) caster sugar
15 ml (1 tablespoon) Japanese soy sauce

40 g (1½ oz) yam
10 ml (2 teaspoons) Japanese soy sauce
pinch salt
4 okra
1 eating apple
4 slices ginger

BATTER

170 g (6 oz) plain flour
200 ml (1 cup, 7 fl oz) iced water, including an ice cube
1 egg yolk

ADVANCE PREPARATION

Soak the sour plums for 2 days in cold water, changing the water night and morning. Then soak in a mixture of 100 ml (3½ fl oz) water and 75 ml (5 tablespoons) caster sugar for the last night. Either on the day you wish to eat or the previous evening, peel and slice the pumpkin into 1-cm (⅓-inch)-thick slices about 6 cm (2½ inches) long. Put into the simmering stock and simmer for about 6 minutes, or until no longer hard. Tip into a bowl and leave to cool in the simmering stock. Peel the sweet potato, cut into slices about 1 cm (⅓ inch) thick and put into their simmering stock. Simmer for about 8–9 minutes. Then leave to cool in the stock in a clean bowl. Cut the bamboo shoots into slices about 5 mm (¼ inch) thick. Simmer in the stock for about 10 minutes, then leave to cool. Soak the dried mushrooms in 150 ml (5 fl oz) warm water for 30 minutes; strain and reserve 100 ml (3½ fl oz) of the soaking water. Discard the hard mushroom stalks. Put the caps with the strained soaking water and the *mirin*, caster sugar and soy sauce in a small pan and simmer for 4 minutes. Leave to cool in the stock. Peel the yam and cut into four wedge-shaped pieces. Soak in cold water for 20 minutes, then rinse and put into a small saucepan with the soy sauce and salt. Cover with water and simmer gently until just soft. Leave to cool in the simmering stock.

AT LEAST AN HOUR BEFORE FRYING THE TEMPURA

Prepare the okra by scraping the bloom from each pod, but leave whole. Rinse well and pat dry. Cut the apple into quarters and remove the core. Cut each quarter into three thin slices. Lift the previously cooked vegetables from their stocks and leave to drain. Prepare the salt-pepper dip (page 24). When ready to cook the *tempura*, dry all the vegetables carefully on kitchen paper and lay out on a plate including the sour plums and ginger. Heat the oil to 180°C (350°F). Beat the egg yolk into the iced water and stir in the sifted flour. Mix lightly; it does not matter if there are some lumps left in the batter, for these make the lacy texture of the batter when it is cooked. Dip the vegetables in the batter, one at a time, then drop into the hot oil. Do not put too many pieces of vegetable into the deep fat at any one time or the temperature of the oil will drop. When golden and crisp, lift from the pan and drain on kitchen paper for a few seconds. Serve arranged on one big dish.

Chrysanthemum leaves with a walnut dressing

INGREDIENTS

250 g (8 oz) chrysanthemum or spinach leaves
50 g (2 oz) walnuts
2.5 ml (½ teaspoon) bicarbonate of soda
30 ml (2 tablespoons) caster sugar
40 ml (2½ tablespoons) Japanese soy sauce

PREPARATION

Wash, trim and blanch the chrysanthemum leaves in boiling water for 1 minute. Refresh in cold water and squeeze dry. Cut the leaves into 3-cm (1-inch) lengths. Boil the walnuts in 300 ml (½ cup, ½ pint) water mixed with the bicarbonate of soda for 3 minutes, then drain. While the walnuts are still warm use a toothpick to lift off their light brown skin. Place in a liquidizer or food processor and grind finely. Add the sugar, then the soy sauce, and mix well. Spoon this sauce over the chrysanthemum leaves and serve in four small dishes.

Lohan's delight

A *lohan* is a Buddhist saint; this dish is so named because it strictly follows Buddhist ruling on food.

INGREDIENTS

25 g (1 oz) tiger-lily buds
2 dried mushrooms
1 sheet dried beancurd skin
1 piece wood ears
5 g (¼ oz) black hair fungus
25 g (1 oz) silk noodles
350 g (12 oz) Chinese leaves
25 g (1 oz) bamboo shoots
45 ml (3 tablespoons) oil
4 squares fried beancurd
25 g (1 oz) canned ginko nuts
25 g (1 oz) frozen green peas
30 ml (2 tablespoons) Japanese soy sauce
600 ml (2½ cups, 1 pint) dashi
salt to taste

PREPARATION

Soak the tiger-lily buds in hot water for 1 hour, then rinse and tie a knot in the centre of each. Soak the dried mushrooms in warm water for 30 minutes, then discard the hard stalks and cut the caps into thin slices. Soften the beancurd skin in warm water for about 5 minutes, then cut into 1-cm (½-inch)-wide strips and place in a pan of boiling water. Simmer gently for 30 minutes. Soak the wood ears and black hair fungus in separate bowls of warm water for 20 minutes, then rinse well. Discard any hard bits of the wood ears and cut into thin strips. Cut the silk noodles into 13-cm (5-inch) lengths with a pair of sharp scissors and soak in hot water for 10 minutes. Wash and cut the Chinese leaves into 8-cm (3-inch) squares. Slice the bamboo. Heat the oil in a large saucepan and stir-fry the Chinese leaves for about 3–4 minutes until softened. Add all the other vegetables, well drained, and the soy sauce. Pour in the *dashi* and bring to the boil. Adjust the seasoning, cover with a lid and leave to simmer for 25 minutes. Serve hot.

Fruit

Serve any fruit in season, such as oranges, peaches or melon. Prepare and cut the fruit into segments or slices and provide small forks for diners.

Tea rice

Follow the recipe on page 154 for plain boiled rice but add 15 ml (1 tablespoon) green powdered tea (*matcha*) and 5 ml (1 teaspoon) salt to the measured water. Cook and dry as directed.

Bibliography

CHINESE

Ham Yuming,
Siji caipu (Four Seasons Vegetarian Cookery),
Hohhot, 1962.

Hu Changzhi,
Sucai xue gelun (Survey of Vegetarian Cookery),
Taibei, 1961.

Xie Yingru,
Nanbei sucai (Vegetarian Dishes, South and North),
Hong Kong, 1981.

Anon.,
Zhongguo sucai (Chinese Vegetarian Cookery),
Dengshi Publishers, Taibei, 1982.

Osamu Harada,
Chugoku ryori sozai jiten (Dictionary of Chinese Vegetarian Cookery),
Tokyo, 1978.

KOREAN

Chong Deson,
Chosen no ryori sho (Book of Korean Cookery),
Tokyo, 1982.

JAPANESE

Eieu Sugai,
Fucha ryori (Temple Cookery),
Tokyo, 1984.

Tsuda, Oshita, Kobayashi, Ito,
Shojin ryori (Buddhist Cookery),
Tokyo, 1984.

INDONESIAN

Penyusun,
Resep Masakan Lengcap (Complete Cookery Recipes),
Semarang, 1963.

Index